East St. Louis

The Way It Is

1990

By Ruben L. Yelvington

Published by Top's Books
Post Office Drawer C
Mascoutah, IL 62258
Phone 744-0094

Library of Congress Catalog Number 90-71151

ISBN: 0-9627453-0-8 11.95

Printed in the United States of America
October 1990

Dedicated to
those who fled East St. Louis
but who can't quit being
East St. Louisans

and today's East St. Louisans,
who deserve better.

May this book make a contribution
to understanding,
cooperation,
and a better tomorrow for
East St. Louis, for all of us who care
and for generations to come

Acknowledgements

This book was possible through the darkroom talents of Leigh Lemke who developed film and printed and screened almost all the pictures the author took for this book, and copied and screened the few that were taken by others. When I told Leigh that I was going to publish a picture book with hundreds of screened black and white photos, she didn't even wince; she just said "What did I do to deserve this?" I promised her I would give her full credit in the book. This is it, Leigh. And at right is Leigh.

Darkroom Technician Leigh Lemke

But the book is what it is because of the cooperation of a great many people. The staff of Yelvington Publications weekly newspapers gave me the time to do write and photograph, put up with my excitement at the concept, read preliminary copy, read proof, helped compose the pages, and helped in countless other ways. We refer specifically to Debbie Sivells, typesetter; Terry Sabaleski, receptionist, billing clerk, tour manager, all-around right and left hand; and Patty Schrempp-Hoover, general manager of Yelvington Publications, who took on some of my chores to give me time to work on this book, fed my ego and did much of the pasteup. And I must add Pat Fogleman, darkroom technican, who printed the final pictures for the book.

Then there was my one-time competitor and business foe Cleon Birkmeier, now a resident of Murphysboro and publisher of a group of Southern Illinois newspapers. He once was Illinois general manager of the Journal newspapers and a New Baden resident. Cleon read early copy, added encouragement and suggestions, helped with the layout and arranged the production details. Unlike most books, this one was printed on a rotary offset press at the American Press plant in West Frankfort, arranged and overseen by Cleon. Cleon helped me generously, but also made a buck for his employers. That is his genius.

Cleon and my staff helped me do the impossible: to take this book from concept to the press in a little over four months. That's at least eight months shorter than normal.

Then there are the people who consented to be interviewed for the essays that intersperse the pictures in this book. It is a great feeling to know that you can call on people from such varied walks of life, power bases and environments and get their immediate cooperation. I am flattered. All — old acquaintenances and new — have talked freely and openly. Each interview has been revealing and, to me, ranged between interesting and fascinating. I have delighted in everyone with whom I have talked, learned to understand and respect their views. I am only sorry I could not have had the time free to do many more interviews. There are many more stories to be told, and people willing to tell them.

There are all those people who helped me with my failing memory, who suggested pictures, who helped me recall names. They include Charles and Mae Baugh, Stanley and Mary Laquet, Ed and Norma Belz, Nancy Macklin, Dick Stanley, Bob Rice, and many others I called at nigh, or on weekends, to ask a question. I owe a special debt of gratitude to Marie Kurkey who did all of the above, and gave a final reading to what she so politely called my "manuscript."

Of course, the contributors include the friends of a lifetime in East St. Louis, black and white, who have shared the experiences that give me the empathy, I hope, to travel throughout the town with comprehension and understanding of what I see; that enable me still today to share in the pride of every accomplishment of East St. Louis, and shudder with compassion at its failures.

When I was editor of the Metro-East Journal I would step outside the door at 425 Missouri Avenue, look up and down the street, take a deep breath and say to myself "This is my town." Taking the pictures revived that emotion. I still feel very strongly about East St. Louis and the opportunities for the people who live there.

Forward

The ghosts of a city that was, tell a story of the city that is

The story of life is the story of death. The new must be born, but it is born of the old who then must die to let the new take hold and grow — and beget its young, and die. This is the story of life, whether of a family or a community.

We must bury our dead, let go, and give the past eternal rest. We must welcome the newborn, the young who can adapt, can find new ways, new roads, new opportunities, new successes. East St. Louis lost its heavy industry, lost it before the white flight; scores of thousands of jobs in industries in the city and on its outskirts that were the economic backbone of the area, and provided the good-paying jobs for the spending that kept retail shopping in East St. Louis; created a tax base for government.

East St. Louis has never finished with its past, has never buried its dead. And its aging loins have not given birth to new ways, to the new jobs of an economy based on communications, computers and the exchange of knowledge.

The shells of the dead city halls, police station and fire house surround the new city hall, hiding it, casting their shadow on its beauty, their broken windows and shabby appearance shouting the message of a city in distress, a message that becomes a self-fulfilling prophecy. When the very seat of government cannot shake clear of its crumbling past, what attraction can it offer to prospective enterprise or prospective residents? And when in desperation it adds to the tax burdens of businesses it would attract, it seems to be shooing away any geese that might lay golden eggs.

The ghosts of the past are evident in abandoned cars, trashed vacant lots, burned out buildings, so many garbage bags, so many piles of trash, of broken glass and old carpet and even old sofas and chairs. The ghosts are so common that after awhile you no longer see them.

And even the schools, burning their trash in dumpsters that do not get emptied, in need of paint and maintenance, tell a sad tale in a period when most men and women, to get jobs in the information age, need the skills that are acquired in the classroom rather than in an apprenticeship.

The derelict business buildings and houses that still stand tell of a city that cannot make it; the boarded up "government property" buildings tell of families with government loans who could not make it; of housing projects that failed because the people who ran them were selfish opportunists. These are stories of defeat, sad stories, depressing stories, frightening stories...buildings vacant, buildings gutted, crumbling; threatening, dangerous buildings potentially housing threatening, dangerous people. And in the streets the children, the hope of the city, play.

In Loisel Village and Loisel Hills and Hilltop, where homes worth over $100,000, even a quarter of a million, can be found, yards are manicured, shrubs trimmed, wrought iron ornate. The wrought iron decorates special security storm doors whose beauty fails quite to obscure their utilitarian function. Here residents with good jobs have been able to accumulate a modicum of affluence, and try to live in an appropriate lifestyle. But they constantly must protect what they have.

The backs of the buildings of the largely decrepit Loisel Shopping Center, adjacent to the fine homes of Loisel Village, are spray painted with the signatures of gangs: The Crips, and the names of the Crips X'ed out. The symbols of the Disciples predominate. The names of gangs are evident in the housing projects downtown, and the vacant, stripped, Orr-Weathers high-rises, where such phrases as "Kill Cops" have been added.

In the less affluent area, iron bars or even heavy wire mesh replace ornamental iron. In the worst areas, the poorest families still must buy and hang doors of steel bars to protect what little they have, and barefoot babes playing in back yards talk to their moms in the kitchen through the bars.

In the areas of typical middle-class Archie Bunker type homes, there are many chain link fences as well as barred doors and lots of yard lights. Throughout the city, churches have seen it necessary to surround their own parking lots with chain link fences.

Every few blocks you will find a liquor store or tavern, and just as frequently, a church. And on Sunday morning, in every part of town you will see people in their Sunday best on street corners waiting for a neighbor to give them a ride, or cruising down the street in clean, shiny cars, going to church; and at the same hour, here and there, a man with a bottle in a paper sack, swigging as he walks.

Are they both symbols of a search for hope?

Meet the Author

Drawing on a perspective from 45 years in East St. Louis

It always brings a laugh when I say my family moved from the Soulard market area of St. Louis to East St. Louis when I was about 2 to get into a better neighborhood. But as a Southern Baptist family surrounded by Catholic Polish families, that's how they felt. And compared to the narrow brick tenements of St. Louis, Oak Park in East St. Louis was more appealing to the former rural residents of Arkansas and Texas, where my parents had lived before they married; and there were plenty of Protestants.

So my roots in East St. Louis go back a long way. I lived there from about age 2 until after my marriage in 1950, when my former wife Ruth and I moved to what is now Fairview Heights. I worked in East St. Louis until I resigned as editor of the Metro-East Journal in 1971 at the age of 46 to publish the Mascoutah Herald and New Baden News. I have been out of East St. Louis 19 years now, but I feel like I never left. And when I'm away and someone asks me where I work, I am just as likely as not to say "425 Missouri Ave., the East St. Louis Journal, Upton 4-2500."

As a youth I lived in Oak Park, for a stint on 27th Street, back to Oak Park and then at 1133 Cleveland Ave., within walking distance of high school and the slots in the drugstores and taverns and bowling alleys downtown. Bus tokens three for a quarter worked well in the dime slots. I went to the teen dances in the YWCA on the second floor over gambling dens on Missouri Avenue, within sight of the old City Hall. I ushered at the Avenue Theater, and I remember the first racial picketing of the Majestic Theater. I ate chop suey in the curtained Chinese restaurant over a downtown dime store (Newberry's?). After I graduated from high school I worked as a machinist helper in the Brooklyn Shops of the Terminal Railroad Assn. I walked each morning to the Relay Depot, past the Second Street Red Light District, and caught the shop train, heated by a pot-bellied coal-fired stove, to the Brooklyn shops.

After World War II and a hitch in India fighting the war in a darkroom, I returned to the railroad job for a few months, until the fall term in 1946 when my high school buddy Clarence Hibbert "Hibby" Raede and I virtually forced our way into the overcrowded University of Missouri. I became deeply involved in the student YMCA, became vice president of the student body, and en route authored a platform that called for a student referendum on the admission of Negroes to the then all-white University of Missouri. It carried 4 to 1. With the

Ruben L. Yelvington

support of some militant Missourians, including particularly one Gordon Parks, the student government was able to lobby through legislation that ended the segregation of Mizzou.

I graduated June 7, 1949, and went to work the next week for the East St. Louis Journal. Tom Duffy was the news editor, Bob Barracks the editor and P. H. "Perley" Wire (who truly was born in a sod hut in Nebraska) the general manager.

One of my first assignments was writing "color" stories supporting the coverage by investigative reporter Charles O. Stewart of the Sen. Estes Kefauver Crime Investigation Committee hearings in St. Louis. Carl Baldwin was among those covering the hearings for the Post-Dispatch. Carl has written much authentic history of the very beginnings of East St. Louis.

After the Kefauver hearings, I wrote some in-depth pieces, drawn from information garnered from the hearings, about Frank "Buster" Wortman, leader of the Southern Illinois link of the Chicago Capone mob.

The old East St. Louis Journal was a vigorous newspaper with a heavy emphasis on investigative reporting. As a new face on the team, Charles used me to verify the continuation of gambling. That is, he drew little maps and told me what I should find in, say the basement of a tavern at 16th and St. Clair. I entered the tavern, followed his directions to the basement (via a door marked "Ladies") and verified that there was a horse betting parlor in the basement with race results blaring from speakers, results chalked on big boards on the walls, and a throng of people their identity almost obscured in cigarette smoke.

I checked for Charles from Brooklyn to beyond Marissa at Harry's Red Horse Ranch on the County Line, and from the Cat and the Fiddle to the Stock Yards and Whiskey Chute.

I saw my share of blood and violence as I reported the "trunk murders" some may remember, including that of Charles Koenig, and the police news over several decades. I can tell you now that it was with the help of Lizzie Nezzlerodt, she of the bright dyed red hair who ran the tavern under the Veterans Bridge approach, that I knew daily how many girls were working in the Valley, and what cop was bag man and how much the girls' pimps paid.

And I wrote the nomination for the East St. Louis All America City Award.

When I became editor, the headline in Clyde Jordan's Crusader black weekly was something like "White Racist Named Editor of Journal." I came to know Clyde fairly well as a man, not a close friend. I had a high regard for him. As a member of the East St. Louis School Board, it was he who called for the "honkey" state police force to be brought into East St. Louis and restore order in the schools — a racially unpopular action but one needed. The meeting was in a secret room at the old Stop Light Restaurant, which later burned. I hope that he also learned to respect me. Bob Rice, then school board attorney, was at that meeting.

I was editor during the great teacher strike, and when the golden tongued Charles Cohen of Cairo, the "Pied Piper" turned out the schools in a racial protest. While I was editor, Sweed Jeffries of the War Lords was a frequent visitor in my office. I was editor of the Journal when the Globe-Democrat ran a daily page one box on East St. Louis "snipings."

I have a million memories of the East St. Louis in which I grew up. They are pleasant memories. I have a million more of the violent years when I worked at the Journal as a reporter and editor: the gangster years, the racial revolution, the white flight. They are exciting memories of turbulent times. I have deep feelings about East St. Louis and the people who live there; the abject poverty that grips so many of the people; the frustration young blacks must feel with a generally inferior education and practically no worthwhile job opportunities. While I celebrate the few who have risen above these odds, they are the exceptions in a rotten system.

I am disheartened that most of us in the "outer county" just wish we could close our eyes and all of East St. Louis' problems would go away. They don't, and they become our problems in the outer county in infinite ways.

Now you know something about the author/photographer who has created this book.

As this is written, there is a disagreement between Mayor Carl Officer and a state study group over how much East St. Louis "owes." The state says that it owes $47 million, while Officer maintains that the city only owes $4 million.

What does the city owe? Who does the city owe? What are the debts?

To pay for past goods and services? Or to restore and repave streets? To repair or replace storm and sanitary sewers that have sunk to the bottom of the American Bottom? To remove derelict buildings, firegutted, stripped of salvagables? To condemn unsafe and unsanitary housing? To restore parks? To bring under control crime and drugs? To make the city safe for businesses to thrive again, providing tax revenue and jobs? To haul away the hundreds of tons of trash and junk dumped on vacant lots and in front of vacant houses everywhere in the city? To haul away the hundreds and hundreds of abandoned junked cars? Are any number of millions enough?

Is money alone an answer?

The purpose of this book is to give its readers a current, realistic eye-view of East St. Louis in hundreds and hundreds of pictures and a few thousand words. We offer pictures of a city in distress, of residents who suffer for the lack of basic services every American deserves. Talk about human rights! But we offer too pictures of the well kept areas, the nice old and some new homes that will surprise you, in a city that could be on the verge of greatness. And perhaps the observations we make will add to understanding and purpose among those who would make the city a better place.

To those who have fled the city, we offer current pictures of the places you knew and loved and left.

We offer something of the efforts to bootstrap; the successes of "survivors" who did not flee, the achievements of some who have overcome, and perhaps, some hope.

No one who lives in East St. Louis likes what has happened to the city.

But does anyone really think the people of East St. Louis can solve its problems alone ?

We "honkies" didn't when we lived there.

I'd like to know your reaction to this book. Please feel free to write to me:

Rube Yelvington
314 E. Church St.
Mascoutah, IL 62258
(Please do not phone. I have a living to make and I cannot spare the time to talk with you courteously)

TABLE OF CONTENTS

Interviews, alphabetical:

Topics in order:

Carl Officer, interviewed during salad lunch in mayor's conference room

City's ship is coming in ...
...and it's a gambling ship

Mayor Carl Officer sees himself as a black Winston Churchill defending his island against the 'Nazi Democratic Party'

Despite his slim athletic body and his tender 37 years, Mayor Carl Officer sees himself as a black Winston Churchill, a bulldog if you will, defending his island against the Nazis. The Nazis in his mind's eye, are the St. Clair County Democratic Party and the lawyers who support it.

There even is an Afrika Korps, he said, comprising the Democratic precinct committeemen that are part of the "Nazi Democratic Party," and the Korps has a Rommel; "Their Rommel is Oliver Hendricks (chairman pro-tem of the East St. Louis City Council), only he isn't the desert fox, he's the desert rat."

Having said all that, and more, Officer claims that for the last two years he has been more careful about what he says.

Things are going to change. The city's ship is going to come in — and it's a gambling ship, with the city's share of the take coming off the top. It will bring with it, in Officer's vision, in addition to $4 million to $7 million a year in gaming revenue, tourism and spinoff jobs, and the poor blacks won't have to go to their precinct committeemen for their five or ten dollars on election day. And the city will be able to provide better services to citizens.

"The party's going to be over, and the boys in Belleville know it. They have consistently maintained control by keeping people on general assistance rolls. By keeping these staunch cutthroats called Democratic committeemen...the majority of them can't read or write past the second grade level...they are some of the biggest bunch of cheesy hustlers I've ever seen in my life." Officer said that in three elections he never had dealt with the committeemen and won without them, because the people do not respect them.

Mayor Officer sees himself as the people's champion against racism and old-time politics that he said are responsible for the city's bonded debts. And he sees himself fighting against immense odds but sees some signs that he could be winning the battle. The most hopeful sign, he says, is that well-educated affluent middle age and younger black people are moving back to East St. Louis. There is some reversal of the black flight for a variety for reasons. Some come back to make a statement about their city and their unwillingness to give up, some because they think they can make a difference, some to take care of parents or businesses. Some because they are tired of the stress of coping with racism in a few integrated communities, with the schools, police, city officials, or with crosses burned in their yards; but racism doesn't have to be all that overt to be felt, to be experienced.

There are those who would have you believe that the people of East St. Louis have lost heart, have accepted things as they are as the best they can be, and are determined to live with the situation. "I think they have miscalculated two things: my leadership and the will and desire of the people. The people in East St. Louis don't have any false images about Mayor Officer. They know he's just as human as anybody else. They don't mind beating up on me, but they sure as hell don't like somebody else coming from outside beating up on me. I think that is what they miscalculated on. I also believe the people do not and will not accept mediocrity and things remaining the way they are. They will demand change, they have a firm resolve."

At the time of this interview, Officer still was opposing demands of the state for a state-appointed fiscal officer reporting to a state-appointed committee as the price tag for a $34 million state bailout.

"This bailout plan...I've heard only two persons tell me 'Take the deal,' and those two are Sen. (Kenneth) Hall and chairman pro-tem of the council, Oliver Hendricks." He said he had met with 45 leading pastors of churches and every head of every civic and social clubs in two public hearings, a total of 110 people, and videotaped the sessions to prove they were not orchestrated. And Officer said they told him, "We haven't supported you on everything in the past, but on this one, don't give away the city."

Lashing out at Hendricks and Hall for supporting the bailout, he said "The difference between Kenny Hall and Oliver Hendricks and Judas is Judas did his betrayal of Christ out of love, he didn't want Him to be harmed when he turned Him over to the Romans. Kenny Hall and Oliver Hendricks are leading us as some of the merchants on the Ivory Coast did, sending their brothers to ships bound for the New World, and they knew what was going to happen to them."

(Eventually Mayor Officer supported the bill, with assurances that the city would be free to manage its own day-to-day finances.)

What is the general image of the city? What can Officer say to whites who fled the city and look back at their former property and ask, "What have *they* done to my city, my property?"

A false image was portrayed by 60 Minutes in the TV program's presentation on East St. Louis. "They didn't show anything that wasn't true," Officer said. "But they boiled down 4-1/2 weeks of filming into an approximately 13-minute piece. They gave the impression that all the people of East St. Louis were capable of doing was producing young men who could play football. Nothing else positive was presented."

East St. Louis High School had a proud football heritage when segregation was in force and no blacks were at the high school, he recalled.

On the other hand, the East Side chess team is a state master team; it and academic and artistic achievements are overlooked.

Officer stressed the close relationship of his family with the Kruta's Bakery family. The bakery used to be on north Ninth Street. He talked about how he liked to go into the bakery early in the morning and enjoy all the aromas of fresh baked goods. "I'm sure they wonder what happened to their neighborhood."

A variety of things happened, he said. The school system began to deteriorate in a lot of different ways. "In 1970, May 26, I graduated from high school. The assessed valuation of East St. Louis then was $169 million. It was still predominantly white. In 1979, May 6, I became mayor, and the assessed valuation was $38 million, and the town overwhelmingly black."

The white flight was followed by a black flight. The city dropped in population from about 86,000 to 40,000. Some people worked hard to maintain their property. "But with the highest tax rate in the state and high insurance costs, for many it was all they could do to hold onto their property, much less maintain it as they should. There were vacant buildings, burn-outs, coming from the social changes that any urban area experiences when there is a flight of jobs."

In some cases, he said, residents were victimized by local government in programs such as weatherization of homes. He said he discharged employees who used "rehab dollars" for friends and relatives and who accepted kickbacks from contractors. "And I am sure these things go on in the St. Clair County Intergovernmental Grants Department and in St. Louis and other places."

He said that the white flight was accompanied by a flight of industry to the Sunbelt and the closing of obsolete heavy industry. He estimated that 25,000 jobs were lost in the East St. Louis area (between about 1945 and 1975.) He cited the railroads, National Stock Yards and its packing plants, industry in and around East St. Louis such as Obear Nester Glass Co., American Steel, Aluminum Ore, two breweries at 18th and Broadway...

Then there is the sewer system. The surface water system handles all the runoff from as far away as Highland, and including Fairview Heights and Belleville. "Water runs downhill. Every time they put in a parking lot or a new complex, more water runs into our system. Not only are we charged with handling it, but it erodes."

For 76 years blood, hair and other debris from the packinghouses in National City ran through part of the city's sewer system. There were tremendous amounts of chemicals from Pfizer or truck cleaning, and from E. J. Dougherty flushing through a system 90 years old. " It was not flushed when the packing plants closed. The city sewer maps are inadequate and sewers are not where they are thought to be. And it is documented that there was no maintenance of the Army Corps of Engineers levees for 35 years. On Oct. 8, 1986 that came home to roost when the pumps completely collapsed and a third of the city was under water. "That wasn't a flood, it was a man made disaster." Flood relief was refused, and a third of our city was under water, people's lives overturned."

Mayor Officer was interrupted by a dozen phone calls as he ate at his lunch during this interview. One call was from State Rep. Wyvetter Younge from the House floor; she put someone else on to talk about financing a project. Officer said he had some entrepreneurs eager to finance it, and they sounded better than the Southwestern Development Authority; "I call that the Ku Klux Klan Development Authority."

A park commissioner was introduced, and we were told that water would be turned on in the Jones Park swimming pool June 22. The city alternates between the Lincoln Park Pool, which had water last year, and Jones Park, Officer said, because the water bill is $200,000 a year. (Actually, because of needed repairs, only the Lincoln Park pool is filled. See Leonard Johnston interview.)

What about the old buildings awaiting demolition? Even the new city hall is surrounded by the vacant old police headquarters, two buildings formerly used for city halls and the old election board offices. The Southern Illinois National Bank and the Union Electric Co. buildings now stand empty with broken windows. What image do they portray? How can you project the image of a successful city among the signs of decay?

"I would not dispute what your eyes see," Officer said. It's like the old saying about the pessimist and the optimist, whether you see a glass half empty or half full. When he drives to work he sees the new addition to the back of the old federal building, and he thinks about the 17 months it took to get it there. He thinks about what it took to get the new city hall finished five years ago (and adds candidly it will look like the old city hall in two years if maintenance isn't improved). He thinks about the miles and miles of streets that he fought to get funding to renew, and declares that the state is illegally witholding motor fuel tax funds until it recoups funds it says were illegally diverted.

What really is happening here, Officer said, is that the city has been denied any help from St. Clair County. There is a county park department, a county health department, and the county clerk administers elections, but there also is an East St. Louis Board of Elections, an East St. Louis Park District, an East Side Health District. East St. Louisans pay taxes to the county but have to run their own departments under antiquated laws, he said. "They should abolish the East Side Health District, the East St. Louis Board of Elections — that is my point. We have not come together to get this burden off of us and ask for professionalism in terms of services." (See John Baricevic article for agreement.)

Officer cited traffic problems and accidents, and said he asked for state police help in patrolling East St. Louis. The city gets 135,000 cars a day across the bridges, he said, and easily could average 14-15 accidents per 24-hour period. The city has more interstates than any other city in the state outside Chicago. An accident on the interstate requires the courtesy truck and at least three policemen, not counting those used for traffic diversion on ramps. "To keep our policemen on the interstate would just lock us up," he said. Normally 10 policemen can handle all the other calls the city receives. But when six or seven are diverted for an accident... He queried the police dispatcher using a speaker phone. She responded that as of June 14 the city had received 15,046 calls.

The city has 66 policemen, "still more than the

Carl spends much of his time on the phone

sheriff's department." In addition to the city's population they must deal with the through traffic, 14,000 commuters who work in the city, and on Friday and Saturday, 11,000 in the entertainment districts, he said. The policemen work under difficult circumstances. "The council talks about hiring more policemen, more firemen, but there's no money — let's get back to who really runs St. Clair County's Democratic Nazi party, the lawyers. Shakespeare was absolutely right when he said to kill all the lawyers.

"In 1986, the city collected $475,000 in traffic fines. Last year we collected $48,000. So far this year (in June) I have only $8,000." Officer said he didn't think traffic offenses had decreased, but rather the judges are "giving credit for time served in the East St. Louis jail" against fines, and that no one spends more than an hour or two before he is taken to court. "The officers get out and write tickets, and the judge dismisses 25 cases. They get frustrated and wonder why they should bother making arrests."

This fine money is used for police overtime, for other departments, to buy tickets to the pool for the most underprivileged children, sending kids to camp.

When East St. Louis blacks get outside the so-called safe boundaries of their own town, they feel harassed by police. But when arrests are made here, they are thrown out. He showed a report that a black East St. Louis woman was arrested in Belleville for failure to have a driver's license. She should have been arrested, but the policeman didn't know she didn't have a license until *after* he stopped her. She was delivering lunch to her mother who has a day job. The policeman said she resisted arrest and kicked him with both feet. She was eight months pregnant and had her hands handcuffed behind her back at the time. "Not many pregnant women can kick with both feet with their hands handcuffed," he asserted, charging that the woman was beaten.

What about the bars on the windows and doors throughout the city? Are they because of drugs? Youth gangs?

Drugs, I think, are overstated. East St. Louis has always been a community of crime. That's a reality going back to the days when there was Bloody Island where the duels were fought.

"Our drug problem comes primarily from Detroit. We've been fortunate not to have a major influence by Bloods and Crips. We've got Disciples and Park Avenue Players, and they are a result of the juvenile system sending our youth to St. Charles instead of the youth camp near Alton for the last nine years. To survive at St. Charles, you have to join a gang. The biggest fear that I have is the Haitians and Jamaicans. They make the Bloods and the Crips look like school children in their enforcement of their territory, much more horrifying than what we are familiar with.

"Drugs account for, I would say, 30 per cent of our crime problem. But poverty and a low educational level in some areas account for a considerable amount of crime.

"With nine or 10 active detectives who have about 53 active cases every day, they're solving the hell out of them. Inspector Lester Henderson has been in charge of the division for about a year and a half. Those so-called child murders we experienced last year, they were not the act of some crazed person. We solved every one of them without outside help."

Again, he attacked the lack of support from judges and the state's attorneys.

"Take the Woodcock case, the one who got murdered at the convenience store in Fairview Heights by those two heathens from East St. Louis. Those boys will probably never see daylight again. I had a personal friend who was killed by her husband at Christmas time and buried in the basement of her home in Loisel Hills. Her husband was back on the streets of East St. Louis in just three years. That's the problem we have. Black crime against blacks is not considered important.

"I can take you on the street and show you a drug deal going down. The dealer will take a package he has been holding in his hand and drop it on the pavement. We can have an assistant state's attorney ride with us and see it, and the state's attorney still won't issue us a warrant. How can we combat it?

"I can document guys we have arrested with bunches of drugs and weapons and money, the judge makes us give the f---ing guns back, and the money! You know why, they say? So they can pay their lawyer! That's what I call the Democratic Nazi Party, damn it! I can give you names, dates and places. Tell me why in the hell we should give these guys their guns back. All they (the court) kept was the drugs, and I'm not so damn sure they're not using them or selling them to dealers."

Officer talked in a controlled voice, choosing his words slowly, if not always carefully. But as he talked about the courts, he raised his voice, almost shouting in the intensity of his anger.

Blacks have been known to pretend ignorance, to put on a sham of being a "dumb nigger" in the white folks' eyes, to test the "honkies." Officer has been known to make some pretty wild statements. Was he playing that game?

"I've been known to do that," he said smiling. In his early and younger days as mayor, he left the running of the city up to a crony and experienced politician, Virgil Calvert. Virgil never changed, he just got better at what he did," Officer said, smiling again, except that city services were not being sold. Then Virgil died, and about the same time Ruby Ivory Woods, a 31-year veteran in the East St. Louis City Hall, sought to run for the Democratic nomination to succeed Tom Elliott as county recorder. But Jerry Costello wanted his brother Mike to have the job. Kenny Hall and Clyde Jordan said they were supporting Michael Costello. Officer was very angry and felt betrayed. A split began that never healed. This, Officer said, was when his political maturity began. "For the last two years I have really watched what I have said."

How about that speech at SIU-E?

"It was designed to stir the controversy. I didn't call anybody else a name, I called myself a nigger. I did that to draw attention. (SIU-E President) Earl Lazerson called my office the next day. I was in Alabama. He was furious. But then some of his own people began to tell the truth. Only 48 black males graduated in the last 10 years out of some 3,000 males who enrolled for a four-year degree - SIU-E only graduated 48 in 10 years! I probably will make a statement like this again before my career is done."

Officer smiled. "Sometimes I feel brilliant." The governor called him about the bailout, he said, and "I told the governor as long as he wants to treat the city as a city according to the constitution of

> *Mayor Carl Officer: "For the last two years I have really watched what I have said."*

1972, then I will treat him with respect as the governor, but if he wants to treat East St. Louis as a colony in the state of Illinois with disrespect for the elected representative of the city, then I'll treat him like any other asshole I deal with.

"He didn't like that very much.

"I think he has been a good governor in a lot of ways, but he has failed us in other ways. What he's trying to do right now is deliver for the Missouri Athletic Club boys who have been good to him over the years...he's pushing as hard as he can to deliver for what I call the VP crowd before he leaves that office. I went to the Missouri Athletic Club one time during the first year and a half I was in office, and they wanted me to form a commission for the development of the East St. Louis riverfront. I could have been taken care of from then on.

"I know, and the forces of evil, as I call them, know there's not much difference between Thompson and the Democratic Nazi party. He's like Stalin, has that kind of alliance with the Democratic Party here. Here's this son of a gun hooked in with Costello and the other bloodsuckers up here and the Republicans can't even get into the governor's office. This helped him retain his stronghold on this area for the last 10 years."

He said riverfront gambling is a reality. The campaign for it began for casino gambling, and Officer said he still can't believe Chicago is not going to get it too. The Saugets "have tried to go through us and around us," he said. The Saugets tried to have the county sponsor a casino boat in Sauget. "I can see there are people, forces outside trying to paint an image of me and the city that we can't handle the riverboat gambling. Bull shit!" he said, choosing the words carefully.

Gambling trips will be just four hours long, and for 1,200 people. The city will receive a cut off the top, not counting property taxes, sales taxes, utility taxes and taxes on service-related industries. "You're talking hotels, restaurants, and one developer has plans for a major theme park. These are not fly-by-night operations, we're talking about major major dollars," he said.

Dollars Officer sees as setting his people free.

Marion Officer discusses humility

Carl Officer's father Marion dressed immaculately, was manicured, wore tasteful jewelry, was very polite and polished, and known for his gracious manners; always a gentleman. He built the Officer Funeral Home into a quality and profitable establishment, and he built a respect for himself and his family among the black and white residents and professionals with whom he had any contact whatsoever. He lived comfortably and graciously.

Then his son Carl ran for mayor, after a humiliating defeat in a county race for coroner where the youthful candidate was buried in the white county precincts. Carl learned the Democratic party's precinct committeeman were selective in their support in the outer county and in East St. Louis. And he learned that racism was not dead. Angry at his defeat and only old enough to have voted in a handful of elections, he ran for the mayor's seat in what still was the biggest city in St. Clair County, black East St. Louis. Carl's victory was exhilarating — suddenly he was John F. Kennedy and the Officer complex was the Camelot compound.

I saw him descend on one school board meeting conducted by Clyde Jordan, not alone but with an entourage of body guards and the favored not-so-few preceding, accompanying, following, ariving in an auto cavalcade and then sweeping uninvited and unannounced into the meeting room. Business stopped while Carl made the rounds shaking hands and beaming his smile on those whom he enriched with his blessing. Then he was gone again, leaving his then-friend Clyde Jordan to resume control of his meeting. Carl was a young king reveling in his glory.

It was against this background that Marion Officer told me that he had tried to restrain Carl. "I told him that it was not he who won the election. It was me and the Officer family who for two decades had built the family name into one deserving respect and confidence; it was his bevy of friends here and from college who came to help him; it was his political friends who gave their support, and all those voters who believed in him — they, not he, won the election."

Marion Officer was concerned that Carl keep his perspective as one elected to serve the people.

"I've always had my wife to help me with that," he told me. "When I went out to make a speech and returned to tell her how great I was, that I had held the audience in the palm of my hand as they hung onto my every word, she would roll her big brown eyes up at me and say 'You ain't worth shit.'"

Officer Funeral Home

Striking view of new city hall (five years old) seen only when entering building

New City Hall from Third and Broadway

Broken windows, neglect mar the once proud Southern Illinois National Bank, seen from Broadway. It was given to the city to use as a city hall before the new one, visible at left, was built

Almost the entire block of Collinsville Avenue between Division Avenue and Broadway is vacant. From right, Division Hat Shop, Dupree Davis law office, Board of Election Commissioners, still used Union Electric office building given to city as City Hall, Southern Illinois Bank Building, also used as city hall. UE building has windows out, trash in doorway. State Office Building is across Collinsville Avenue. New City Hall is hidden from the east behind the abandoned buildings.

The old East St. Louis Poilce Station stands vacant now, another abandoned building, and masking from the north the new city hall and police headquarters. Police cars jam Division Avenue. The author spent the better part of two decades reporting police news here. Up the front steps to the right was the desk sergeant, behind him the dispatcher and traffic office; to the left the chief, a training room. Upstairs were the record room, the detectives' office, interrogation room. The back (Third Street) side was Engine House No. 1, photo lower left, with the men sleeping upstairs. Across Third Street was Smitty's Tavern, where you'd find Globe and Post reporters on a dull day. Hose lays in front of a fireplug — the hose is abandoned too — just outside the old Firehouse No. 1. Today they are ghosts of the past hovering oevr the new city hall.

A few law offices remain on Main Street across from the old police station. Once the Arcade Building reached from here to Collinsville Avenue, was filled with justices of the peace and bail bondsmen's offices, and a marriage license office. In lower picture, the walls remain of a city garage binding the abandoned police headquarters to the new city hall complex.

First Illinois Bank has cleared all the buildings between the bank and Third Street and made a large parking lot, top photo. Across the street the old Illini Federal Savings and Loan, now Fidelity, has done about the same thing. The old City Hall is gone, leaving a clear stretch from Missouri Avenue to the abandoned police headquarters. This "open space" will greet motorists who take the Third Street exit westbound from Interstates I-70, I-64, giving a largely unobstructed shot to the Fifth and Missouri site of the planned Metro Link terminal. Missouri Avenue also leads to the fedeal court, St. Mary's Hospital, Illinois Bell offices and Post Office complex. With even minimal police protection it should be a secure area.

The State Office Building, seen above from Broadway and Collinsville Avenue, originally was planned for the city of Collinsville. The old Metro-East Journal campaigned to have it built in East St. Louis, closer to the people most in need of service. Gov. Richard B. Ogilvie listened. The building looks better from the backside, right. Below, a park replaces the old Arcade Building, but it gives a splendid view of the abandoned police headquarters.

State Representative Wyvetter Younge

"We have the escalation of hate by the newspapers, I mean the newspapers writing in such a way as to promulgate hate. We need a program that gets us down emotionally from all this bad feeling among racial groups."

Common issues supercede race

Wyvetter Younge, state representative for 15 years, calls for a coming together of black and white people to solve economic and social problems without reference to skin color — on either side. The people of St. Clair and Madison counties have more in common than they recognize, and they need to sit down and realize what East St. Louis is and isn't, she said.

"The area has an interdependency, and its problems can be solved only by sitting down together as people, or peoples, and beginning to look at our problems together, depending on what our perspectives are. And one of the biggest common assets we have, and one that should be used to the benefit of all of us, is 4,200 acres of riverfront from Madison County to the end of St. Clair County.

"I think part of the (future) prosperity of the region is directly related to our capability to see that riverfront as one tract, one development opportunity," she said.

"Our big challenge is to be able to work together to come out to the highest and best use of the riverfront area.

"We have the escalation of hate by the newspapers, I mean the newspapers writing in such a way as to promulgate hate. We need a program that gets us down emotionally from all this bad feeling among racial groups. I don't think

East St. Louis can recover until there is general agreement to the market share in this region, and that can't happen until people begin to feel better about each other."

Issues are more important than the color of one's skin or anything else, she said. Both sides have got to quit talking about the white man wants or the black man wants, and start talking about what "we-all" want. Leadership in this effort, she said, has to come from the church, civic and social areas in addition to politicians. "It is absolutely clear that we have people problems, environment, economic, that we have to solve as a region.

"Economically, East St. Louis is dead," she said. "We have to redefine its market. The people who are here came here to work in the smokestack industries of the past. Now what is its new use? I think this region has to say 'This is the market share we are going to locate in East St. Louis.' It is as simple, and as complicated, as that. And what is keeping that from happening is our attitudes."

Wyvetter Younge was the legislator that held out to the ninth hour seeking amendments to the governors "bailout bill" for East St. Louis and other distressed cities — a bailout that would give East St. Louis a $34 million loan. Her action was called treachery to her people in a News-Democrat editorial. Her holdout was daily page one fare in the same newspaper and the St. Louis Post-Dispatch. She said she held out until it was untenable to hold out any longer, but she finally was given 45 minutes with the governor in which she said she reached important agreements — agreements that make her say now of the revised bill, "The sky is the limit as to what the total package can do for East St. Louis if certain things happen locally."

The "coming together" is one of those things.

In her meeting with the governor, she said she told him that piling on $34 million in debt for the city to repay did not solve any problems. The problem is the economic base. It is gone, absolutely fallen apart. The issue is one of economic development, restructuring to increase the capability of the town to pay back its debt while it provides essential services. The governor listened, said he thought her proposals were a reasonable addition to the bill, and agreed to have citizens of East St. Louis sit down with the Department of Commerce and Community Affairs and to work on a redevelopment structure.

"What can come out of this could be the economic revitalization of East St. Louis. What can come out is the restructuring of quality environment. What could come out of it is much more than they were getting at. They were getting at just fire, police and trash pickup. We need fiscal integrity in the City Hall plus those essential

The Eads Bridge, dedicated by President U. S. Grant, and the Mississippi River, both part of our common heritage

services, but we need too to do something about the environment, hazardous waste, flooding and unemployment. What I am saying is that when you talk about economic development, these other things can't be put off. Anytime you are going to do something, you have to talk about all of that. It's complicated, yes, but I think after the negotiations we will come up with a plan to handle all those problems, and that's what East St. Louis has got to have."

On an immediate basis, she said that because of the governor's anger with Mayor Carl Officer, all of the state's resources have been frozen to East St. Louis. She said the governor promised her to have all the departments look into their budgets for additional monies for East St. Louis, and hopefully motor fuel tax funds and other assets will be freed so the town can get on with the business of rebuilding itself.

The general assembly gave the city the power to raise sales tax and sent to the governor a license for riverboat gambling and ways to raise payback funds.

Asked what faith she has in DCCA - the Department of Commerce and Community Affairs, the representative said, "DCCA has to be completely restructured, DCCA has testified on many occasions that it is a total failure in East St. Louis, and that's why I was very anxious that the governor personally agree that the citizens will sit down with DCCA to draw up a redevelopment plan.

It doesn't have the capacity even to understand what is good for East St. Louis much less do it; it doesn't have the will, it doesn't have the competency, it is a total failure not only in East St. Louis, but so far as small business is concerned, all over the state."

She said that she has other feelings about the system, especially in terms of public aid. She wants public aid recipients employed. "Isn't that best for people?" She said that East St. Louis is in a depression that may be the forerunner of a national recession. "Paul Simon is right, there is a government responsibility to the jobless." We need WPA, CCC type projects where public facilities would be built and people put to work. We are at a phase in our history where we give people checks without their having to work. I've always felt that we could combine the work to be done with the resources of government and have people working."

A petition for city manager government was ready as we talked. She said the mayor and aldermanic council agreed that a city manager is needed, and that she hoped the people would provide for city manager government and that a blue-ribbon committee would look nationwide for the best accredited city manger, someone familiar with budgets and financial records, which are city weaknesses. She said that the governor has promised that if this happens the state will give the city manager cooperation.

Younge thinks it is important that the first money from the bailout goes to improve the police department. She wants it to meet national accreditation standards, to be the best there is, the pride of East St. Louis, and to give assurance of street safety in East St. Louis. "The question of crime is close to being resolved."

Light rail will help the city, and it should give immediate attention to development in the area at Fifth and Missouri for the East St. Louis terminal. She does not think the perception of safety will be a major problem. When the Martin Luther King bridge was closed, white people were driving all over East St. Louis finding their way to Eads bridge, she said, and they really know there is no trouble. But she agreed safety needs to be demonstrated.

As to the Jefferson Memorial, she said she wished someone beside the Southwestern Illinois Development Authority were handling it; that it needed more involvement by the citizens. "Economic development has to involve people, I work for economic democracy too."

As for the riverboat gambling, the state will have its money there too, and it will protect it. "The boat and the parking lot probably will be the safest place in the world."

> *Our job is to lessen tension and bring about good will. We are in a psychological war. It's very much like the Jews in Warsaw, people who don't know you hate you because you are from East St. Louis, you know. We must take it very carefully, first a successful police force, trash collections, clean up the city, do the riverfront right, then people can begin to come in and have pleasant experiences.*
>
> —Wyvetter Younge

She was excited too about the return of Dr. Cleveland Chandler of Howard University, who has worked with ghettos and come up with an economic model for growth in the local economy. It involves five sectors: household, business, finance and banking, public, export and imports. Move in these five areas and the whole economy will move, Chandler said. East St. Louis needs new financial and banking resources, she said, charging that there is hard redlining. You can't borrow money in East St. Louis for residences or new businesses, she said. She hopes to have the city council, the DCCA and local citizens working on the Chandler program. Younge has been working with a group of citizens since Chandler's visit here a year ago.

Returning to her central theme, she said "The big problem is how to work together to improve this region, a part of which is East St. Louis, to see how it is to our common advantage as a section of the country to move forward economically and get beyond this whole question that race is the cause of everything. There are civic and economic questions. We must become more sophisticated as a group of people.

"I'd hope that in the early part of the 1990s we'd plan how we were going to be the latter part of the century. I've just got a good feeling about it, really. I have faith that it will turn in the right direction."

And that's a high note to end this discussion.

Will McGaughy

Will McGaughy: Better to be inside with the action than outside hollering

Will McGaughy thinks East St. Louis will be one of the greatest cities in Illinois.

But he wants to make sure that the black people of East St. Louis will be there to enjoy it and to participate in the prosperity.

McGaughy suspects a master plot to run the blacks out of East St. Louis by building Section 8 housing in the O'Fallon, Belleville, the other outlying towns, and by making the housing in East St. Louis untenable. Then there will be a flip-flop and the whites will move to East St. Louis and the South End where they can sit on their decks and watch the Arch.

"But Will McGaughy will be right here, watching the Arch from his deck," McGaughy said as we sat on that deck at 1402 S. H St., just north of what used to be called Rush City.

McGaughy said the first East St. Louis economic bailout legislation offered by the state provided for overseers to govern all city finances; part of the conspiracy to take East St. Louis away from the blacks. It was State Rep. Wyvetter Younge who forced the changes in that plan and made it acceptable; she did what she was there to do, McGaughy says with conviction. He writhes with anger as he discusses Belleville News-Democrat editorials that criticize her for endangering the future of the city with her holdout against the bail-out bill. She may do some foolish things sometimes, but she is for the people, and she forced the changes that made the bailout bill acceptable, he said.

In the process she also obtained pledges by Gov. Jim Thompson to follow through on authorizations and appropriations that have been passed years ago, but which have been bottled up, including money for sewers and a housing manufacturing plant.

Some people call Will McGaughy crazy. They mean he does things they consider irresponsible.

Sometimes Will McGaughy calls himself crazy. He means he takes chances doing things he thinks need to be done.

He's not crazy.

McGaughy, 57, first burst into the attention of the citizens of outer St. Clair County back in the '70s when he brought a truckload of dogs from the East St. Louis dog pound to Belleville and turned them loose in the new county courthouse. He was commissioner of health, education and welfare for the City of East St. Louis, and had found that it was the county's responsibility to impound strays. Vic Canty was County Board chairman, and had made promises, but nothing was happening. Will said children in East St. Louis had to carry clubs to beat off the strays. He found a way to focus attention on the problem.

"Some of those dogs went right into the offices and up to the women working there. One of them patted the dirty, mangiest dog on the head and said "poor thing." Hell, they thought more of the dogs than us," he said, his blackness showing.

Will never forgets he is black, or his "brothers." He's not a racist, he doesn't dislike whites, nor does he try to use them. But he thinks black.

"How, Will," I asked, "can you get people to come down into East St. Louis? White people are afraid to come here."

Will's son Felix Xavier answered for Will. "I'm afraid to go to Freeburg at night, or Pinckneyville, or lots of other towns."

That's the difference between thinking black and thinking white.

But as a matter of fact, Will, his son and other guests on that porch agreed that whites in East St. Louis, minding their business, seldom have a problem; when they come looking for drugs, or white men looking for black women, or messing around doing something they shouldn't be doing anywhere, then sometimes they "get their heads blown off." But most crime in East St. Louis is black against black. Thousands of whites still drive through East St. Louis on Bond Avenue, Missouri Avenue, State Street, even past 15th and Broadway, once thought the worst intersection in the city, unharmed every day.

McGaughy cited the author's experience driving and photographing throughout the city for months with no problem, few even paying any attention.

McGaughy is the East St. Louis Township supervisor. He also has been a member of the County Board of Supervisors since 1978. He serves on important committees, and he affects what happens in East St. Louis and in all of St. Clair County. But he started out a "street person," a hustler, who never finished high school.

Will had only an eighth grade education when he went into the Army as an infantryman. When he got out he was what he described as a street person hustling dollars shooting dice, playing cards in a tavern at 19th and Wilson. At 21, he was in a car outside the tavern waiting with some others for the shift change at Monsanto Chemical Co. on payday — waiting for the workers to come and be hustled. Another driver bet the driver of the car he was in that he could beat him driving to the Monsanto gate and back. Will said he had no bet on and he wasn't going to get killed in a drag race, so he got out of the car. As they were returning the railroad crossing gates came down and he thought the race was over, but they shot through the gates; the first car stopped, the car he had been in skidded into it then came down the hill and ran over Will and three others. He lost his right leg at the knee.

He studied and took a test to obtain a GED (general educational development high school equivalency certificate), and studied accounting at Mildred Louise Business School for two terms. His grammar is not the best, he sometimes drifts into the street language that helps him communicate so well with "the brothers," and yet he is just as apt to use technical terms he has picked up in government service of one kind or another. One recalls that Congressman Mel Price was a terrible public speaker; that former East St. Louis Mayor Al Fields, as shrewd a politician as Mayor Charles Daley, was almost incoherent in conversation and that Red Foley, when he was East St. Louis township commissioner, would have sounded like a noon factory whistle if his cuss words were beeped out. Whites have trouble understanding Will, but if they listen closely enough to understand, they will hear straight talk. He may be wrong, but he claims that as his right, too.

Will took a job with Charles Merritts driving a cab, became shop steward of Teamsters Local 971. They were in negotiations over pay, terms for leasing cabs. He was driving home one night when a shot was fired at him. He called a 10-50 on his radio — a call for the cabbies to rally — and took off in pursuit. The cars raced through the South End and Monsanto to the man's home. Police came, but did nothing to him. Will wrote a sealed letter telling what he thought was happening, took it to the East St. Louis Journal to be opened in case of his death, and found a man with a shotgun to ride in the back seat of his cab. But the other cabbies urged him to back off, saying he should quit before he was killed. He decided that if they weren't willing to fight for a better contract, neither should he, so he quit driving a cab.

McGaughy was anti-government, the guy on the other side. He got up in city Central Democratic Committee meetings and told them what they were doing wrong. He was among activist demonstrators in the '70s, but came to the conclusion that there was no point in being "outside hollering when the action was going on inside." He ran unsuccessfully for township supervisor, but was elected to the County Board in 1978. When Township Supervisor Clyde Jordan died, he succeeded him in that post. As a County Board member, he was appointed to the St. Clair County Mental Health Board while this writer was president of the board, and while the Specialized Living Center in Swansea was being completed and staffed.

He established a predecessor to the WIC (women, infant and children) program providing surplus food to pregnant women and lactating mothers in East St. Louis in the '70s, the first in the nation, and set up the Metro-East Health Services Center at 15th Street and Broadway which was a predecessor to the health maintenance organizations (HMOs) of today. He was ousted by the board for lack of education and a professional hired — a high-flying expert who flew to his California home weekends at the agency's expense. He was indicted for stealing funds, Will recalls, but never served time. Meanwhile, the center closed and the building still stands empty.

McGaughy said that he went into politics "to try to make some changes within the structure. I haven't been able to make all the changes I want, but I have been able to effect some changes, you know."

When the Model Cities urban renewal program was started about 1972, Will was to be relocated across town. He refused, buying a house for $1,000 and spending the $15,000 allowed by HUD and a great deal of his own money to reconstruct it. Now he is building a waterfall and fish pond in his back yard. He said he wants to show you don't have to leave the ghetto to live comfortably.

So here are some of Will's views:

1. Crime. There are maybe 30 tough criminals in East St. Louis. The other criminals are "punks," who would change their ways if there were alternatives; jobs and opportunity and law enforcement.

East St. Louis has some excellent policemen. They solve murders without the Major Case Squad, and as part of that squad go into other communities and solve crimes. The police force overall needs equipment and encouragement.

Newspapers make East St. Louis sound like the capitol of killing. Some of the most gruesome murders have been in Belleville.

2. Drugs. They are largely local; significant but local. People from East St. Louis go to other urban centers, buy drugs and bring them back to turn over to dealers who pass them on to peddlers.

"The average young brother out there is selling dope because he don't get no money any other way. Other brothers out there are using that dope because he don't see no future. If they see a future, they got some other avenue, they can be changed.

"If I've got jobs, alternatives, I can stop 98 per cent of this crime myself.

"If you get the sellers out of the picture, the men who bring in the dope will have to sell it themselves, and they'll get caught. Now as long as they don't get caught bringing it in, they turn it and the chance of arrest over to the sellers.

"I can go anywhere in this city and I don't worry about dope. I've never seen anyone selling it or using it. I don't know why. Maybe they respect me, maybe they're afraid of me because I'm crazy and they don't know what I'd do.

"I gave a picnic in Orr-Weathers Homes, where they say dope is the worst. I invited the brothers to come, and the old folks in the project too. After all, the brothers are their kids and grandkids. I had 2,000 weiners and barbecue sandwiches, snoots and all that. There was not one incident, not one. People sitting in chairs eating with their kids and grandkids, maybe some were dope dealers, I don't know, they all looked alike to me and they don't do it around me.

"One dope dealer come to me, told me he needed to be locked down for treatment. I couldn't help him. I gave him $20 I had in my pocket. He said he needed help. I found out he was selling dope to kids. He got sent up, doing seven years now. He begged for help."

3. Jobs. McGaughy said he can't count the calls he gets every week from people looking for jobs. "I can't help them. I could run 'em around, I don't do that. I tell them I don't have anything and I think they respect me for telling the truth."

Factories need to be attracted. To get them we need good schools for the children, good police protection, decent city services, fire protection, tax incentives, a shopping district. We have a prime location, we should offer the incentives to get the plants and get more taxpayers.

4. Taxes. The key to bringing taxes into line is code enforcement. Property owners tear down old housing rather than repairing it, taking the buildings off the tax rolls. The city could make the owners repair or sell the buildings to someone who would repair them and offer them to the people. As the housing is removed, tax rates climb. Property owners also could be forced to keep their weeds cut,

McGaughy says his home, top photo, once looked like his neighbor's, below

improve the appearance of the city. It would take a whole staff of lawyers, but in the long run, it would be worth it, he said.

Tax rates are too high, but those who are "all right" get certificates of error, other ways to reduce their taxes; those who aren't "all right" pay too much.

5. Development. Exciting breakthroughs are coming because of location, riverboat gambling, the airport (Scott joint use), light rail, the Arch. People come from all over the world to see that Arch; "Look down the street, you look right through the center of it from here."

6. Housing. The federal housing officials and the East St. Louis Housing Authority seem to be working against the people of East St. Louis. The public housing is taken off the tax rolls, making the city poorer. There are houses boarded up all over town because the tenants are suing the Housing Authority and the buildings are tied up legally. The people sue because they pay forever and never get title to the houses (See related article from the Housing Authority). Other buildings that could have been turned into apartments or condominiums by HUD or some other federal agency have been left to deteriorate. The old Christian Welfare Hospital is an example; so was St. Teresa's Academy. "Some vacant public housing could be turned over to tenants for a few dollars and they could fix them up." Instead they stand vacant.

7. Population. The census will show a big loss, but that's because the Census Bureau is not doing its job. McGaughy did not send in his return, and in July no one had contacted him. "If they can't find me, how are they going to find the other brothers." Many of the housing units have more people staying in them that are authorized, and the residents are not about to turn in papers saying they are staying there. The blacks that have left East St. Louis and are paying rents of $500 to $600 a month in O'Fallon and Belleville are being urged to return.

8. Politics. Will is for Carl Officer's re-election as mayor, period. Officer is not a people person, he's a businessman, " but that's just his nature."

Bob Kassing

Kassing says he's the original cynical pessimist

You've got to have leadership. There's no leadership down there. Anytime something goes wrong, it's whitey trying to take over.

Bob Kassing is president of the First Illinois Bank, 327 Missouri Ave., on the northwest corner of Collinsville and Missouri avenues. His uncle was Ollie Briedecker who was president and chairman of the board of the bank when it was First National.

Interviewed in his office next to what once was the busiest retail street in Southern Illinois, Kassing said "I dunno, I don't see any hope if you want the truth. I guess I'm the original cynical pessimist around here, but I've been here ... I'm not from East St. Louis, but my uncle was president of this bank at one time, and I've been coming here since I was a child. Lived in South St. Louis. I've been here in my capacity now for 24 years, and I always thought maybe 10 or 15 years ago we were at the absolute bottom, but I don't see a bottom."

"You sound hopeless," I said.

"Maybe I've been here too long. I don't see any hope with that gentleman in City Hall running it. Nor his council."

But Kassing also is on the board of East St. Louis Junior Achievement.

"We run a Junior Achievement center at 72nd and State Streets, probably one of the most successful in the entire Mississippi Valley. We've got kids that we have to turn away because we can't get enough advisers. We're out there three nights a week, have four bays. We have trouble getting advisers for obvious reasons, a hard time getting women to go out there. Two nights we have four bays; we are trying to fill the fourth bay the third night.

"We're probably serving several hundred kids

out there. They show up, they're very respectful, you don't have any problems. And if there are problems, the center manager takes care of them right away. And it's all volunteer work. Monsanto, Union Electric, Illinois Power, the banks and so forth.

"We also run a program at the high school. The kids in the high school, some of them really want to be taught; they want to know how they can better themselves and get out, I guess. I don't know whether we help them or not. If you've ever been privileged to go to an annual banquet, they always have two speakers, a boy and a girl who are achievers. And it is an outstanding evening. It makes you feel good."

"You are not as pessimistic as you say you are, you find good in the people," I suggested.

"We've got a lot of good people here."

"I have heard there are blacks who won't take a stand because they don't want to be involved in politics," I suggested.

"I've had some people tell me that.

"I dunno," he continued, "I don't even know who could run for mayor that I would give strong support. We have always hesitated to throw our support behind anybody. You always run the danger of being called a racist trying to control whoever with campaign funds, etc."

As for Carl Officer:

"He and I haven't spoken for years. I can do without him very easily. We lost the bank accounts years ago; we just recently got them back, but we get nothing but garnishments. (City Atty. Eric) Vickers called the other day when they (the city's firemen) had the garnishment and wanted to know if we could hold off 30 days before we filed our answer, and I told him no, and asked him 'Why in hell don't you pay the firemen the agreed upon amount and you wouldn't be garnished.' He said 'quit telling us how to run City Hall.' I said 'Then quit trying to tell me how to run the bank. If you don't like it, take the deposits out right now. We did well without them before, and we'll do well without them now.'"

The bank doesn't have a large loan demand, but "makes do" with other investments. Housing loans mainly are FHA, 90 per cent guaranteed by the federal government. Stan Sieron, one of the biggest private owners of real estate in East St. Louis, is on the bank board.

Is there red lining?

Kassing said every house is looked at individually, and appraisals, for a quick sale are made on all houses. A problem occurs when the house may be good, but there is a burnout in the block, empty lots grown up in weeds, poorly maintained houses that affect the resale value of the house the buyer is seeking. And there are relatively few blocks without a burnout or a trash-filled lot.

"There are some areas worse than others. Go around Pfizer (Chemical Co.). That's really bad," he said.

Is the tax burden a problem for East St. Louisans?

"I imagine the taxes are somewhat significant." He said people pay as much in East St. Louis as in Fairview Heights or Belleville, but "for half a house." The city's plummeting assessments result in climbing tax rates.

Will Metro Link help the city?

"It can't hurt, but I can't see anybody coming down here and park their car and take the Metro Link to St. Louis."

Are you afraid to come down here?

"No, I'm down here all the time though, that's different. We have a hard time getting help to come down here unless they are from the area or worked down here in the past."

Does the perception of danger exceed the danger?

"Yes, I think. Once we get people to come down here we don't have as big a problem because we are right off the highway and bang, right into our parking lot. We've got a guard downstairs."

The Metro Link parking lot will be just two blocks down the street.

"I know, but you can walk two blocks down and get accosted to buy crack, too. You know how Belleville people feel about East St. Louis, there is no way they are going to come down here and park their cars. I live in Chesterfield. That link isn't going to do a damn thing for me."

If it goes to Scott?

"I don't see them moving out there."

"I hear blacks are begging for work. Couldn't it take them to jobs at Scott?"

"Who are you hearing that from?"

"The people they are asking," I responded.

"There are people who want a job and people who want to work. There is a difference. I think Metro Link will be super for people wanting to go to St. Louis, but it will be a helluva long time before it gets to Scott. They have more problems there because there is a natural rail line from downtown St. Louis to Lambert," Kassing said.

Will the gambling boat help?

"I agree with Mearl."

(Mearl Justus opposed gambling on boats saying it will bring more crime.)

"How many people are going to come over and spend $1,000 a day to gamble on a riverboat? You've got (gambling at) Fairmont Park. Are they making big money? If they are depending on riverboat gambling to pay the $34 million loan (governor's state bailout) back, I don't want to buy

Bob Kassing

A burnout or a poorly maintained house, destroys the loan value of every house in the block

any of their revenue bonds.

"Something's wrong with our society if we think gambling is the only answer, an alternative to hard work, good ideas — and it's not Illinois and East St. Louis, look at the country, everybody wants to have a lottery, and what's it done for education in the State of Illinois?"

What about the riverfront and expansion of the Jefferson National Expansion Memorial?

"I'm on Target 2000 and we support development of the riverfront. But he confided that the site being below the levee wall doesn't help."

He isn't aware of any interest by investors in condos or other large-scale developments on the riverfront.

"One of Carl's pipe dreams."

No, Jerry Costello's.

"Jerry's been talking to *** ****. He doesn't have any money, any of that kind of money. He's more of a developer, needs financing.

"Jerry has been extremely good for East St. Louis. He has done more than lip service. We have had him talk to Target 2000 several times.

"Unfortunately, they won't let the city have federal money unless they funnel it through somebody like Target 2000." Target 2000 is composed of a mixture of blacks and whites, businessmen and labor unions, and is working to get East St. Louis on track by the year 2000.

The federal government required multiple signatures including Target 2000 representatives to pay for the repaving and sidewalks for Broadway, Collinsville and Missouri Avenues.

Target 2000 solicited $60,000 form St. Louis corporations to fix the Jones Park swimming pool, and operated it for one year, hiring the life guards and concession stand operators and supervising the operation. For the only time in its history, it actually made money. The city took it over the second year. It is closed in the summer of 1990.

Target 2000 has plans to build a subdivision of moderately priced homes near 72nd and State in an attempt to get school teachers to move back into the city. The project has been plagued by many problems, the latest being the discovery of a "damn piece of Indian pottery" that added $20,000 to the cost.

Target 2000 has its own financial problems. You can only go to the same financial sources so many times, and there are few corporations left to carry the cost. You go to Rotary, Junior Achievement, Target 2000, we're all the same guys. We sometimes don't know what meeting we're at, there are so few of us.

"Basically, without Monsanto Chemical Co. all the organizations would be in trouble, because they contribute quite handsomely to all of them, either with time or people or money."

Target 2000 was 10 years old a year ago. "It wants to go out of business before 2000."

You don't want to see if your goals are reached?

He half-smiled.

Union Bank President Ron Wallace

Ron Wallace

Wishing on a star dangerous

If East St. Louis is going to turn around...if Southwestern Illinois is going to continue to expand, somebody has got to come to grips with the cancer right here in the middle of it, and what we've got is a bunch of general practitioners trying to cure a cancer patient. They all have varied opinions, they are parochial in their attitudes, so we're not getting the pulling together by a team. We need specialists that can get to the root of the problem and possibly come up with a cure for it.

This is the view of Ron Wallace, president of Union Bank in East St. Louis.

"I don't see a cancer specialist on the horizon," he said. "I don't see the cancer specialist in the form of a city manager who is hired by local elected officials. I see a continuation of the same parochialism that is to a large degree responsible for us being where we are today."

The prospects for the city are very difficult, Wallace continued. "We hang our hopes from time to time on a few bits of good news — like the extension of the Jefferson National Memorial to this side of the river as a catalyst. Well, I don't know that's the catalyst. I don't believe riverboat gambling will be the catalyst for anything. I've been reading an article in the Christian Science Monitor. Here's Atlantic City still awaiting its jackpot as a result of casino gambling. If you get a few steps away from the Taj Mahal and those other casinos, it's absolutely a shambles there. This (and he shows a picture of a rundown house) is not atypical of East St. Louis."

Wallace refers to efforts to develop new housing, and a housing factory, "all worthwhile projects except you have to have jobs to make them work." Some say you need housing before jobs, and the other side asks "How can you have housing if you don't have people gainfully employed so they can pay for the housing?" He said he understands a housing factory has to be able to manufacture and market 200 units a year to break even, and the nature of the product requires the market be nearby. "Can East St. Louis absorb 200 units a year? I question that."

He is a member of Target 2000 which plans a new subdivision to bring school teachers and other professionals who have moved elsewhere back into the city. "I hear a good deal about some of those folks out there," he said. "They are professionals, middle-income wage earners and on and on, who are waiting to get back if someone can come up with the kinds of housing and the kinds of amenities that would make it worth their while to come back to their first love. But I don't know if there are enough of those kinds of folks to fill 20 units of new housing, or 50, or more."

Robert Vancil's plan to us tax increment financing to reduce the effect of high taxes on home buyers has merit, Wallace said (see Vancil interview). "The burden of the real estate tax is beyond a burden, its unthinkable. Even the TIF doesn't do nearly enough just to relieve that burden. A $60,000 home would be assessed at $20,000 and at a $20 tax rate, would be taxed at $4,000 per year. If TIF gets it down to $3,000, it would still be too much, and the home could not be resold for $60,000 because of where it is."

Getting private enterprise to replace some public housing would be a lot better, he said, "if you could get private enterprise to come in and run it."

"Public housing has proved what it isn't, and that's at the very painful expense of this city and to cities all over the country. It is something that happened well intentioned, but it doesn't work. The sooner you can get East St. Louis and all cities in this country shifted to a privatization of housing the better off we are going to be. But I don't see that happening overnight; not anytime soon."

(Some 14,000 East St. Louisans live in public housing — 35 percent of the preliminary 1990 census figures. They pay no real estate taxes to support the city and its school system.)

Wallace sees Metro Link of benefit to the community in creating construction jobs and as long as its terminus is in the city, but once it is extended to Belleville or Scott "I don't see the stops at this terminal as meaningful anymore. It's not a panacea.

"One of my concerns is that we have been down so long in this community that we hang our hopes on stars, and that can be a very traumatic, disappointing experience when the star plummets and you go down with it. That concerns me a lot."

There are things that can help in the short run, but they shouldn't be mistaken for long-term turnarounds, he said.

"I guess the single most important thing that is in my mind is coming to grips with the political problem of this community, and I call it a problem because I think it is a very, very strained, very hurtful political problem. Unless we get the principle of strong fiscal management, it is going to be pretty much of the continuation of the same. We may see some neighborhood pockets gussie up, we may see some low to moderate income housing begin to spring up, probably in clusters in various parts of the community, but I don't know that beyond that we are going to see business return to the community. We have very little to offer in terms of basic services such as sewers, public works, police, fire..."

"One of my concerns is that we have been down so long in this community that we hang our hopes on stars, and that can be a very traumatic, disappointing experience when the star plummets and you go down with it. That concerns me a lot."

Like many East St. Louisans, Wallace would like to see more appreciation of the academic achievements of the school system rather just that it produces fine athletes. He said that his bank sponsored an essay contest with a $1,000 savings bond as a first prize, $500 second and $100 third. "We were absolutely blown over by the quality of the essays. These kids write well, they think creatively, they think with some depth. They were a real credit not only to East Side and Lincoln, but they would be a credit to Belleville West, Belleville East, O'Fallon and on and on. We are doing more here than training football and basketball players."

Some of the divisions are caused by a lack of communication, and leaders are not communicating because they are not making the effort, he suggested. That is probably compounded by some of the media throwing a roadblock to open and honest communication. If there's a bone of contention between (John) Baricevic and (Carl) Officer, I guess I don't see the News-Democrat doing anything to allay that, to bring the sides together and say "Fellows, aren't we really saying the same thing?"

Carl Officer, Wallace said, is charismatic, bright, has a quick mind, but "he is changing. He's not the same guy who was first elected."

Sen. Alan J. Dixon enthusiastic speaker

Riverfront key

Economic climate for business investment vital

Alan J. Dixon of Belleville has lived close to East St. Louis and its problems all of his life as he progressed through a series of state offices to the U.S. Senate, and he has seen East St. Louis decline with the loss of smokestack industry. He sees the restoration of an economic climate that can attract private sector businesses as the most important single thing to help the city and its people.

"Even if one would assume that East St. Louis has the most productive government climate given its situation — and I don't assume that, incidentally — you still couldn't make the grade on the tax base it has," he said. "You need an improvement in the level of government services, but beyond that you need a support system that works," and he said there is none. "I would like to see us try to find methods through enterprise zones and other avenues to bring private sector investments back to East St. Louis.

"You know, to the extent that I've been able to do that, for instance, on the Armed Services Committee, we've done some things for one business that has a defense contract. That sort of thing is something we could do that could help significantly.

"Obviously if we could get waterfront development in final shape in such a way that it would be a significant tourism attraction, like the Arch is across the river...the Arch has really worked. Tens of millions of people have come to St. Louis for no other reason than to visit the Arch, and as a consequence of that you've seen this remarkable renaissance, this recovery of a downtown section of St. Louis," he continued.

"Obviously the ball park had part to do with it, and other things, but you can see when you get some kind of an anchor, it's almost like a shopping center, you get a good anchor and other stores will follow. I think that's what we need in East St. Louis. If it has that and then we had some really fine housing along the water, and some restaurants, bars, theaters, other things, I think that would be a beginning," he said.

On riverboat gambling, he said he hated to see gambling promoted, and did not see it as a good solution, but "maybe some riverboat gambling there will bring in some people, will help a little." But, he added, "A boat on the river isn't going to

The river is a special thing

help much unless you've got some restaurants, theaters, bars, shopping areas and other things."

The river, he said, is a special thing. "I'm reminded of my own experiences out here (in Washington) where I lived for awhile.

"I live on the Hill now, but when I first came to Washington I lived in a condominium in what they call Crystal Gateway Condominiums, in Crystal City, across the Potomac, by the National Airport. There had been nothing but junkyards there for old abandoned automobiles. There was a brick yard there and a sand place where they dug the sand for highway construction and other uses, and a trashy motel with short-term services; just all that kind of stuff.

"A fellow by the name of Charles E. Smith took that Potomac waterfront and redeveloped it with hotels and restaurants and bars and theaters and an underground shopping center and these condos and other things and now literally he has gone all the way to the end of that section, to the 14th Street Marriott, there at the bridge, and torn that down to build new structures.

"The whole thing is an absolutely renovated area that was nothing but a slum. Obviously the riverfront on the East Side of the (Mississippi) River presents the same opportunities. We see that all along the river here — we see it not only by Arlington in Crystal City but in Washington where they've taken those old warehouses and put in what now amount to million-dollar apartments. It wouldn't be for those prices, but with the immediate access to St. Louis by the bridges, that area (in East St. Louis) could be a tremendous area for profoundly important renovation with pretty expensive housing" and the rest. "Then," he said, "if we could get some private sector businesses of other types into the community," he could see how the good economic effects could spread across the city from the river.

Asked how all this might come about, he said he thinks there has to be private sector involvement by somebody like Charles E. Smith. In Washington, there are several "big shooters" who do that sort of thing. "When I came to Washington 10 years ago, Pennsylvania Avenue was a junk street; now it's gorgeous," and there are other sections in Arlington that have been rebuilt by these big investors. There's that kind of opportunity for the east side of the river, he said, if you can find the right kind of entrepreneurs.

"Government needs to play its role as well. The problem we have now with the...federal budget is such that there isn't a lot that you can do, but don't forget light rail is functioning; light rail is coming from the airport right into East St. Louis and on from East St. Louis to Belleville, O'Fallon and Scott Air Force Base, believe it or not. So you have the transport system in place. You just have a lot of things that'd make it work..."

Dixon is working with the congressional delegation for an expansion of the Jefferson National Expansion Memorial to the East St. Louis riverfront and the development of a major ethnic

Quality brick homes boarded up by HUD, removed from t he housing market and never on the tax rolls. Some want HUD Secretary Jack Kemp to come see the extent of the problem in East St. Louis

cultures' museum there as a tourist attraction. It could be the first anchor for riverfront development.

Dixon said that with the East St. Louis government's recent record, he'd like to see the state involved in the development. He recalled a Pete Fox with the old Department of Business and Economic Development — now called the Department of Business and Community Affairs — who recently was putting together a bond issue for a stadium for a ballpark in Milwaukee. There are lots of people who could make it work, he said.

Dixon said he is supporting several bills, including one by Sen. Paul Simon, to help provide job training that could benefit East St. Louis; that could help make sure that the unemployed citizens could participate in a restored economy. He said that the junior college could and should be providing basic educational support systems for any emerging job market.

Dixon also supports joint civilian-military use at Scott Air Force Base and this could help provide job opportunities for East St. Louis.

Regarding the city's housing stock, he said congress has passed a new housing bill supported by Jack Kemp, secretary of the Department of Housing and Urban Development (HUD), with a "very definite tilt toward renovation of existing housing stock." It particularly would focus on houses recaptured by the government for failure to meet commitments by owners and occupiers of those houses all over America, he said. Sylvia Thompson, a very well-qualified black member of Dixon's staff and his specialist on urban housing, said the bill definitely could fit East St. Louis' situation. Renovation keeps buildings on tax rolls, as opposed to public housing. Kemp even has proposed that selected public housing be sold to its occupants to get them back on the rolls, provide pride of ownership and reduce the federal government's obligations.

"There's housing stock in East St. Louis that you can buy for almost nothing...Let me tell you something," Dixon said. "I live on the Hill in a 94-year-old house that cost me in six figures that sold for something like $15,000 or $16,000 in the 1940s. So don't say areas don't come back; you see that all over the Hill here in Washington, where every house is either remodeled or in some stage of it."

Dixon said he would talk with Kemp about making a personal trip to look into the housing situation in East St. Louis, and perhaps could accompany him to the city.

Front Street New York Central "Big Four" office building gutted, above; intermodal warehouse crumbling, bottom photo

Hundreds of trailers remain from piggy-back operations, but weeds and grass surround the wheels; abandoned GM&O freight warehouse stands between Cargill and planned park site

Tracks have been removed from former rail yards, even the bricks are broken; abandoned platforms, rusting trailer remain. East St. Louis once was nation's second largest rail terminal

A nest of houses in 100 block of B Street, once called Bloody Island, next to Five Star trailer repair

Railroad car repair business at Trendley and Front Street has closed

Ramp once led through wall to levee, but dirt has been dumped inside the gates

Flag shows proximity of park site to Cargill. Lower picture is of modern grain truck dump at Cargill

Restaurant and bar at Broadway and Front Street still operating

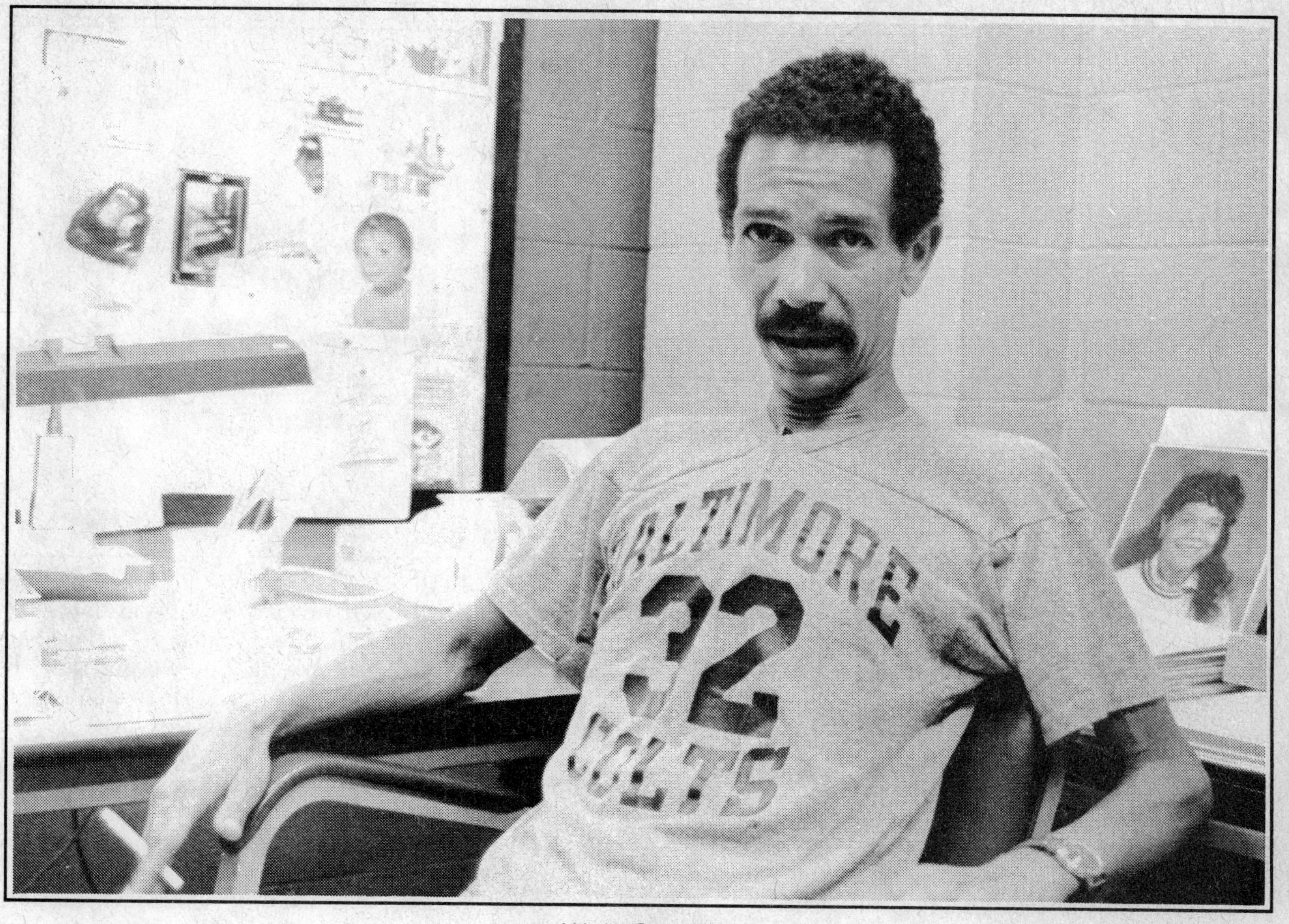

Wally Carson

Cultural Museum on riverfront, a dream to marry Metro East, West

Wally Carson is the executive of the East St. Louis Area Development Authority, and he has a dream, a dream that he feels must come true.

It is a multi-cultural ethnic museum "smack dab in the middle" of the Jefferson National Expansion Memorial extension on the East St. Louis riverfront, and accompanying it, a large amphitheater. It would complement and complete the Jefferson Memorial with a world class museum celebrating the contributions of the various ethnic groups that shaped our nation and moved through this area going west: French, English, American Indians, Germans, Polish, blacks, others.

"There is nothing in the country that I know of that celebrates that great event from 1730 through the end of the 1800s," he said.

"This could be an anchor development that could marry the whole region," Metro-East to Metro-West, and could provide the spark for riverfront development and East St. Louis redevelopment.

It could be financed — $30 million to $40 million — with revenue bonds then turned over to the National Park Service to manage and maintain. That way it wouldn't even show up in the federal red ink.

It would be complemented by Metro-Link which could shuttle Arch visitors across the river to see the rest of the memorial, and to enjoy the spectacular view from the East St. Louis riverfront of the Arch and downtown St. Louis. It could be given a sense of security by architectural design. It would open the door to East St. Louis' participation in the United States' fastest expanding industry — tourism.

Carson would like to see a park of 100 to 200 acres. U.S. Rep. Jerry Costello sees the park coming in 1990, but it might be as little as 17 acres to start. He thinks it is better to start with whatever

New National Food Store at 25th and State streets

can be donated. He favors a smaller park — the Memorial in St. Louis is only about 80 acres — so as to keep more of the riverfront taxable. Mayor Carl Officer also wants to avoid removing more land than necessary from tax rolls.

The riverboat gambling "is not going to be the financial salvation of East St. Louis," in Carson's eyes. Revenue must come from real estate taxes and sales taxes. "Or an increase in population living in privately owned (taxpaying) housing." The riverfront park can bring direct jobs, but more importantly can spark investments and developments that will bring real estate and sales tax revenues, and many more jobs.

The East St. Louis Area Development Authority comprises the mayors of East St. Louis, Alorton, Centreville, Brooklyn and Venice, the directors of the Illinois Department of Commerce and Community Affairs and the Illinois Finance Authority, and one gubernatorial appointment. It was created in 1986 to do overall comprehensive planning and economic development activities in the five communities. It has office space in the East St. Louis City Hall. However, Carson also works for the City of Centreville and as a consultant for other cities, and spends about 10 hours a week in City Hall.

Funding is by the General Assembly primarily on a piecemeal basis, which has impaired the comprehensive planning that was contemplated at its inception. However, it claims a record of $6 million in private investments and 250 jobs created in its first 2-1/2 years. Its biggest project has been the clearing of acreage including the old Kurrus Funeral Home and the building of a new National Food Store at 25th and State streets in East St. Louis, with developer Don Soffer. "We essentially gave away some state property to a developer and we worked with that developer to relocate families and businesses and to build that store. We had a few problems, but we got the job done." That store accounts for 150 of the 250 new jobs the authority cites. It seems to be thriving.

Carson would like to see the agency funded for its original concept of regional planning. "We think East St. Louis, Centreville, Alorton and Brooklyn are going to be the key to the economic health of this region by the year 2000. The area simply has to grow because of its strategic location and we want to help prepare the community for the growth that we know is going to come. In order to do that, a lot of planning will be required and a lot of money has to be spent."

While Carson doesn't see East St. Louis exploding into a new era, "I do think it is on the brink to a new era, and the direction is going to depend on how well the state cooperates with the city and the city cooperates with the state. I see some changes coming, both in the structure of city government and the approach that's going to have to be taken."

"That approach needs to be 'back to basics,' in police protection, fire protection and city services," in Carson's opinion. And streets and sewers are basic to city services. "The city itself can't handle these problems with existing revenue. Through the state and federal governments' help, in three or four years the city could be 'back to snuff,'" Carson says.

"If the state and federal governments are willing to make the investment, then the city will be back almost as good as it was in the late '60s in terms of making it an All-American City again, maybe by the year 2000. That gives us 10 years. But someone has to risk a substantial investment in order to get the city back on track."

St. Louis skyline seen from East St. Louis riverfront

Federal authorities have taken over the East St. Louis Housing Authority for mismanagement of funds, the state has reclaimed motor fuel taxes for misuse of funds and community development grants are funneled through Target 2000 to guarantee responsibility in the use of the money. So who will risk that "investment?"

"We're going to have to get some people in city government who are responsible professionals, planners and administrators," Carson responds. The city has a poor vertical staff. A third of the city workers ought to be replaced for laziness or incompetence, but many are entrenched.

Carson favors city manager government, being pushed by State Rep. Wyvetter Younge and endorsed, according to Younge, by Mayor Carl Officer. Carson thinks a strong city manager could clean house of inefficient or corrupt personnel where it is politically impossible for elected officials.

From his planning perspective, Carson's other dreams include a unified storm water and sanitary sewage system and treatment authority with the cost spread over the entire drainage basin. The present system is far too costly. Carson worked for the last tax increase for the Metro-East Sanitary District, but said it is not the long-term answer.

Carson does not think crime is as bad as it is perceived to be, but acknowledges that there are places to avoid. However, he doesn't see a cop on every corner as a solution. He sees a need for jobs and alternative life styles and programs to deal with some of the social problems that police face, including drug abuse. "Our municipal police forces are simply not equipped to deal with that. It is a social problem that should be taken away from the police department and put somewhere else. I don't know where, but I think we should devise some experiments and see what will and won't work," Carson said.

He sees Metro Link used from East St. Louis if it offers value. Thousands of white motorists already drive through the city on local streets every day, he said. The area of the East St. Louis terminal and Fifth Street and Missouri has to be cleaned up, look safer, he said. New sidewalks are being poured on Missouri Avenue from Collinsville Avenue to the Federal Building and Post Office, but some of the buildings along the way are in sad disrepair.

Carson thinks St. Clair County should rethink its taxation policies and work more with the city for a fairer distribution of county services and costs.

More decent housing is needed, but not necessarily new housing, he said. Many buildings have been torn down that could have been renovated; as a result the housing goes off tax rolls. The assessed tax valuation goes down, and when the cost of services remains the same, tax rates must go up. Many people don't understand that, he said.

Maybe things will change, and maybe that change will start with a dream on the riverfront.

Since public bodies own a levee right of way, why not build an esplanade atop the levee wall? The upper picture is taken standing on the wall at Trendley Avenue, the park site. The lower picture is from near Eads Bridge. The auto parked against the wall shows how far it is from levee top to the cobblestone levee.

Crime, taxes and revenue are three problems East St. Louis must solve — Jerry Costello

A question for those who want to get rid of Carl Officer: Who do you want in his place?

U. S. Rep. Jerry Costello

Jerry Costello, former St. Clair County Board chairman and now congressman, sees the possibility of a bright future for East St. Louis if cooperation can be achieved, the brightness working its way from riverfront development and following the tracks of Metro Link to Scott Air Force Base, with the betterment of the entire metropolitan area resulting.

But no financial bailout alone can save East St. Louis, Costello warns. For East St. Louis to be saved, the crime problem must be solved, the problem of the highest tax rate in the state must be solved, and there must be continuing funding sources for city services.

Costello and Officer have exchanged heated words, but Costello recognizes "You have to have revenue to run a city. I don't care if Carl Officer is mayor or Jim Thompson is mayor of that city. The problems in East St. Louis are not totally Carl Officer's fault. Or this city council's fault. The problems go back for many years, and the problems have grown progressively worse instead of better, despite the rhetoric about things getting better or 'We are turning the corner.'

"That city needs a lot of help. And it needs a plan with the federal, state, county and local governments working together.

"I don't think the state has any business trying to run East St. Louis, nor does the federal government, nor the county. The people of East St. Louis elect their local representatives to the council and as mayor. But when the federal and state government comes in to financially bail the city out, and that's what they are doing, there have to be some strings attached and some checks and balances. You can't just throw in the money and say 'when this is used up come back for more.' You must ask for accountability."

There are many people outside East St. Louis who want to get rid of Carl Officer. Officer's arrogance in television interviews, his inclination to take different positions on different days, his reputation for presumably shooting from the hip (not always a correct presumption) and his verbal attacks on the white political structure have won him few friends outside the city limits. But Costello answers Officer's critics with a question: "Who do you want in his place?"

There is a lack of a strong leader. Sen. Kenneth Hall and Charles Merritts say there has not been a strong leader of the people since the death of Clyde Jordan. If Officer runs for re-election as he probably will, "I'm not sure he won't be re-elected," Costello said.

There is little question in the minds of most politicians that Officer will be elected to his fourth four-year term.

With East St. Louis featured on 20/20, Nightline and 60 Minutes all in six months, the image of East St. Louis as a poverty-stricken city has been imprinted on the minds of TV viewers nationwide.

Many of the more affluent people of East St. Louis, including many teachers, have fled the city, and others are thinking of leaving. But still Costello finds there are plenty of people in the city who have something to contribute, good people who care.

Important events are happening in East St. Louis, and other events are on the horizon. The national attention from the television probes and the print media heighten the excitement. The state bailout can be the beginning, not the end.

As County Board chairman, Costello said he never was asked about East St. Louis when visiting the outlying towns or in St. Louis. But when he was elected to congress and as a freshman was asked to address, in Washington, a group of chief executive officers of major Illinois corporations including Illinois Bell and Caterpillar, the first question at the end of his presentation was "What are we going to do about East St. Louis?"

Whether it is because the blacks are fleeing from East St. Louis into outlying communities, national attention or just awareness, in town hall meetings as far away as Highland and Hillsboro and Marine, they ask "What about East St. Louis?"

The plan by Gov. Jim Thompson for a state bailout has made every taxpayer in the state aware of the city's problems, and the cost to other taxpayers.

East St. Louis must have outside help; no city in East St. Louis' condition can pull itself up by its bootstraps, Costello said. It will take a combined effort of federal, state, county and city government working together. However, in the past the East St. Louis leadership, and specifically Carl Officer, have taken the attitude "Give us your money, but not your advice or accountability. Keep your auditors and inspectors out of our City Hall."

The county has to account for the community block grant funds it receives, for state and federal monies, to open its books to auditors and its projects to inspectors. East St. Louis can expect to do no less.

Costello said that when he was County Board chairman that on two occasions he worked out a plan with Sen. Kenneth Hall, State Rep. Wyvetter Younge and the Operating Engineers union for its members to use St. Clair County trucks, graders and other highway equipment to do a massive cleanup in East St. Louis of burned-out buildings, trashed vacant lots, and dilapidated buildings. But it was left up to East St. Louis to organize, and nothing happened either time.

Again, Costello became enamored with Operation Brightside in St. Louis, sent staff to St. Louis to learn about it, and offered to Officer to hire up to 500 youths in East St. Louis for an Operation Brightside there. Again, Officer dropped the ball.

St. Clair County has acted as the entitlement body for community grant funds for the entire county except East St. Louis. East St. Louis is its own entitlement unit. Therefore, most county federal funds could not legally be used there. When the city's demolition program was shut down by the federal government after some fraud and indictments involving contractors, Costello, over the objection of some County Board members, used discretionary county funds to continue the demolition program. He also filled the Jones Park pool for the free use of East St. Louis youngsters.

Costello's successor County Board Chairman Francis Touchette said there is no way he would permit county equipment to be used for a cleanup program in East St. Louis. Touchette is not running for re-election in November. State's Atty. John Baricevic is most likely to get the post.

Officer has been vague about city finances, Costello said. One day he says the city is $50 million in the hole, the next day $5 million. The governor did the right thing in appointing an investigative task force and pinning down the debt at $47 million, and for making a proposal for relief. "We need to move forward from here," Costello said.

Moving forward and revenue to support the city both start, in Costello's opinion, at the riverfront. He has his fingers crossed that the House of Representatives by the time this book sees print will have marked up the budget to provide $2.25 million for the cleanup of the Jefferson National Expansion Memorial park on the East St. Louis riverfront.

That park, he predicts, will trigger the development of the entire East St. Louis riverfront if the city cooperates.

Back in 1984, U.S. Reps. Mel Price and Paul Simon (now a senator) were able to pass legislation for an extension of the Jefferson National Expansion Memorial, the site of "The Arch," to the Illinois riverbank, but the legislation was very restrictive. It provides for the park to be 100 acres or less, for the land to be donated, and for any annual maintenance costs above $350,000 to be paid by local sources. More recently, Sens. Alan J. Dixon, Simon and Costello met with the Secretary of the Interior and obtained an agreement that he would designate the land as a national park providing the land were donated and was found environmentally safe. The state has taken test borings and the preliminary findings, Costello said, is that the soil is environmentally safe.

Costello asked Earl Lazerson, president of SIU-Edwardsville and chairman of the Southern Illinois Development Authority, to see if he could get the land donated. About 50 acres had been donated at the time of the interview in June.

"We want to lift the restrictions" in the enabling legislation, Costello said, but he and the senators feel it is better to get the designation and initial funding, then seek to amend the enabling legislation. Costello said some people want to see a 250-acre park, but Officer does not want to see that much land taken from the tax base, "and I agree." The memorial in St. Louis is only about 85 acres, and 100 acres on the Illinois side should be ample, in Costello's view.

The park and a Metro Link stop on the riverfront could be the key to spectacular riverfront development, it seems. St. Louis interests have assured Costello they are ready to build condos, apartments, even a golf course, on the Illinois side with assurances of safety, reasonable taxes and the anchor of the park. The developments could provide the revenues the city needs to provide services after the bailout, Costello said. The developers want to make money, but there is no problem with that if the city also benefits. East St. Louis has home rule and could give any incentives it needs for development to cooperate with programs.

The Jefferson National Expansion Memorial draws 1.5 million people annually and is the second or third busiest attraction in the federal system, Costello said. East St. Louis could participate in the revenue derived from this major tourist attraction.

Riverboat gambling, which Officer sees as a key to city income and jobs and a spur to development, obviously could contribute to the tourism value of the riverfront.

The presence of park rangers on the riverfront would add to an overall sense of security that can spread through the city.

Metro Link will have a positive impact. It will be safe and fast and give another sense of security in the city. It is being planned carefully and modeled after the best. Costello said he rides the Washington D.C. Metro from his Crystal City apartment to the Capitol every day, and feels more secure there than anywhere else in Washington, which may have more murders per hundred than East St. Louis, as well as an acute drug problem. When people from Metro-East visit Washington, they are amazed at the Metro. It's clean, safe, fast, not the New York City subway system — and neither will Metro Link be.

Scott Joint Use also will improve the job market for East St. Louisans. Costello said he hears of quotas and he doesn't know that he accepts the need for percentages, but he agrees that many of the jobs for construction and operation should go to the people who need them most.

If the city, county, state and federal governments can find a way to work together, the state bailout, riverfront park, riverfront development, Metro Link, Scott joint use, and yes, riverboat gambling, all can help East St. Louis overcome the problems of high taxes, high crime and the lack of revenue, and to provide decent services for the residents and businesses.

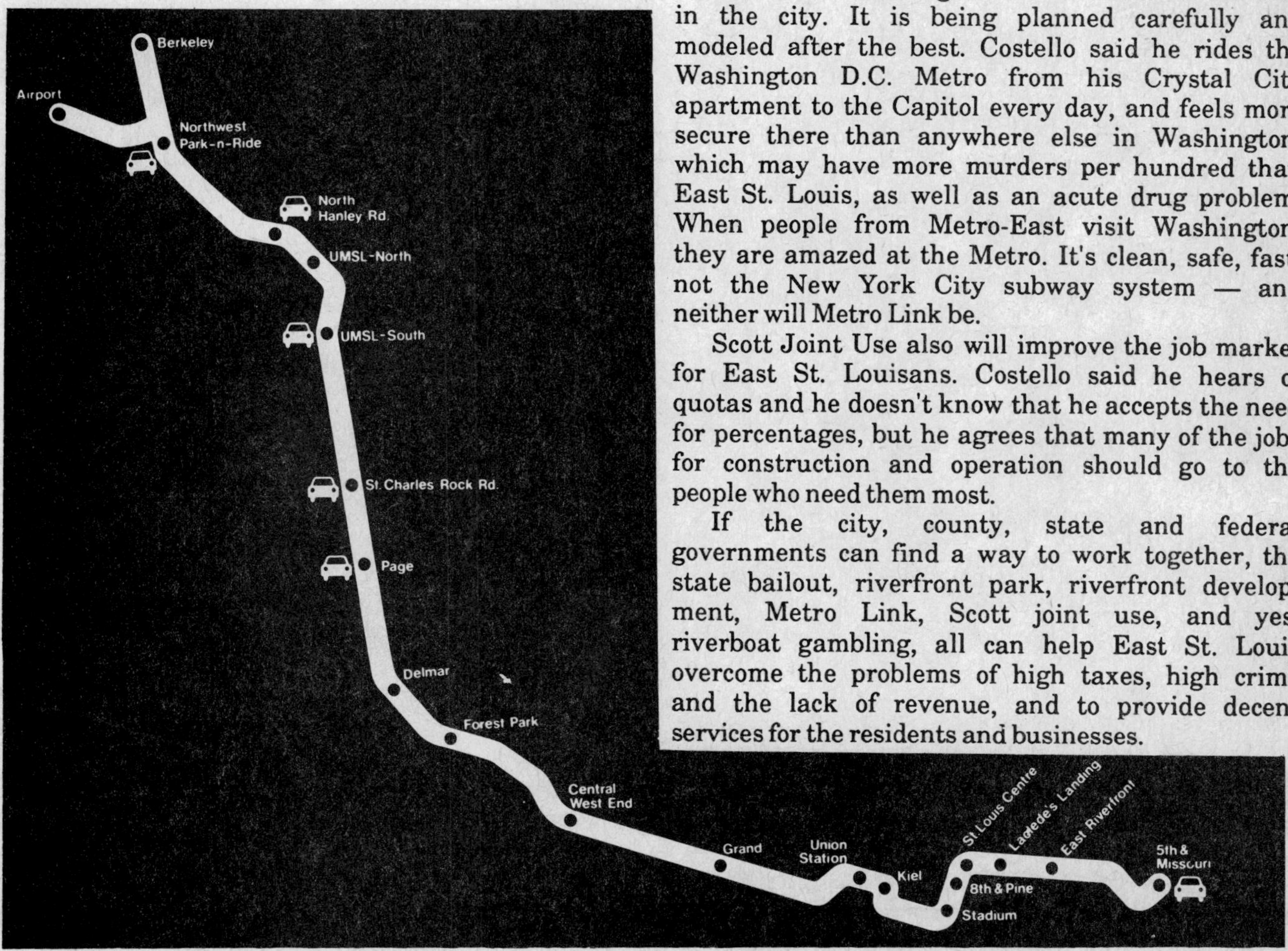

Metro Link stop will be on this site at Fifth and Missouri, where First Federal Savings & Loan once stood; only vault remains next to former Metro-East Journal building at 425 Missouri, now used by Rex Carr's law firm for storage

With grant money, city is replacing sidewalks between Collinsville Avenue and the federal buildings on Missouri Avenue and side streets. Spivey Building entrance once led to news stand, offices and a basement bowling alley

Lawyer Rex Carr, according to the New York Times, draws more than a million dollars a year from his law firm. He still maintains these offices in East St. Louis, across the street from the Metro Link stop

Century Cigar Store, a downtown landmark, in its relocated site at 507 Missouri Avenue. Lawyer Bob Mays now has his offices here. The Century always had a friendly card game in t he back room

State Rep. Wyvetter Younge says the city must clean up the Metro Link area. Spivey Building has been boarded up since its use by the State Community College

Northeast corner of Fifth and Missouri - across Fifth Street from Metro Link stop, is the former Skye Drug Store, which also sold trusses; behind it was a bar said to be frequented by gays

Former site of Paddock Tavern, restaurant business home of Frank "Buster" Wortman who controlled the gangland underworld in the '50s and '60s, at northwest corner of Fifth and St. Louis

Though empty, Spivey Building still dominates downtown area

Sidewalk project unearths original doors to businesses before Mayor Stephens raised the streets to halt flooding

Old Post Office Building is now "old" federal courts building, with new courts building added to rear in 700 block of Missouri Avenue

New Federal Building in 600 block of Missouri Avenue

St. Mary's Hospital, viewed across parking lot behind Federal Courts Building. Only hospital in East St. Louis, its poverty patients make its survival difficult. It is among city's major employers

Illinois Bell Building across street from old Post Office/Federal Courts Building

New Post Office takes up 900 block of Missouri Avenue on south side

Only the restaurant of the City Centre — once a Holiday Inn — is open

Across parking lot is once-prestigious Illini Club, with arched panels. Here East-West Gateway was born when SIU's Gene Graves was directing Community Progress, Inc. — one of the organizations that made East St. Louis an All-American City. Parking lot is empty, guard house unneeded.

Rear of Broadview Hotel, Fifth and Broadway, now home of SIU-E in East St. Louis. Out of camera range to left is fenced playground operatedby the college. SIU-E has been deeply involved in the city ever since its inception in the Morrison School. Hotel lot backs on Illini lot, above

The old Broadview Hotel — SIU-E's primary physical presence in East St. Louis

Precursors to city turn-around

Fiscal credibility, sound infrastructure, quality school system

Fiscal credibility, a sound infrastructure and a good school system are necessary to turn East St. Louis around, in the opinion of Earl Lazerson, president of Southern Illinois University at Edwardsville, founder of many programs that impact on East St. Louis.

Lazerson conceived the Leadership Council Southwestern Illinois, midwifed Target 2000 in East St. Louis, led the legislature to create the Illinois Development Authority with the dream of extending the Jefferson Memorial to the east bank of the Mississippi, chaired a committee that recommended the Martin Luther King Bridge be part of the interstate highway system and served on another committee to make it happen, and most recently served on the governor's financial advisory board that led to the $34 million loan "bailout" plan passed for East St. Louis in the summer of 1990.

SIUE has spent millions on its East St. Louis center, now located in the Broadview Hotel, and the dental clinic operated there.

Asked what East St. Louis needs, Lazerson spoke easily on a topic obviously deeply considered:

"Realistically, there are two things that in a concrete sense would be precursors to turning the economic situation around. One is you've got to guarantee the fiscal credibility of the city. Nobody in my view is going to invest unless there is a sense that the city is prepared to handle its obligations and responsibilities appropriately.

"When I am talking about fiscal responsibility I am talking about preparing balanced budgets, seeing to it that the appropriate accounting takes place, audits are run on a regular basis, the way that in a normal sense you run any municipal corporation.

"The other aspect is that you've got to guarantee the basic infrastructure. I'm talking specifically about safety and security, health, roads, sewers, that sort of thing. Those things have got to be (provided). Speaking as a member of the (governor's) financial advisory board (on East St. Louis' fiscal problems), our report I think clearly lays out the situation of the city in both cases. There is in my estimation no way for these two things to happen, that is the re-establishment of fiscal credibility and the kind of work that needs to be done on the infrastructure — none of that is going to be possible without the kind of remedies that we suggested in our report to the governor.

"Since then the legislation has passed, the aldermanic council has triggered that legislation by voting in support of becoming in effect a distressed city under the legislation, and that would enable the governor to appoint his oversight commission, and move ahead with the work that needs to be done there. But I think that is one set of things that needs to occur.

"Another thing is that the public school system, which is the backbone of any community, needs to be strengthened and every child in the City of East St. Louis needs to be guaranteed that he or she will get a proper education. I see that as the foundation on which everything else rests.

"Now, I am an optimist. I am an optimist about the future of East St. Louis based on a number of facts, the most central of which is it sits on key strategic ground with regard to the entire metropolitan area. It is perfectly sited for the future development of Southwestern Illinois. If that can occur, I think the entire region will benefit. If it does not occur, conversely, the entire region will suffer.

"This is not simply an East St. Louis problem. It is a problem for the whole metropolitan area.

"How it came about, the historical nexus of events that led to it, that is something I don't know very much about, in an extended sense. But I do know that the issues that I have laid out on the table, education, fiscal credibility the development of sound infrastructure, those are crucial to the development of that city."

Asked whether he sees racism on the part of blacks, the opposition to white "interference" in black city affairs, is an obstacle to turning the city around, Lazerson responded:

"I think that what we are talking about here varies dramatically depending upon whom you are encountering. I have had the privilege of working with people like Sen. Kenneth Hall and Oliver Hendricks, Percy McKinney and Roosevelt Malone. I don't detect any of that in those relationships. It seems to me they are four-square attempting to resolve the issues of the city and it is color-independent. In my working relationship with them I have never had a feeling of a barrier between us.

Earl Lazerson, president SIU-E

Aug. 30 Gov. James Thompson signed the Distressed Cities Act in East St. Louis and appointed Earl Lazerson to head the East St. Louis Advisory Authority, to oversee the city's handling of state loan funds, city budgets and fiscal responsibility. Also on the authority are Ron Bean, executive direector of the Illnois Development Finance Authority, Ronald Thompson, president of The GR Group Inc., Claudia Thomas, retired East St. Louis schoolteacher and Rev. Jerome Jackson, minister at the Southern Mission Baptist Church.

"I'm not going to sit here and tell you that you are wrong about your perception, because it screams out from the newspapers every day. I have always taken a very pragmatic view of things; I sort of put that aside and attempt to make progress where I can and where I'm welcome.

"The mayor (East St. Louis Mayor Carl Officer) for example, on a number of occasions has engaged in that kind of rhetoric; on the other hand, I have seen him in other situations where there is not a hint of that. I chalk that up in part at least not so much as an ideological perspective but as a political one. I think it gets in the way. I think it confuses people. I think that we all have a responsibility to stick to the facts."

Asked about a speech Officer made on the campus that startled many people, accusing the

Interstate network just one of East St. Louis' advantages

university of not meeting its obligations to black students, Lazerson said, "I don't really want to get into a situation where I am talking about what the mayor says or does not."

Explaining the role of the Southern Illinois Development Authority, Lazerson said, "We were created by legislative mandate back in 1987, the governor signed legislation, with the intent to promote economic development through certain specific tools in the two-county area, St. Clair and Madison; that's our jurisdiction. We have the power to issue bonds in support of projects that are covered by the legislation. The mandate is very broad. It also speaks directly to our being involved with regards to the question of riverfront development.

"On that score, the specific that we are currently involved in has to do with the expansion of the Jefferson National Memorial across the river to the east bank. In August of 1989 the Secretary of the Interior indicated that if a parcel of land of up to 100 acres were to be donated and found environmentally clean, he would then move ahead and designate that as the national park complementing the Arch park. The role of the development authority is to, one, attempt to secure the land through donations or other means and two, to provide the environmental certification that the secretary talked about.

"It is our hope that if we can accomplish that then he will move ahead and make the designation."

Lazerson continued that Officer "came to me as chairman of the authority several months ago and asked if we would take on the general responsibility for riverfront development, and my response to him was that our role was as a participant as part of park expansion, but we were not in a position to take on that general responsibility. We would work in cooperation with the City of East St. Louis to do what seemed feasible and prudent within our powers."

The authority has only 17 acres at the river's end of Trendley Avenue. Fifteen of those acres, where the huge flag flies, had been acquired by the Gateway Center group in St. Louis. The titles have been transferred to the authority. The authority is about to do an environmental assessment of the general area between the Poplar and Eads bridges, where siting would take place.

The secretary's 1989 letter spoke of up to 100 acres. Lazerson said his view is to move to as quickly as possible get him to designate, following certification of environmental soundness, what has been acquired. That land would be the nucleus of the park.

The National Park Service also wants a 300 acre protective zone. Lazerson said that the intention from the beginning and the State of Illinois and others have indicated that they would help out in creating the 300-acre zone with other state and federal funds.

Fast food restaurants flourish between Seventh and Eighth streets on old St. Louis Ave. (Martin Luther King Drive), despite $20 tax rate. But Arthur Treacher's nearby didn't fare so well. Below, Marty Miller, the old East Side Shade & Fixture Co., is a survivor in the Ninth-Tenth street complex on MLK/State Street. Marty, who says he won't even tell himself his age, says he is in business because he doesn't know how to get out. He had varied investments. Marty said he died five years ago when his beautiful wife passed away.

The old Sears Roebuck store, top photo, at 10th and State streets. When TV came in, Sears put a set in the store window and speakers outside, and crowds gathered at night in the parking lot to watch and hear the Ed Sullivan Show. Now it is the headquarters for East St. Louis School District 189. Across 10th Steet to the west sat Kresge's and a National Food store. Now that is the Crusader typesetting and printing and school supply firm. The Crusader and the Monitor are the two weeklies serving East St. Louis

The Mollman Building at 710 St. Louis Ave. once housed the Mixon Buick agency; it now is Behrman Auto Sales. The author once lived upstairs. Dick Stanley founded Miller Finance and Senate Finance in the Buick agency. It now is Miller-Senate Finance, still in the same building. Stanley now operates Miller Chrysler Plymouth Inc. in Belleville. The Odd Fellows Hall, once on the corner is gone

At the other end of the 700 block of King Drive is Senate Auto Parts, once a printing company run by Max Hill, who became a "reform" sheriff, and later Al Geiger

The Ainad Temple in the 600 block of Martin Luther King Drive remains the headquarters of Shriners throughout Southern Illinois. During meetings, Shriners patrol the area to make certain autos are protected

A classic car sits in a show window across from the Ainad Temple, once the Plummer Pontiac and later Carnody Pontiac agencies

Braun Auto Electric, top photo, at 720 Martin Luther King Drive (formerly Illinois Avenue) still is thriving and draws customers from throughout Metro-East. Remember Montgomery Ward, lower left, its store windows closed up now. And at the northeast corner of St. Louis Avenue and 10th Street, below, was Saeger Wachtel Hardware.

East St. Louis Public Library has gained an addition on east side at Ninth and State streets

Barcroft Motors, between Seventh and Eighth on Martin Luther King (Illinois Avenue), later was E.B. Jones and then Bundy Olds. Sign says "East St. Louis Christian Community Center"

East St. Louis Township Office at 1210 State St. is former tire store

Bradford Electric Co., 925 Missouri Ave., left, has grown markedy, taking over former Park District office building on northwest corner of Ninth and Missouri, adding on and expanding westward to Eighth Street.

Former Sherwin Williams paint store, Ninth and State streets, is vacant. It is just west of Crusader

When President Herb Littlefield moved Southern Illinois National Bank to this location on 10th Street at State, he thought he was moving to the new center of retail trade. It is vacant; Southern moved on to Fairview Heights, is now Central Bank

John Baricevic

Baricevic will seek solutions, but they may bypass Mayor Officer

The likelihood of the election of John Baricevic as St. Clair County Board chairman and the re-election of Carl Officer as mayor of East St. Louis in 1991 could spell some rocky roads ahead unless unprecedented accord is reached.

Baricevic, state's attorney and likely St. Clair County Board chairman after November, 1990, is not looking forward to working with Carl Officer on East St. Louis problems, calling him a liar. But he says that upon his election he will wipe the slate clean and offer the hand of cooperation as long as it is met in kind.

If they are not, Baricevic said he will seek solutions around the obstacles, because "It is critical that all of us take on the problems of East St. Louis.

"I guess I see (East St. Louis) as a place that can improve, that can grow, but unless a lot of people choose to really care, it could continue to simply be a legally constructed ghetto where there will be no hope, and no good government, and no police protection, and I don't know that I am as optimistic as you are about it changing."

"I have drawn an analogy arguing politically and philosophically...it's like a toothache, the smallest tooth in your body hurts, but when you have a toothache you are a miserable person. St. Clair County's toothache is East St. Louis, and it is hurting the rest of the county.

"We can't pull it, it is impossible to remove

East St. Louis from our county, so we've got to improve East St. Louis and the quality of life and the government services, and that's not just 'we' St. Clair County government, that's 'we' churches, businesses, everybody pulling together to help our fellow man.

"If you don't do it from an eleemosynary point of view, the worst bigot in the county ought to want to improve it just from a selfish point of view. That person's property values are going to decrease, his tax are rates going to go up, the quality of life of his neighbors and friends is going to go down. Absolutely it is critical that all of us take on the problems of East St. Louis."

Baricevic lists the problems as unresponsive and irresponsible local government, poor police protection, limited fire protection, little public service — streets, sewers, lighting. Parallel with that, an effective school system. Baricevic says to put them all at the top of the list.

And one of the problems is that government itself is "legally constructing a ghetto; because of the corporate limits of the city we are forcing poverty in on itself and it is just multiplying."

Baricevic referred to separate housing authorities, election mechanics, health districts, grants departments, taxing districts. Real estate taxes — a rate of more than $20 per $100 assessed valuation and that on a tax base for the whole city less than that of St. Clair Square — are a major problem.

"There are a lot of problems the black community inherited. There was deficit spending, a lot of other things, and I have never blamed all the problems on Carl Officer.

"Take the problem of housing where the federal government will not allow one to tear down a housing unit, you have to replace it, which is one reason why the units remain unimproved and vacant Improving the units or adding units is only going to increase the percentage of people living on poverty in the city.

"They pay no taxes, the housing authority pays no taxes. How is Carl Officer supposed to supply services where one third of his community pays no taxes?

"How are we to solve that? We are two different housing authorities, the East St. Louis Housing Authority and the St. Clair County Housing Authority. For anyone to suggest that we ought to absorb the East St. Louis Housing Authority would be met with cries of racism. But I think that is one step. We ought to be one housing authority."

And Baricevic thinks there should be one county health authority, and one election board, and one grants authority. Baricevic said that if the city were part of the county grants department, through savings in administration costs it could receive more money for city improvements. But he thinks any call for such mergers would bring cries of racism.

(Interestingly, Mayor Carl Officer in his interview complained about the cost to the city of having its own separate districts, including the election and health authorities — not the grant authority — and Officer would have the county take over the city's parks. He also complained about the administration of the housing authority, which was taken away from the city by the federal government because of mismanagement.)

Baricevic blames the state and federal government for part of the lack of credibility of the local government because they have not required the audits they legally can. He says the state comptroller, who happens to be black (William Burris), has refused to call for the audits that he has the authority to order. He said the federal government is owed nine or ten million dollars in federal tax dollars, but it won't give Sen. Paul Simon the records.

"They won't respond to my requests," Baricevic said. "They will not attempt to collect it. Until this office started filing some actions on the misuse of motor fuel tax money, nobody in government took any action. Nobody in government has forced the City of East St. Louis to be responsible, to audit — it's not just East St. Louis' fault..."

Baricevic spoke reflectively, pausing to gather thoughts, beginning positively, finishing his train of thoughts skeptically:

"I see East St. Louis as a city with a lot of potential. I think we tend to ignore the positive a lot, and there are lots of positives in East St. Louis. A lot of people have a lot of pride in the community and a lot to work with, but in my opinion we have systematically taken away resources. 'We' are a lot of people, a lot of agencies, a lot of organizations, a lot of governments...been taking away resources, taking away assets, prohibiting the development, and that 'we' includes the city and its leaders — it's been a very destructive process that actually is prohibiting development and there has been an insidious inbreeding so that the slide of government, the decline of the city, has been progressing in geometric proportions, becoming more difficult to stop.

"So I guess I see it as a place that can improve, that can grow, but unless a lot of people choose to really care, it could continue to simply be a legally constructed ghetto where there will be no hope, and no good government, and no police protection, and I don't know that I am as optimistic as you are about it changing."

The decline of East St. Louis has included a population decline. Much of the public housing even stands empty. Some Orr-Weathers high rise buildings are boarded up. Turnkey housing units, for whatever reason, are boarded. Some public housing units appear to never have been completed and now are fire-ravaged, vandalized.

"You and I have lived through the white flight, and now (the city) is experiencing black flight," Baricevic said. "I am very anxious to see the 1990 statistics, see what it actually turns out to be. I'll be surprised if it is over 40,000 people. Certainly the population will decline. Where it will settle I don't know. With such a large geographic area, it could decline to 25,000 people, something of that magnitude."

The decline of East St. Louis is eroding the tax base of the county as a whole, while it increases its expenses.

On the positive side, Baricevic joins such black leaders as Sen. Kenneth Hall in having hope that the governor's "bailout" plan will bring the fiscal controls that can in turn begin to restore fiscal responsibility in city government.

"I am an advocate of the governor's bailout plan. We have the means to solve the problem and maybe the difference is the governor's bailout plan has strings attached, not to run the city, but to require responsible audited government.

"Why did the motor fuel tax problem go on for 20 years? If the state would have stopped them from misspending the money when it was a thousand dollars, and said look, do this and this and this, the problem would never have got there. When they misspend the federal dollars, take the problem away from them. Now, I am as critical of the federal government and the state government. The feds did take away the East St. Louis Housing Authority. It is the only housing authority in the nation taken away from a unit of local government. Finally there is good response there. Yes, there still are a lot of problems, but they have the state police in, they have rehabbed some units, these are all factors that other people have to control.

"There are lots of problems outside the City of East St. Louis that have helped to create and perpetuate the problem. So it is a white problem, some of the problems are white generated, some are ..."

Baricevic at this point seemed to realize that he was falling into the mental trap of equating East St. Louis as "black" and everything else as "white." He continued "You know, government isn't really black and white, a comptroller who will do nothing is black. There are a lot of white officials who could do things and who have not."

Baricevic was asked about the view of some blacks, mainly those political leaders who were never part of the political system in East St. Louis when it was dominated by whites, that there is a white conspiracy to draw and drive the blacks out of East St. Louis so the whites can take back the city with its geographical advantages on the riverfront and in the shadow of downtown St. Louis. The author suggests leaders of this train of thought are Mayor Carl Officer, State Rep. Wyvetter Younge and East St. Louis Township Supervisor Will McGaughy. They view with suspicion any program that they see coming from "white government."

The worst bigot in the county ought to want to improve (East St. Louis) just from a selfish point of view. That person's property values are going to decrease, his tax rates are going to go up, the quality of life of his neighbors and friends is going to go down. Absolutely it is critical that all of us take on the problems of East St. Louis.

Baricevic called this a self-defeating attitude. He said there are many young black leaders willing to work with white leaders for the benefit of the city. "There certainly is a group of new young black leaders that don't fit that category, but there are some that do...those who scream racism for their own particular benefit. If they can't get what they want, it is a racist attack. They don't care about the city, they don't care about anybody but themselves and they are using it (racism charges) to keep themselves at the top of the list. There is another group that sincerely believe that (the white conspiracy theory). I put (State Rep.) Wyvetter Younge in that group. I believe that Wyvetter sincerely believes that scenario.

"It is such an outlandish scenario that anybody with any desire to sit down and work with the system, or against the system, cannot construct any set of facts to show how that could happen. It is pure ignorance leading the blind, and Wyvetter Young is a very well-meaning individual only hurting her city by passing that out.

"Wyvetter wants gifts and nothing else... It is people like that who really hurt the city. But I absolutely do not challenge Wyvetter's integrity — I don't think she has ever stolen a dime from the City of East St. Louis. She wants to help the city. She truly cares about people.

"Wyvetter has brought people to my office and complained that we are not doing anything about crime. Wyvetter then brings another group of people to my office and complains that we are putting too many blacks in jail. She has stood right here, with other leaders from East St. Louis, and argued two different things to me: I prosecute too many black people, so I must be racist. The next week, figuratively, they come back with another group and complain that I am racist because I don't care about black victims of crime. None of it makes any sense. No matter what I do, to some group of leaders in East St. Louis, I'm racist. The same leader will be on both sides of the issue, and I have not figured out how to solve that problem."

Recalling his football playing days, "There's an old football saying, 'You find solutions.' I am not going to try to change Wyvetter's mind, or to convince her that she is wrong. I am going to go out and try to find solutions. I am going to do what I can to get problems solved, and I am not going to worry about Wyvetter's or Carl Officer's or anybody else's opinions except the voters.

"You have to look for solutions, and if you continue like Wyvetter and Carl Officer to blame other people for problems, you are not going to get anything done. I am not going to blame Carl or Wyvetter for the problems of East St. Louis or the problems I might be having. I think we need to ask leaders in St. Clair County to find solutions. If somebody is causing a problem, then we've got to find a solution to get around that particular problem.

"Everybody wants to point a finger. Let's not point blame, let's get solutions done. Now, as state's attorney, I don't do anything without pointing a finger, When I file an action, I name a defendant. So I guess I could be accused of doing the same thing, but that's in a professional capacity and my main goal, I hope in retrospect, is to get a problem solved."

As county board chairman, a post Baricevic anticipates, "my focus will be dramatically different by definition. As a legislative and executive leader, I'll have to encourage working together to solve problems. Although I will not relish it very much, I will have to work with Carl Officer or whoever is the elected official of East St. Louis."

Baricevic said he thinks county government historically has not allowed blacks to rise to department head levels. "I have trial attorneys that are black, (County Clerk Janice) Delaney's chief administrator is black, (Sheriff Mearl) Justus' guy who runs the jail is black, but they have stopped there. We have to let blacks rise to a public position where the black voters know they can look to a black in a position of responsibility.

"It's a lot easier for my office to try a case if there is a racial defense, and have a black lawyer prosecute the case. We try to keep blacks on our juries. We want to let black America have a say in how the county is run. I think we have done it, but we need to do a better job of it.

"We have to overcome a lot of negative publicity and encourage St. Clair and Madison counties to become a part of the metropolitan area, and get St. Louis looking east instead of west. Jerry (Costello) started it; before Jerry there was not much of an East Side presence. We were on all the boards but nobody went to East-West Gateway and those things. It mostly is just hard work convincing people to work together.

"Most of the solutions we could work on with East St. Louis would require them to acknowledge that we have to work together so I can open the door and attempt to work with them, but if East St. Louis does not want to accept some responsibility, it won't happen.

"For instance, we can take a quarter million dollars off their budget by running the elections, but that won't happen unless it is voted on by the citizens of East St. Louis. They would have to want to give it back to us, dissolve their electoral board. It would be an added burden of St. Clair County but we would do it, I would be for doing that. But in spite of that, there are things I would be for.

"We probably could absorb all their grants (work) without any addition to our personnel, and in essence take the portion of money they spend for overhead and put it back into the City of East St. Louis. But that would require one of two things, the federal government forcibly taking it away from them, or them voluntarily giving it to us. I'm not asking for it. A number of people would interpret that comment to me and say I am trying to take over East St. Louis.

"The amount of public services available to the city are not exorbitant. That's another problem with some of the community leaders down there, they think we have the authority to pick up their trash and police their streets, and we don't. They don't understand that."

On a broader plane:

"You know, America is changing. There is not a community in St. Clair County — there might be a subdivision, but there is not a community in St. Clair County that does not have a substantial taxpaying black population. A significant number of blacks live outside the city limits of East St. Louis in what East St. Louis would like to say is white America. Those black people are getting police protection. Those black people are getting government services. Not that there is no racism in St. Clair County.

"If East St. Louis wants to label Mascoutah as white government, they are still providing services to black people. I think that (attitude) is one of the problems we want to work around, that is an example of East St. Louisans, in my opinion, trying to isolate themselves for their particular benefit. They are not the only blacks in St. Clair County anymore. After the next census returns,

I'll bet (they'll show) there are more blacks outside the city limits of East St. Louis than inside. But we have an obligation to solve problems for all citizens. If we can solve them for blacks outside East St. Louis, we ought to be able to solve them for blacks inside East St. Louis.

"We've got enough problems with racism without us trying to have different classes of black people.

"There's another example of 'I want it both ways, I want to be able to yell at whites and get things, I want to be able to blame whites.' In some cases they are right, there are bigots in our communities, but that (yelling) is self-defeating. We can't allow that to happen (from) the black leader that does it solely to perpetuate his own particular position, his self-interest."

Baricevic was asked about economic development in East St. Louis. His response:

"We have got to convince the leaders of East St. Louis and the leaders outside East St. Louis to work together for a common goal if we are going to get anywhere. Otherwise, if we are fragmented, nobody from outside St. Clair County is going to want to work with us. That will require some give by the leaders outside East St. Louis, but it also is going to require some give by the leaders inside the City of East St. Louis, and at this point the Carl Officer administration, the Wyvetter Younge candidacy, will not accept any give by the city of East St. Louis. Even if quid pro quo, we back off here, you back off there, we meet somewhere in the middle. That's not good.

"At this point they want us to come over to them. I will not throw tax dollars down that rat hole. But I do want to put a lid on that rat hole, because there are a lot of good citizens. I have a lot of friends living in the city. It is easy to say it's going to be hard to do, but we've got to get together and find solutions. So which problems am I going to address first? I don't know."

But Baricevic sees accountability as the basis of any improvement. "A balanced budget with responsible accountability — the state government has the ability to make that happen. The state's attorney can prod, but it is primarily the responsibility of state government."

Is there a lack of commitment to solve the problems of East St. Louis?

"Where there has been commitment," Baricevic responds, "there has been from that same group of leaders a locking of doors. Carl Officer gets on KMOX and says that there are no black employees in the state's attorney's office in St. Clair County. That's a patent lie. He gave some figures, eight per cent or so employees of St. Clair County were black, where it is 22 or 24 per cent.

"Carl wants to count only blacks from East St. Louis in those figures. If we hire blacks from O'Fallon, those are not black persons. When I filed an action against the City of East St. Louis to get sewers fixed to draw raw sewage out of the homes of Villa Griffin. Carl Officer labels that as a racist attack on the city and called me more racist than the regimes of South Africa. Well, I tried to get sewage out of black homes and away from black children – how is that racist? For the life of me I can't understand that. I know racism has to be viewed in the eyes of the person that it is directed at, and not by me, and I don't pretend to know what racism is, but it is those kind of things that prohibit people who attempt to help from staying involved."

Baricevic cited another example. He said that during the severe snow storm of 1983, when the area was snowed in for three or four days, Jerry Costello and county board chairman "called Carl and said 'our major streets are clean, we'll send some truck to your city if you will tell us what streets you want plowed.' Carl Officer's response was 'If one of your trucks hit my city limits I will commandeer it and you'll never get it back.' His reason? It's his city and by God stay out of it.

"On one level we get criticized for trying to take over the city. Then we get criticized for not doing anything.

"To me it is obvious their tirades are simply designed to keep them in power and not to help their citizens, because we get criticized for being racist whether we do or not. If we try to hel,p we're racist; if we don't, we're racist. This is not a label by everybody, but some leaders, and they shut doors for people trying to help the City of East St. Louis."

What is the crime situation in East St. Louis? How bad is the drug problem?

Drugs, according to Baricevic, are not syndicated. "We have not as yet seen major ties to international drug dealing, the street gangs in Los Angeles. There is some of that, but our drug trade primarily is a retail drug trade at the street level. We have had a number of arrests with connections with Detroit, Chicago, St. Louis and Memphis, and those are necessary for the drug trade to exist. But at this point we are not a Mafia or Los Angeles Street Gang outlet."

The Crips and the Bloods, despite poverty, are not in East St. Louis, at least, not yet. "The Mississippi River is a major socioeconomic barrier. We have little crime connections with St. Louis for anything. We have had some Blood and Crips connections, but not to the point that St. Louis has. If something isn't done, eventually it will get to us, and I suspect it will get to us, but it's not here yet."

Mayor Officer has charged the county does not care about black crime victims and cites a case where a black man in Loisel Hills murdered his wife, also black, and is now free. Baricevic agreed "That was a travesty of justice. That person should have been in jail forever and ever and ever."

But he added "We were lucky to get what we did because the constitutional violation by the East St. Louis police department in taking the confession. If we had gone to trial we would have lost it and got nothin'."

Officer says the county will not prosecute drug dealers. Baricevic replies:

"He has yet to give me or anyone that I know of one name of a case that wasn't prosecuted except one — we had two cases against the same individual — we prosecuted the guy on another case and he is in the Department of Corrections; he's off the streets. There are five or six (East St. Louis Policeman) Lester Anderson cases I won't prosecute because I think Lester was not worthy of belief in the cases. Those are generally possession of 20, 30, 40 grams of drugs. They are not delivery cases, there was not one dealer involved.

"Outside of those few cases, Carl Officer will make that statement every opportunity he gets but he will not tell anybody the case, give me the name of a defendant who the police came up here and were turned down for a warrant, unless it is because of constitutional violation by the police department.

"Of the first 100 drug cases this year, only 15 were made by the City of East St. Louis. Yet we prosecuted 80 people in the black community. That's because white people care, other police departments, Illinois state police uniform division, Department of Criminal Investigation plain-clothes division, sheriff's department, metropolitan enforcement group, secretary of state's office, are all making drug cases in East St. Louis. Those are not all white cops. In fact most of them are black cops, but those are the same organizations the city wants to label as white."

What about the quality of the police department?

"They have both the best and the worst in St. Clair County," Baricevic said. "The police department cannot make a move without the mayor. Good police departments don't operate that way. I have tremendous faith in (Chief) Isadore Chambers. I think he's impeccably honest.

"I sued the city for making a criminal act for putting their cops in police cars with holes in the floor, with seats that go up and back when they want to. I'm trying to force good equipment on the police department so they can respond to calls. Carl calls that racist. Tell me what's more racist: trying to get a good police car under a policeman, or Carl perpetuating no services to blacks? Who's being more racist, Carl or me?

"We have a higher percent of criminal defendants who are black who commit crimes against blacks going to jail than anywhere else. We have more people going to jail from East St. Louis than anywhere else. We have more people going to jail from St. Clair County than from anywhere but Cook. Carl Officer cannot...it is impossible for him to show any consistent situation where I don't care about black criminals.

"I will not work with a liar, and Carl has been. I will not work with somebody who says one thing behind the scene, and something else to the media.

"For instance on light rail, Carl Officer was asked, invited and encouraged to attend every meeting on the development of light rail. When the light rail contract was awarded, on the riverfront, Carl got up and criticized it as a racist attack and said it was not going to get to the city because he was prohibited from having any input, when we had begged him to get involved. I won't work with a person like that. You can't work with him because you can't trust him.

"If Carl Officer wants to be a man of his word, his honor, let him be aggressive, be tough for his city, fight for his citizens, not let people who are racist have any foothold into his community — I don't want somebody who is not going to aggressively support the interest of his community. But I've got to have somebody with integrity and honesty to work with.

I'll give everybody a chance, and whoever is the leader, whoever is voted in by the citizens of East St. Louis, I will work with until they convince me they are a liar and have no integrity. From Deember I will be putting on a different hat, and I will give Carl a chance and I hope Carl gives me a chance, and we start off fresh. It is up to us if we want to work together, but ... it is a two way street."

Will he work politically for or against Officer in the East St. Louis 1991 election?

"I have never attempted to influence anybody's election except in Caseyville Township, where I am a citizen and pay taxes. But I never shut doors, you never know who's going to come around."

(Baricevic is being opposed for County Board chairman by Ted Farmer, who did not have time to talk with us as this book was being prepared in August. Although Farmer may do better against Baricevic than previous Republican candidates against the Democratic nominee, his election would be an upset. The News-Democrat reported Sept. 2 that Officer, Centreville Mayor Riley Owens and Washington Park Mayor Sylvester Jackson revealed they have been meeting to discuss supporting Farmer. Baricevic spit back that he did not want Officer's support, and cited a track record of caring about the problems of blacks. He said he has no respect for what Officer has done to East St. Louis.)

St. Clair County Board Chairman Francis Touchette

Touchette talks about 'we' and 'them' but sees jobs as key to city rejuvenation

It's obvious that the problems of East St. Louis have not been the principal concerns of Francis Touchette, aging Centreville and St. Clair County Democratic party political boss and successor to Jerry Costello as St. Clair County Board chairman. He's the last of the oldtime bosses who wielded power in the Alvin Fields era of East St. Louis. He was a Fields opponent and ran a distant second in power as long as Fields held the reins as mayor, and moved to the forefront of county politics when Fields dropped those reins.

On the one hand, as Touchette talks about "we" and "them," equating East St. Louis with its largely black population, and "we" with the whites, he says the only thing *we* owe *them* is concern about their hunger and health, those things we as

Americans don't think anybody should have to do without. He said he gives tens of thousands of dollars in food to the poor from his charitable trust, set up with leftover "profits" in his political fund.

On the other hand, he sympathizes with the plight of black East St. Louisans hooked on dope, with no jobs, nothing to do, no future.

"What is the Devil's workshop? — Christ, I sound like a preacher. It's an idle mind. I don't know, if we don't got a goddamn thing to do, and I say this in a lot of my speeches ... I don't know if I were one of them and didn't have no place to go or no future or nothin', I wouldn't be one of them too. I honestly feel that way.

"I have people beg me to get a job, and I say shit, you can't work, you're loaded with that stuff (drugs). They say 'Yeh, I know Mr. Touchette, I wants to get off.' Now how sincere they are, I don't know. But I do believe there would be a chance to rehabilitate them."

On the one hand, regarding East St. Louis' future, "I don't think anybody has got an answer what to do about East St. Louis. I think it'll peter itself out. The answer might be don't do anything at all."

He estimates the population of East St. Louis today at under 40,000. Many buildings are gone. You can see the blacks sitting on the lawns on West Main Street in Belleville.

On the other hand, he sees Scott Air Force Base joint use, Metro Link light rail, and the expansion of the Jefferson Memorial if it is done with a giant cooperative effort of government and business, providing some of the jobs that are vital to any turnaround in East St. Louis.

On the one hand, he says somebody will "take a f---ing" on riverboat gambling in East St. Louis. "I just can't see people coming from other parts of the country, putting up that kind of plant (boat and dock) and making money out of it. I can see people gambling, but what are they going to come to East St. Louis for? Not just to gamble. There ain't nothin' here to see. Shit, they can go to Vegas, they can go to other states. There ain't nothing to see here when you come to East St. Louis. There's legalized whores in Las Vegas, there are lots of clubs, decent clubs, a lot of things to see there. Here what would you go see besides shoot craps?

"They're gonna have a helluva time just because of the City of East St. Louis itself. People are scared to go down to the damn place."

On the other hand, less than a week later he urged the St. Clair County Board to support a riverboat gambling license for Vincent Sauget in the Village of Sauget, which adjoins East St. Louis on the south. The Belleville News-Democrat quoted him in its June 26, 1990 edition "Whether the county passes this or not, there is going to be riverfront gambling in Sauget. I can't disclose all I'd like to about that at this point, but I think we should vote for this."

"This" was to let nightclub operator Vincent Sauget detach to the county part of the village on the riverfront so Sauget Properties' gambling boat corporation, Arch-View, Inc. could apply for a gambling boat license in the county's jurisdiction, since the Village of Sauget was not large enough to qualify. The County Board voted 28-7 to notify the state that it supported Arch-View's application despite opposition from the East St. Louis black board members, several outer county members and the county sheriff. (The question became moot when the state eliminated the size requirement to allow Sauget to apply.)

Touchette has thought about the problems of East St. Louis, and says that jobs are critical to any recovery. He has his own plan for East St. Louis and all other depressed cities; it is to put up factories and train people to work in them, give them incentives and profit sharing, let them join unions, wear hard hats and pay income taxes. He sees this as far preferable to dumping welfare money into the city, especially without accountability, "thousands of millions of dollars."

You couldn't spend too much money this way, he said. Giving poor people jobs, a way up, a way out would curb crime, save countless dollars in police protection, crime losses, court and prison costs. "We can't keep operating the way we are because our prisons are all full."

The plants could manufacture goods needed and even given away abroad, if necessary, so as not to compete with private enterprise. That would have to be worked out. Right now, he suggests, recycling plastic might be a possibility, in keeping with current environmental concerns.

Behind the plants would come schools and help for people to get off drugs. Right now, "I don't think the federal government is interested in putting anything down there any more because of the way it has been handled."

Touchette said he has talked about his factory plan with Adlai Stevenson when he was senator, to Sen. Alan J. Dixon and Sen. Paul Simon. "I must be wrong in my theory because I've never been able to get it though."

(Touchette said he wishes he had had the education to be a lawyer. His language may be crude, but he is shrewd and should never be underestimated.)

Francis Touchette cites health reasons for not seeking re-election as St. Clair County Board chairman. Ironically, as he retires the Supreme Court has issued a decision that political patronage is a civil rights violation, ending a practice on which he and many other political leaders built

This sign west of Obear Nester Glass Co. and American Steel Co. off Broadway, near the old C.K. Williams & Co. plant, struck us as darkly humorous; whole plants were "dumped"

Obear Nester Glass Co. — chemical and metal firms use part of the grounds, but not the buildings which are quietly decaying

their power bases.

While patronage still has been practiced in East St. Louis, only the school district has enough jobs available to be of importance. The buying of votes through jobs has been limited by the city's destitute finances.

Touchette thought Carl Officer would be re-elected mayor for a fourth term because there was no viable opponent with the backbone to run.

(Sen. Simon wrote a book in 1986 "Let's Put America Back to Work" in which he cites the frustrations of the jobless in case histories in support for a plan for "guaranteed job opportunities for everyone who wants to work." It doesn't propose government make-work industries, but it defines the problem and suggests remedies, which like those from Touchette, have not been tried.)

Charles Merritts in the spacious back yard of his Edgemont home — and near his motor home

Charles Merritts

He thinks East St. Louis and he both lost in his bid for mayor

East St. Louis refuses to die. There'll always be an East St. Louis. It will revive because of its highways, its location near airports, Scott Air Force Base joint use, river gambling, expansion of the Jefferson Memorial and because of the river and the riverfront.

Besides, St. Louis needs some place to dump its bodies.

This is the view of Charles Merritts, 72, the man who wanted so much to be the first black mayor of East St. Louis, the man who trained under Al Fields and John T. English, and Tom Lewis and Esther Saverson, who helped make Leo Dougherty a political boss, and who once ran a cab company in Belleville as probably the first black Belleville businessman, back under Mayor Charles Nichols. He can tell you how the election judges marked the ballots to elect the first black school board member. He knows about the smoke-filled rooms, patronage, and trading promises for votes. He played the political game the old way.

Merritts never got to be mayor. He lost to James Williams in 1972, though he had the support of the white Democrats. He expected to win. He wanted to win so badly he could taste it, and the bitterness of that defeat still lingers. Soon thereafter, a U.S. district attorney prosecuted Merritts for taking kickbacks as president of the School District 189 Board of Education and for putting a contract out to kill Clyde Jordan, a fellow school board member and publisher of the Crusader black weekly newspaper. He was convicted and sent to a federal penitentiary in Texas.

Forty-two days after he started serving his time, Merritts said he was told the federal government had gotten what it wanted; Merritts was an ex-convict who could not hold public office and his name was smeared, so he could go free the next day if he would give evidence to convict his white friend Bob Rice, who had been school board attorney, William Mason, who succeeded Williams as mayor of East St. Louis, Francis Touchette, Centreville Township supervisor and now county board chairman, or school board member Claude Bush, father of Gordon Bush, a black now prominent in county politics. "I told them I didn't know what they were talking about," Merritts said.

Merritts said he was guilty, but the prosecution had no evidence against him. What they brought out were lies. But "Hell yes I wanted him killed," he said of his former friend Clyde Jordan, "I hated the son of a bitch."

Merritts said he accepted donations from contractors doing business with the school district because he needed it for "the organization," but he never had anyone pad a contract, as was charged, in order to pay him a kickback.

Merritts was a strong black politician raised in the "old school." He recalls the mayors Doyle, Harrison, Crowe and Connors, before Al Fields; and he served the political organization under Police Commissioner John T. English, who then lived at 1421 St. Louis Ave., and Street Commissioner Leo Dougherty. He said he sometimes chauffeured English about town at night so he could check on what was going on in the taverns and in the Valley.

White politicians made money, he said. He talks glibly about a safe jammed with so much money that it fell out when you opened the door. The money, he said, came from payoffs on gambling and prostitution, not out of taxes.

Merritts recalls when the blacks were required to live south of Missouri Avenue, and in each precinct the committeeman was king. He could decide who could have slot machines, dice games. "I had two crap games, 20 slots." Merritts said he kept the slots, got part of the proceeds from the crap games.

And Frank "Buster" Wortman oversaw the whole thing," Merritts charged. The gangster was "another police force" who kept other gangsters out of East St. Louis. If they wanted to go to Fairmont City to see the races, they went by way of Granite City unless they had Buster's permission. Buster had his good side, Merrits said; there was organization. Today there is no organization. Today, there is no money from gambling and prostitution to finance the political system. There is even very little patronage as most government bodies are on the verge of bankruptcy.

The white regime would have collapsed years earlier if it had not been for World War II, which kept some of the industry and the packing plants alive, Merritts said. Merritts worked on the fifth-story killing floor at Swift's. "Nobody had a fifth story killing floor," he said. Industry was obsolete. The white politicians turned over to the blacks a city laden with old buildings, old debts and no jobs when obsolete heavy industry in the area closed or fled to the Sun Belt states.

"When I lost the election for mayor, East St. Louis lost," Merritts said. He wanted to give the city an honest administration, one politically oriented, because it takes a good business head and political connections to run a city. "I think I had both," he said, as well as a dream to make good as the first black mayor of East St. Louis.

I expected to win," he said. He said Congresssman Melvin Price took him to McDonnell Douglas Aircraft and asked as a favor to Price for the big defense corporation to set up a small plant employing perhaps 100 men in East St. Louis and teach them to build carburetors and fuel pumps. McDonell agreed, he said. But when Merritts was defeated, nothing happened.

When Merritts was sent to prison, a phone call to Price won him a reassignment to a "country club" prison in Texas. He hit a speaking circuit before church men's groups. "You had to have an appointment to see me." But many East St. Louisans made the trek, including at least one bank president. Some said he ran his businesses and politics by telephone. He admits to long telephone conversations with his son Charles Jr. and his wife. But he made the calls at night out of courtesy to his fellow prisoners, since there weren't very many phones. However, he had his stereo and TV, and he ordered how he wanted his eggs cooked in the morning. When his wife visited, he got a pass to town and a motel. "I told my wife," he said, "if I didn't know what this place was, I'd pay to take a vacation here."

As a child, Merritts picked up spilled coal along the railroad tracks and sold it for money. He worked at Hogan's Grocery at 15th and Piggott for 35 cents a day — raised to 50 cents when he started going to St. Louis and buying the produce. He worked at American Steel for $3.69 for a nine-hour day until he signed up for the CIO union and was fired. By 1970 he owned a fleet of taxicabs, a string of liquor stores, a night club and a construction company, and was earning $75,000 to $100,000 a year in addition to the money he accepted for his "political organization."

Today, the people of East St. Louis have given up, he said. They think their lot is the best they will have. They think their vote is worthless and they let others run their town. Only by leaving the city can they expect to do better. Teachers do not live in the city. People with ambition and skills move away from the city. Merritts said were it not that he owns so much rental property, and cannot sell it because the banks and savings and loans won't make loans in East St. Louis, have "red-lined" the city, he too would be gone.

(He gets in his 36-foot motor home and travels away from the city frequently. He likes to leave without a destination and let his whims guide him.)

As a result of the people accepting their fate as the best they can have, since the death of Clyde Jordan there is no leadership in East St. Louis, he said. And there is no organization, and no order. Drug usage and crime are rampant. "We kill enough of each other," he said, but most crime comes from St. Louis and St. Louis uses East St.

Ana Estates is just across Summit Avenue from Charles Merritts' home. The developer started the big house for herself, built the townhouses to market, then bogged down. The project is included in a citywide housing plan advocated by Robert Vancil

Louis as a place to dump its bodies.

Twenty-seventh street is "drug alley," and you can drive down the street and get curb service, Merritts said. He said mothers send their children to take orders from motorists, to deliver the drugs — police can't send the children to prison. The church at the corner of 27th Street and State, the old Winstanley Baptist Church, held a prayer meeting in the street over drugs. Gov. Jim Thompson sent a representative.

He called his longtime foe Mayor Carl Officer "the problem" with East St. Louis, and says the city cannot recover with him as mayor. He said he doesn't think Officer is taking money as mayor, but that he is careless and doesn't realize those around him take payoffs. But he predicted that somehow, Officer will be removed. He expects to see Officer indicted over his preacher friend charged with using his church to launder drug money. If the power structure wants Officer out, they will find a way, is Merritts' view.

Meanwhile, speculators are buying up property in East St. Louis. He said he sought to buy a vacant lot next to a liquor store to add to his parking, and the St. Louis owner said no, that he was going to call Merritts to buy his property as an investment.

Right now, you can't buy a lot between 15th Street and the riverfront, he said — not unless you want to pay three prices. The property has been bought up by speculators, including a lot of whites.

Will the blacks flee the city and the whites return to take over? Will we have the white flight in reverse? There are those who believe the whites are sitting by waiting for East St. Louis to crash so they can take over the valuable site so close to the Arch, the riverfront, downtown St. Louis. There are those who think the bailout plan was part of such a scheme, and that it will be followed by heavy investments in city property.

Merritts is watching. If he were mayor, he is sure he could handle it, turn it to the city's advantage.

Philip Cohn

"You can't just label it down there and up here, you've got to say 'It's all us, what can we do?' Side A can't fight side B. This isn't the Civil War. Side A and Side B have both got to come off their horses and forget that the white man thinks like this and the black man thinks like that, and one's out to get the other, and say 'These are our people "down there" that are suffering, and we've got to get our heads together and do something, or you're going to keep hating me and I'll keep hating you and they're going to keep suffering" – Phil Cohn comments on residents "on the hill" talking about the "up here" whites and "down there" black East St. Louisans.

To rebuild a city, look to the people

Philip Cohn, 28, is energetic, articulate, self confident, the third generation in a real estate family that has done well renting and selling houses to the poor who couldn't otherwise finance a home.

The Post-Dispatch in May, 1990, reported that Philip and his father Arnold were among the two families that are the largest owners of private property in East St. Louis, with 523 parcels valued by the assessor's office at a total market value of

$1.65 million — an average of $3,154.88 per property. The other father-son team is Edwin Sieron and his son John.

Arnold Cohn is turning the business over to his son, who wants to add a new emphasis on commercial properties. He has had some success in renting commercial properties and has sold two office buildings to investment groups, one involving European and New York interests, and another to other investors. Both buildings are occupied by doctors, lawyers and accountants.

Cohn said frankly that he is in East St. Louis to make a living doing what his father and his grandfather have done for 60 years, buy, rent and sell homes, but on the other hand he does care about East St. Louis and God willing, he would give what he could to programs to help the people of the city, especially educational programs. He does not look forward to the "dawning of a new era," not to say he would not welcome it nor be willing to make a contribution to it, but that he can't look to that for his business future.

However, Philip has some frank and different ideas on the needs of East St. Louis.

Asked, for instance, what help he thought would come for the city from the expansion of the Jefferson Memorial to the Illinois shore, Metro Link, riverboat gambling and Scott Joint Use, he said they might help, but "You're sort of building your house on a foundation of toothpicks. You need a sturdier foundation. You need the people. Those things are not going to teach people to care, teach them to read and write, help them get jobs — they might help them get a job, but not help them keep a job. I'm proud they're coming in, they show people care, but that's only half of it."

So what would help more?

"You're not going to do anything without money and you are not going to get money without being a diplomat with the governor and other politicians willing to give a helping hand."

Be a diplomat, get government support, and start all kinds of programs, especially with adults, have classes for them, out in the neighborhoods, class after class, "educate people and I think you can turn them around," he said. "I didn't say it would be easy. We've got ourselves in a mess here in East St. Louis and it is going to be difficult; but that's why we've got to work on it."

We need leaders, he said, to go to businesses, industries, and say "Let's get my people working," bring them into East St. Louis. Give tax abatements, free parking lots, police protection, whatever it takes, as long as they are willing to hire X number of East St. Louisans, Cohn said. Use the money to upgrade the police department, but then you've got to erase illiteracy. You've got to take those kids and teach them. "If there's anything I could do to help, I'd be happy to."

Cohn said the city has leadership, but that leadership needs to take a look in the right direction. "Fighting isn't going to help anything. You've got to fight for what you believe in, there are exceptions, but you can't fight with people who want to come in and help you, call them racist."

Some things have changed over the last decade.

"The attitude of people has settled down, they've grown older and calmer, and they realize the only thing they have is each other; in many ways they cling to each other. You come in here (at McDonald's, where we were talking over lunch) and you see everybody be friendly with everybody else. I think they've learned from their mistakes, they don't want to shoot any more."

"East St. Louis has been symbolized perhaps by a bottle in a paper sack, and the proliferation of liquor stores and churches: Comment?" we asked.

"Churches are going to do a lot more good than the bottle." In the last 10 years, he said there has been a swing toward religion among the people he deals with; people who have been on alcohol, uncaring, dishonest, now are God-fearing. "It has changed them; they work harder, you don't have to chase them down to see why they didn't finish a job, they're chasing you and saying 'Come look at it, I'm finished.'"

But don't look for political leadership necessarily from the churches. A political leader "must be a politician, but also a businessman. Maybe the church or even the streets can provide a leader, but just being honest isn't enough. Carl is a politician; I don't know what kind of businessman he is."

On leadership, Philip continued "Every summer for the last 23 years I have been going to a summer camp volunteering to help kids. I always said to myself when my time comes to step out and let somebody else take over I would, because the camp, or any institution, is larger than one individual, no matter how big that individual is in that institution. East St. Louis needs somebody who realizes that East St. Louis is bigger than that one individual, and you just cannot make all the decisions on how it is going to help you instead of how it will affect the majority."

His business philosophy: "I'm not foolish enough to think that one 28-year-old person can do everything on his own. What you've got to do is learn as much as you can from everybody then assess the situation and do what you have to do."

"My father's generation ... they were never sure where their next dollar was coming from," he said. While he has to work hard and keep tight controls, still, as one employee puts it, "Whether we make the deal or not, we'll still eat at McDonald's."

"I've got 60 years experience behind me," Philip said. "I have a better chance than they (his father and grandfather) did." And he has enough security to perhaps care a little more about the people.

In his business, he has learned that East St. Louis is a rare animal. The people have their own attitudes. They don't seem to feel that their house payments are as important as a lot of other things — things that would surprise you. Some do, a lot don't. So Cohn makes thousands of calls a year himself to collect payments He sees a lot of cases where fathers are illiterate, spend their time drinking, playing cards... "It's got to have an effect on the next generation," he observes.

But many East St. Louis families have been on welfare for two or three generations. They don't have work habits.

"That's right, and it will be four or five or six generations if we don't do something about it, get some programs in here, not steal the money, piss it away," Cohn said

Cohn would have people on public aid — three-fourths of the population — form work squads and clean up the city for their aid checks. He said his company takes people off the street and teaches them to paint properties. The good ones he keeps. Some leave to go to work for others, to go into the painting business. He recalls the proverb, give a man a fish and feed his hunger today, teach him to fish and feed his hunger forever.

People need to learn to care about their city, be taught to take pride in it. It's morale.

Cohn is close to the people in his houses, and he is irritated when people in Belleville talk about things "down there."

"Tell them to come to my office and go to 50 houses with me every month, see how people are living. They don't have enough to pay their gas bills, kids are sleeping on couches with roaches crawling on everything. I don't feel like I'm up there and they're here — I'm here, it's a fact, I am with these people, whether they like it or not, I am and I live it. I may go home to a house (in Belleville) where there are no roaches and my air conditioner works, but the fact is the people here don't know better, and I can't in good conscience turn away from that and not do anything about it if I am able to."

"You can't just label it down there and up here, you've got to say 'It's all us, what can we do?' Side A can't fight side B. This isn't the Civil War. Side A and Side B have both got to come off their horses and forget that the white man thinks like this and the black man thinks like that, and one's out to get the other, and say 'These are our people "down there" that are suffering, and we've got to get our heads together and do something, or you're going to keep hating me and I'll keep hating you and they're going to keep suffering.

Cohn would have aid recipients clean up messes like this in 31st Street north of St. Clair Avenue

Beulah M. Penry, president, National Stockyards Co.

Changes in marketing, industry methods cost area jobs

National Stockyards Co. President Beulah Penry can look out her office window and see the trucks unloading hogs every morning, and she can raise her eyes and see the ruins of the Armour Packing Co. plant — the old Swift & Co. plant where she worked as a secretary for 16 years has been torn down.

The stockyards supplied thousands of jobs from runners at the bank to those who wrapped hams and stuffed sausage in the packing plants. Then times changed — packers closed the plants at the yards: Swift, with about 4,000 employees, Armour, with 4,500, Hunter, with maybe 1,500, and hundreds more at Royal and Circle. The big packers built new plants, more efficient plants, elsewhere, and began buying their animals directly from the farmers, at 50 cents or a dollar a hundredweight less than current prices at the yards, or contracting for the animals even before they are conceived.

Beulah Penry is president of the National Stockyards Co., with some 650 acres, and vice president of the Oklahoma City, Okla., stockyards. She flies back and forth between the two yards. There still is lots of activity here with 2,000 heads of hogs sold every day, and a few hundred head of slaughter cattle. These "private treaty" sales still determine the market price that is paid by the packing plants when they buy on the farm. But the sales are dwindling every year — about 12 per cent this past year. There is a feeder cattle every Thursday with 500 to 600 animals, and a feeder pig auction each Tuesday, with 600 to 1,000 pigs.

The marketing system has changed.

With it went...how many jobs? The yards themselves 20 years ago employed 100, now employs 34 full-time. There were 12 commission houses, each with several employees; now there are six. The packing plants employed probably as high as 10,000! Now there are none. There were drovers handling sheep and goats as well as hogs and cattle. The farm supply stores still are there, but their business is not the same. Then the farmers hauled their cattle to market, supplies home. During World War I, the yards was the biggest mule market in the world. There were scores of satellite businesses, including the fascinating Chicago Curled Hair Corp. It bought, cleaned and

New Stockyards Inn and Cafe

curled hog hair to upholster furniture. There were hide companies, and companies that bought cripples and dead animals for dog food. North American Cold Storage was big business. There were several fertilizer firms employing hundreds of workers.

In the heyday of the yards, cattle came by train, and with them real cowboys with manure on their boots. They sauntered down Collinsville Avenue on Saturday night, spending their money there, or back on Third Street. The tracks at teh yards are gone, the unloading sheds rotting away.

Thirty years ago most husbands worked and most wives stayed home and kept house. The jobs in the yards easily supported 25,000 people! The jobs are gone because of a change in the way animals are marketed and slaughtered.

The yards story is illustrative — Aluminum Co. of America, 1,500 to 2,000 jobs lost; Alcoa Research Laboratories, 500 more, American Zinc Co., another 1,000 or so, Hill Brick, Obear Nester Glass Co., American Steel, Moss Tie, Walworth Valve, Socony Mobil, Phillips Pipeline, Continental Can, C. K. Williams & Co., on and on. Smokestack industry jobs, lost to changing technologies, new ways of doing business. Alcoa tried to bring bauxite freighters from South America up the Mississippi River to East St. Louis (really, Alorton). When that didn't prove efficient, it moved its aluminum ore reduction plants to the mine sites, which made sense for Alcoa, disaster for East St. Louis.

At the same time, after World War II, trucks and planes displaced the railroads. East St. Louis had been the second largest rail center in the United States (Chicago was No. 1). But the cows and hogs came to the yards by truck over farm to market roads, then interstates. So did many other products. People went by plane. And the once thriving Front Street warehouses and loading docks turned into ghost buildings which, one by one, were torched. Jobs lost? One thousand, two, thousand, more? Who has an answer? I rode the shop train from the Relay Depot, now gone, down the street from the hotel on Missouri Avenue, now gone, to the Brooklyn backshops of the Terminal Railroad Assn. where several hundreds of us labored over steam locomotives. Now less than half that many repair diesels. The Alton & Southern Railroad closed its doors, and it was a major employer.

The number of jobs lost in the East St. Louis area was something above 25,000, maybe as high as 45,000. Obviously they were held not only by East St. Louisans, but also by residents of Belleville, Granite City, Fairmont City, Cahokia, Dupo, East Carondelet — many other towns. But the residents of these other towns have found, since then, new employment. The residents of East St. Louis, poor and black and many uneducated, have been less fortunate. For East St. Louis, the biggest industries provided jobs only; for tax purpooses Alcoa, Monsanto and the stock yards were located in small incorporated commnities bearing their names, and in the case of National City, literally owned by the company.

The union halls went silent as jobs went to the non-union sunbelt states, or evaporated completely to new technology.

The stockyards really is an anachronism.

From her window the Stockyards Co. president can see the First Bank, bottom left, the trucks at the hog barn, a corner of the restaurant at right, and above it the ruins of the Armour & Co. plant

Every slaughter animal sold there has to be hauled somewhere else to be killed and butchered. That it has survived so long is a tribute to sticktoitiveness, and perhaps the fact that farmers know somebody has to set prices or all producers will be at the mercy of just three big packers. Twenty five years ago I asked Gil Novotny, then National Stockyards Co. president, how many years the yards had left. He said 10.

When the whites fled East St. Louis 20 years ago, the plants already were closing. The companies were "generously" giving their plants to the city; it saved the cost of tearing them down.

Penry is a native East St. Louis who now lives in Belleville. She has driven through East St. Louis to go to work for 42 years. As vice president and later president of the yards company, she oversaw the erection of a new stockyards company building after the disastrous fire Feb. 13, 1986, a new restaurant that is doing quite well, thank you, and is a great place for lunch, watched a new bank rise, and is controlling 650 acre of prime real estate in sight of the arch, 38 acres of it riverfront property. The present yards operation needs only a hundred acres. As president she does about the same thing she did as secretary to Novotny, including answering her own phone.

She belongs to the East Side Associated Industries and the Leadership Council, Southwestern Illinois.

Pemry has hope for the yards, for its survival, not revival. She has hope for East St. Louis and its riverfront development, for revival. While she's not much on pie in the sky, she believes East St. Louis is going to turn around.

"There are a lot of first tier people working on this that are truly concerned," she said. This is what is going to turn it around, whether its riverfront development, new housing, new industry or whatever. These people, black and white, have no axe to grind other than see the area make a comeback, that's their only goal, nothing personal, nothing selfish, and that's what it takes. If anyone has a selfish motive, it's not going to fly."

St. Louis National Stockyards Co. office building

Falling Debris sign cheaper than repairing failing North American Cold Storage Building. Bi-State Cold Storage does all regfrigeration now needed

Sign at entrance to yards pushes restaurant. First and Last Chance bar prophetic; all that is left of Whiskey Chute. Back entrrance to Swift, Armour is fenced and locked

Hunter Packing Co. plant, above; partial rear view at left shows bombed-out appearance. Hunter was third largest packing plant at the stockyards

Above, Circle Packing Co. Building; sign advertises used vehicles. Below right, pens at back of Circle Packing, a few cars inside fence. Above right, former Packing House Workers union hall, now Faith Miracle Temple Church of God in Christ

Serum company building on St. Clair Avenue is being demolished. At left, Robertson's Farm Supply is holding on.

O'Neil Lumber Co., always a commercial firm dealing with builders, has expanded east of First Street with O'Neil Buildings — within sight of the St. Louis Arch

Heitman Poultry Co. at First and Pennsylvania not only is guarded by dogs, sign warns they are pit bulls! At right, Free Spirit hot tubs and massage parlor in Brooklyn; Beulah Penrod said National City speeders include men hurrying home from "rub-a-dub-dub" before Mama misses them. Below, Brooklyn backshops of the Terminal Railroad Assn. Steam roundhouse has been torn down, turntable, inset below right, now is out of doors. Below left, a few diesels outside apparently are waiting repairs. TRRA once built its own 300 series steam locomotives here.

St. Louis Auto Shredding at 1200 N. First in Goose Hill big business

On Sunday, trailers of crushed cars wait to be unloaded Monday morning

Shredded metal, shredders' own Mack truck fleet

On Old Route 3 north of the stockyards, Greenspon Pipe and Edison Pipe use part of the LaRoche Industries ag chemical plant

Gutted remains of Corno Feeds mill backdrop for Parsons Avenue dumping near 20th Street

Bi-State Truck Repair, 1100 N. First St.

Commercial Truck Transport trailers, N. First St.

Industrial Track Supply, 2901 Missouri Ave., Alorton — just outside East St. Louis — makes landscape ties

Fluorspar piles sealed as "strategic materials" for the federal government by Alcoa

Part of Alcoa plant. Signs are for Helmkamp Construction, General Railroad Equipment Service

Alcoa buildings: small one signed Universal Air Filter, larger one East St. Louis Skill Center, State Community College, 3300 Missouri Ave. Welding, similar courses were taught here

Chemtech, 3500 Missouri Ave., former Alcoa building. Hydrogen fluoride also was made here

Skeletonized remains of Alcoa Research Laboratories. Behind it are LanChem, 2904 Missouri, and Stahly Cartgage stainless steel trailers

Lowry Electric Co., 3000 Missouri Ave., a survivor

Former Alton & Southern Railroad headquarters, now United Steel Drum, Inc., 3105 Missouri Ave.

C&M Services overhauls diesel locomotives for the Army

Upchurch's Atlas East St. Louis Readymix & Building Materials Corp., 29th and Missouri

Sauget, known now for nightclubs and girlie shows, is the home of Monsanto Chemical Co., which East St. Louis civic leaders say is a major contributor to civic projects. The town's name was changed from Monsanto to protect Monsanto's trademark. Thousands of jobs have been lost in the village with the closing or cutbacks of plants including American Zinc, Moss Tie, Cerro Brass, Midwest Rubber, Phillips Petroleum, Socony Mobil Refinery. Many industries located just outside East St. Louis in Monsanto, Alorton, and National City to keep from paying city taxes.

Jul Fischer Distributing Co. on Martin Luther King Drive has been abandoned

New Illinois Bell Telephone Co. service building, 4200 State St.

New Bi-State bus garage on 49th Street near Summit (whole building bottom photo, closeup of entrance above) is immense

Former Key Boiler Works Equipment Co., from rear, in Alta Sita. Five Star Metal Frabricators and Cadwick Can Co. have used parts of the facility. Other industries in area lost include Walworth Valve (formerly Wescott), Dixie Mills. The A&S yards are nearby.

American Steel Co. off Broadway, south of Obear Nester, closed

Skeletonized industrial building in near South End off Eighth Street. Vacant industry sites abound, boggle the memory

Sam Flood

They haven't written the book on assessing East St. Louis

How can you establish the fair market value of property in a town with no city services, no police protection, little fire protection, poor streets, collapsing sewers and high crime? This is the problem St. Clair County Assessor Sam Flood says he faces, and there is no book to tell how.

"We have people from East St. Louis coming in here crying on our shoulders asking for relief," he said. "They are poor people and they can't pay the high taxes and they are in a position of losing their homes. So we in turn have been sympathetic and have lowered the assessment of the properties down there. All that does is give a lowered assessed valuation in East St. Louis, then the city fathers, because they have home rule, again raise the rates. So it is a vicious circle that has to be stopped.

"The National Food store has just opened a nice new

"I was a big supporter of Carl Officer the first time he ran. I can remember how he jumped on the back of a garbage truck and helped dump the garbage. That lasted for half a day and he hasn't rode a garbage truck in the past 12 years" — Sam Flood

supermarket at 25th and State. This is the type of thing that we need to do. You can remember Collinsville Avenue, when there was never a vacancy, clothing stores, men's stores, furniture stores, they all thrived. By thriving, they were able to generate sales tax and the city didn't need the enormous amounts they now need from realty taxes.

"What I am saying, I guess, is that until East St. Louis turns itself around and changes its reputation, getting law and order back in there, getting city fathers who will be productive, we're not going to see anything."

Flood said his staff is in the process of reassessing East St. Louis. "What we intend to do is gather all the physical facts in East St. Louis, measure all the properties, make any changes on the property record cards, enter new properties — there are very few of these — and then sit down with the people I have here and some outside people experienced in real estate in East St. Louis and the surrounding areas and try to put some values and come up with a system of reassessing these properties..."

"Before we put these values on the books, we're going to have to have an agreement with the city fathers down there that they're not going to adjust their rates, and will hold taxes down. All we're doing is creating a vicious circle in that people won't pay, can't pay, and so they abandon the property, it winds up on the county tax rolls and we have the problem of reselling the property and try to give money back to the taxing districts.

"We'd certainly be more willing to do some things down there that would entice people to not only stay there but to develop down there, such as enterprise zones, abatements and tax adjustments and tax free lands for a period of years to draw industry and commercial properties, to increase the sales tax if nothing else, and aid employment..."

The tax rate in East St. Louis is the highest in Illinois, running more than $20 per hundred dollars equalized assessed evaluation, about four times the rate in most St. Clair County cities. "We've had several small firms, national firms, come into East St. Louis, but once they checked into property taxes, they decided to abandon their projects or establish just outside the city limits to avoid the tax rate down there," Floodsaid.

Crime is a major problem, Flood said. He said he was born and raised in East St. Louis, and was never afraid for his safety there, but "I'm a little skeptical now in some areas. You see whole neighborhoods that are gutted and burned out and piled high with old tires and trash, big piles, one house maybe sitting in the middle of a block with maybe an old couple and that's all they have. They can't give it away or don't want to give it away, and have to remain there."

Flood looks to the river, too. "As far as the tax base in East St. Louis, I don't think we are going to see a resurgence until the riverfront starts to develop, and until we get some credibility in the offices down there."

Flood wears another hat as the representative of he 21st Congressional District on the Democratic State Central Commitee — Democratic state central commiteeman. This gives him state party stature and makes him the key figure

The tax rate in East St. Louis is the highest in Illinois!

in Democratic state political patronage — what there is left of it — in St. Clair, Madison and portions of Clinton counties. It also gives him considerable voice in the selection of Democratic slate candidates in St. Clair County. Finally, his voice is a important in the distribution of party funds to precinct commiteemen at election time.

Flood was irritated by the charges that the Democratic Party in St. Clair County, dominated by whites, use the black vote to win elections.

"If you look at the county offices, most of us have won elections without the vote in East St. Louis. It certainly helps to have East St. Louis and know they will vote heavily Democratic. They know they can rely on the Democratic Party to assist them in any way we can. Carl Officer would like to blame the white persons for the problems of East St. Louis, but they have had black mayors in East St. Louis for 20 years now and they've had the black school board for over 20 years."

Flood said large portions of Canteen Township, and Centreville Township, which are all white, and Fairmont City which he said is white, vote strongly for Democrats; Fairmont City is probably the best Democratic precinct in St. Clair County, he said. "So to label black East St. Louis as the people who carry the election is not true. We welcome their support, we have asked for it many times and they have given it to us many times, and in return we've been very helpful to them, and we will continue to be helpful to them as long as they are responsible.

"There are some responsible people in East St. Louis, and we are not denying that. I have the utmost respect for Kenneth Hall. I think he's down there fighting a battle that I hope he lives long enough to see won. Years ago we tried to entice him into running for mayor of East St. Louis and he wouldn't do it, he wanted to stay in the senate. Things might have been different had he been down there.

"I think the people of East St. Louis have to take charge of themselves and quit blaming the white people above the hill. There's only so much you can do for people unless they want to help themselves."

Unlike most politicians and office holders, Flood was not sure Officer will be re-elected. He named four or five potential candidates. "I would think that if you are going to beat Carl Officer, you're going to have to mount a united front; you can't have four or five or six people running. Whether or not they'll get together and decide to do that, to mount that kind of campaign — I can't answer that. At the moment, Flood said he was more concerned with winning re-election in November himself.

Approaching Collinsville Avenue from the interstate bridge, shoppers are welcomed. Does mayor's name seem an afterthought wedged into award sign?

Roy Weiss Building, north of state office Building, is shabby. Remember Uncle Dick Slack?

Plattners is modern store across from Roy Weiss in 100 block. The block between Divison Avenue and Broadway is shown in section on municipal complex

West side of 100 block up to where Arcade Building once stood

Where Arcade Building stood, viewed from main Street. On Friday nights downtown nightclubs fill this parking lot and every other parking space near Collinsville Avenue

The Terrace, last building in the 100 block before you reach the former Illini S&L Building, and the entertainment complex across the street (bottom photo), are among the popular weekend nightspots. Nightclubs have heavy security guards, seldom trouble police

Walgreens, at Fifth and Missouri, has changed little

First National now First Illinois

Banner hanging for more than year

Dollar General in old Kresge Building in 200 block. Pictures taken on a Sunday means bars, no cars

On down the 200 block on west side

Empty storefront old school election headquarters

Marty Seidel's women's fashion store looks fetching

East side, 200 block, Union Bank north to LaBelle

Night Spot next to LaBelle, since renamed Emerald City for green front

Lots of wig, hairdressing shops

From B-J Clothing (230 N. Collinsville) to entrance to Murphy Building

Queen of the 200 block, and all of Collinsville Avenue, old Redmon's Majestic Theater

Stanley's is now Star of India at Collinsville and St. Louis as we enter 300 block

Across the street is Lurie's Home Furnishings, the Sears store before it moved to 10th and State streets

Moving north, street degenerates fast

Top photo., children from Gompers Homes play hide-and-seek in empty refrigerators at Collinsville Avenue second hand store. The game could be fatal. Matador Night Club in 400 block has reopened. Remodeled building at right looks pretty good until you see doorway is filled with rubbish and building is abandoned. Thrift store below brightens 300 block.

Just off Collinsville Avenue, on Broadway, top photo, is the Union Electric Co. Building, more secure, and more efficient than the building the utility turned over to the city for use as a city hall — which now stands vacant. Scotia's always has been on Broadway, and Treesh Neon Signs is one of the few businesses that have survived the civil rights revolution and the disintegration of the city of East St. Louis as the white population knew it.

Bottle in bag typical Monday morning scene on Collinsville Avenue, looking south from King Drive

Loss of sales tax revenue adds to city's many woes

Robert Vancil of LeRoy, Ill., tax increment financial consultant for the City of East St. Louis, April 10, 1990, wrote to Mayor Carl Officer in part:

"While the city has been studied to death, no report seems to focus on the real problems. Hence, most proposed solutions fall short of the mark. The single most important fact in the city's decline has been the loss of sales tax revenue.

"This loss came because of the flight of retail businesses in the late '60s and early '70s. Rebuilding the stock of private housing and retail businesses is the double task at hand."

He reports that typically a city the size of East St. Louis garners two-thirds of its income for the general funds from the city share of sales taxes. In the 1960s and '70s this was true in East St. Louis, then the white flight was followed by the business flight, complicated by the growth of Fairview Heights as a retail center. "For 15 years the city has lived with a loss of 50 percent of its income," Vancil says. Federal revenue sharing helped, but it has been cut off.

Comparing sales tax revenues for Belleville and East St. Louis, in 1965 Belleville received 75% as much as East St. Louis; in 1990 (really 1989), Belleville received 500 per cent of East St. Louis. The figures:

Year	Belleville	East St. Louis
1965	$727,291	$1,007,429
1970	$1,259,932	$1,189,003
1975	$900,338	$1,074,039
1980	$3,830,968	$1,091,691
1985	$4,005282	$1,988,533
1990	$4,633,828	$933,073

The Collapse of Collinsville Avenue as a retail trade center for Southern Illinois contributed to the sales tax revenue collapse. So did the loss of the major automobile dealerships to the suburbs.

Vancil proposes that the city pursue with the state legislature distribution of sales tax revenues on a per capita basis rather than to the cities in which the sales were made.

Public Housing mess attacked

$40 million renovation program under way

Ruth A. O'Sullivan

There's a core of people, black people, committed to this town who, for whatever reason, love, loyalty or whatever it might be, are working very hard here to get this town to turn around. I don't know whether they will be successful. I admire them tremendously for being committed because I would have walked years ago. — Ruth A. O'Sullivan

Some one third of East St. Louis' 40,000 residents live in public housing. There is a waiting list of over 2,000. A third of the public housing is vacant, including at least 200 units in the senior citizen high-rise Lansdowne Towers. Of the units not occupied, half are not fit for occupancy.

The East St. Louis Housing Authority is being operated by Quadel Consulting Corp. of Washington, D.C., for the Department of Housing and Urban Development (HUD) which took over the authority in 1985, declaring a breach of contract by the local housing authority. The previous executive directors are "serving time," according to Ruth A. O'Sullivan of Quadel, who helped oversee the project here for two years and now makes frequent inspections here.

There was fiscal and general mismanagement, maintenance was not done in any organized way, properties deteriorated. And there was a class action suit filed by the Land of Lincoln Legal Assistance Foundation against HUD that pretty well forced it to take action.

The authority operates three programs: rental housing, generally in projects; a home ownership program of "turnkey" housing in which the occupants eventually own their homes and Section 8 housing rentals. The authority is allocated 250 certificates or vouchers that families can take to find their own private sector housing, with HUD helping with the rent payments. This housing must meet HUD guidelines and is inspected by the authority. With the exception of Section 8 housing, none pays real estate taxes.

The Housing Authority is supposed to reimburse the city for city services. The county, spurred by Township Supervisor Will McGaughy, found the authority had not been doing that, asked for $800,000 in back payments, and according to O'Sullivan, collected a negotiated settlement more like $300,000. However, she said these are not in lieu of taxes, but are for services, and East St. Louis supplies few. Consequently, that settlement may be the last the city receives until it at least provides garbage pickup. However, she adds, the authority is giving the city "tons of money for construction permits."

As of Sept. 1, there had been an agreement to settle, as yet unannounced, the Land of Lincoln suit regarding the home ownership program, affecting 580 units. The settlement is occupant-

Ruth O'Sullivan, housing authority consultant

Lansdowne Towers

oriented, O'Sullivan said, with long-time tenants given ample credit toward ownership. It was not an easy problem because of the lack of adequate records. The authority has no way of knowing how much many of the tenants have paid toward home ownership, she said. Not only are records missing, but whole houses were "lost" in the transfer of housing from the St. Clair County Housing Authority to the East St. Louis Housing Authority when the latter was created in 1954. She said the settlement provides procedures for settling cases where records are missing, all very much in favor of the homeowners. "Most of those people unfortunately have not been able to get anything from us, because it was in the lawsuit and we had no way to settle."

But most of the turnkey housing will become rentals, because the tenants were not qualified as homeowners to begin with. They were somebody's mothers — not people able to qualify on an income basis and other criteria.

The turnkey housing was bought from private contractors. "You may see 10 houses alike, but only one or two will be ours;" the others, private sector housing. She said many of the homes were poorly constructed, and this has contributed to the deterioration of such housing. Somebody, she said, "and we've never been able to point a finger at anybody — somebody made a killing."

White?

"Oh, yeah."

The rest (of the deterioration) was pure negligence on the part of the housing authority," she said. "They put in people who did not meet the definitions of home buyers. Not only did you have to have sufficient income, you had to be able to make payments, all sorts of requirements to be eligible to move into those units. Many were not qualified."

Buyers made payments into a reserve fund for maintenance. If they were able to maintain the property, make repairs like a new roof themselves, they could draw money for materials from the reserve; excess could help them pay off the units earlier. If they could not, the housing authority could tap the reserve to maintain the buildings for them. The system sought to encourage "sweat equity."

We met a man who lived south of Summit Avenue in Oak Park in such a home for 16 years. He had no idea where he stood on payments. When it rains, his end of the street floods. He has a pump and two-inch hose to try to pump the neighborhood drainage over the railroad track right-of-way nearby. He has a heart ailment and wears a medication patch on his chest constantly, so is not able to do many repairs. The sills of the house near the outside door are deteriorating. Who should do

Boarded up Orr-Weathers high rises

something about that?

"We're still the owner of the property," she said. "It is the responsibility of the home owner but the authority too. The location shows negligence in the initial purchase, a total lack of management. Years went by and no one looked at those houses or responded to tenants who were responsible enough to call and say there was a problem that needed fixing and they didn't have the ability to fix it. You had to know somebody to get work done. As a result — and this is why the lawsuit — this went on for 15 to 20 years, people living in horrible circumstances, and they still are in some cases. All we have been able to do is a lot of bandaid."

The lawsuit involving rentals probably will not be settled right away, she said, because the Land of Lincoln Legal Aid wants to keep control and make sure HUD continues its level of funding.

"Money was being stolen, maintenance not occurring, some people not charged rent, it was unbelievable," she said.

Rent collections in 1985 were at 50 per cent — half the tenants weren't paying rent. Today collections are at 90 per cent. "We try to offer the assistance needed for them to meet their obligations, help with budgeting, social service referrals to agencies. In the absence of that, then we are in some sense quite mean. We have very strict rent collection policies, very strict lease enforcement policies; we educate the tenants from day one what we will do. We've gotten to the point where tenants will tell other tenants 'You'd better be good, better pay your rent because they will kick you out.' People generally have fallen in line."

The housing authority is at 67 per cent

A few weeks earlier, Orr-Weathers had looked like this, with all boarding stolen from the windows. With open elevator shafts, housing authority risked major liabilty

Ruth O'Sullivan, housing authority consultant

Rehabilitated Gompers Homes

occupancy right now, which is consistent with HUD goals for East St. Louis, "but that's 33 per cent not occupied, and half are not fit for occupancy."

The vacancies primarily are among the elderly units in Lansdowne, built in the late '50s and early '60s. "We've done a marketing study and found we don't have a market." East St. Louisans old enough to meet HUD standards (62 or over or handicapped) tend to be the frail elderly who require care rather than just housing. "We provide some level of services, the emergency bells, some social service programs, nutrition programs, but we are not a nursing home or intermediate care facility; people have to live somewhat independently."

Quadel has lowered the age limits to the "near elderly" — 50 and older — to attract more people, and it is working but "we have several hundred units to fill, and this is a town in which people are leaving, anybody who can is leaving."

Are tenants frightened?

"Crime is a problem throughout the city."

No worse there than anywhere else?

"I would think not."

Is Lansdowne the worst neighborhood?

"It keeps shifting. For awhile it was the Villa Griffin project, which is right next to Lansdowne Towers, so it is from that the (senior citizen) high

John Robinson units fenced for rehabbing. Housing Authority is administering $40 million in rehab funds

Federally insured, perhaps never finished, vandalized, but probably not public housing

rises get affected. We have brought in the state police who are very effective there, and that moved it over to the John DeShields. We keep chasing it back and forth."

The housing authority is paying nine undercover state police to fight crime, especially drugs, in the projects. There are 16 other state police assigned to the city. The authority has applied to HUD for funds to assign two city policemen, in uniform, to work under the state police direction in the housing projects, to give visibility.

O'Sullivan praised the East St. Louis Police Department. "They really try." She said this is one service the city is providing to the authority and meeting its obligations.

"We have a number of other agencies in the community providing services, providing drug treatment programs and providing educational opportunities, but when people are afraid to walk out their front door, they're not helping anybody."

Are they afraid in the daytime?

"Yes, but it is easing. There's a visible difference. Violence does occur. It's heavier at night, no question, but during the day one of our employees was shot in broad daylight, working on a vacant unit. He was caught in the crossfire of a gunfight.

"That's what tenants are afraid of, crime within our property. It is almost always not our tenants. The people who are victimized are our tenants. When people are afraid of becoming

Some turnkey housing is this bad. Is this turnkey? Possibly

Midtown units north of St. Clair obviously abused

victims, we wonder what they are involved in.

"We have improved evicting people, left and right, when we identify them as involved in drug activity. We have won every single case. We are very happy to have a court that will cooperate with us.

"Since April (four months), when state police came on board, there have been 55 arrests. We've evicted 15 families, many more are in process, and 10 moved out once they were notified of the eviction procedure. People are starting to get the message. Our message is that if you want to keep your house, get those people (into drugs) out of your house, take control of your family.

"We come across to some people as being very mean, but most tenants are sympathetic and agree with us that if they are going to tolerate this in their homes, then they are going to have to suffer the consequences."

The Housing Authority is involved in rehabilitating rental units. It just has completed Gompers Homes, downtown, at a cost of $9 million. A $7 million rehabbing project at John Robinson Homes is about completed (Sept. 1). Villa Griffin is next, also at a cost of about $7 million. "We are administering $40 million in rehab funds."

Orr Weathers is scheduled for various work items, elevator work, rewiring, replaced boilers on hot water heaters, but not comprehensive rehab. Two of the high rises are vacant, two in operation. The two vacant ones have been boarded up for the fifth time, but people steal the boards. This time the replacements are welded in. "It has been a frustration, a lot of money has gone down the drain from that. With the elevator shafts, the buildings are a tremendous liability too. We have to keep people out."

The authority is prohibited by federal law from tearing down any units without replacing them. So the two will stay boarded up.

It does not have to replace, however, units sold to occupants as in the home buyer program.

It has applied for authority to demolish 76 units of houses beyond rehabilitation. None can be demolished until funds for the demolition and replacement units have been approved. The replacement units probably will be the acquisition and rehabilitation of existing housing in the private sector.

There is all kinds of housing here, she said. It would be silly to build more public housing. The replacement units may be smaller apartment houses, maybe some single family.

There are several HUD-subsidized Section 8 apartment projects around the area. One sizeable one is in Alta Sita, but it has deteriorated and the housing authority has canceled it as an option for its certificate holders.

O'Sullivan said the mayor and other public officials get a lot of press, but "there's a core of people, black people, committed to this town who, for whatever reason, love, loyalty or whatever it might be, are working very hard here to get this town to turn around. I don't know whether they will be successful. I admire them tremendously for being committed because I would have walked years ago."

She said there is a consortium of social service agencies that meets monthly to serve the elderly, a variety of folks from the town, not with government in any shape or form. It is "one of the reasons we feel very good about what we are doing, it is not a hopeless cause or effort.

"The tenants make our lives worthwhile," O'Sullivan said. "The kids really get to you. The kids are the ones who will come out of this somehow. The kids are a joy, the kids are what really get you going. Their parents are helpless, but there are a lot of people struggling to get ahead, going to school, working a couple of jobs, trying to make a life for themselves and their kids.

"For that reason, we hope to stay three more years, a total of seven years. We have no promises from HUD. We'd like to stay until it is time to turn the authority back to the city, and the city is ready to have it turned back. HUD doesn't want to continue to operate the program, but it doesn't want to see it slide back once it has gotten it straightened out, either."

We recalled Carl Officer's concerns about the housing authority, and commented:

"You don't sound like such bad guys."

"We don't think we are," she responded. "We think we're sort of saviors, in a way. We do a good job of trying to make things run correctly. We feel that we are very pro-tenant, and we do what makes the most sense and will benefit the tenants the most."

There have been many "housing projects" in East St. Louis built under many different programs. The mistake often is made of assuming all are "public housing." Many are private housing, but constructed with federally guaranteed loans of one sort or another, some offering federally assisted rents. There is no one trying to sort out all the housing in East St. Louis, including housing that is vacant while hundreds are homeless

Jones Park Pool dry concrete

When you're fighting for survival, beauty takes a back seat

If you visit Jones Park, you'll find the toilets locked and portable outhouses in their place. They've turned the water off — the Park District cannot afford the sewage treatment fees charged by American Bottoms Sewer District.

There is no water in Jones Park Pool for two reasons: the pool leaks. It leaks through the bottom. It leaks through the sidewalls. And if it didn't leak, it would take 600,000 gallons of water to fill. And each hot day, the district would have to add 50,000 to 75,000 gallons for evaporation, and the overfill necessary for the skimmers to work. And it would have to pay sewage fees for the evaporated water, because the treatment charge is based on water metered in, not out.

It would take a million dollars to renovate Jones Park pool, Leonard Johnston, park district superintendent, said. It was built in 1958 — the same year as the Lincoln Park pool, back in the days of segregation. The Jones Park pool was bigger. Five years ago there was $700,000 spent on Lincoln Park pool in repairs — from a grant. It evaporates perhaps 30,000 gallons of water a day. There has not been a grant to fix Jones Park pool. If there were, the district couldn't afford the water.

Leonard Johnston, park superintendent

Leonard Johnston, park superintendent

Jackie Joyner Park is well-used

Johnston has been with the district 10 years, and says his job is a frustrating one. A citizens beautification group headed by Francell Morgan volunteered to plant flowers in the park. They died, for lack of water. and maintenance. With so many people out of work, he sought to enlist volunteers to work in the park. But he said he guessed they were more concerned with the basics of survival; when you are fighting to live, "beauty takes a back seat."

This year the Park District budget is $249,000. Sixty per cent of the budget is fixed costs. Twenty years ago the budget was $500,000. Decreasing property assessments have brought the revenues down, at the same time costs have skyrocketed.

In all candor, he said, all the district can hope to do is keep the grass cut below knee height at Jones Park, the diamonds cut so the high school, little league and an adult baseball league can play, and a couple of tennis courts in shape, and water in the Lincoln Park pool.

With the cooperation of the Department of Conservation, from an Urban parks fund the district got $300,000 to dredge the lagoon and the department stocked it with fish, including rainbow trout, but two years ago it filled with philominous algae, apparently brought in on the feet of a bird. It grows in the sun, and because the lagoon was shallow and the sun reached the bottom, it filled the lagoon. Last year over the winter the district used a grant to deepen the lagoon by three or four feet to an average depth of six feet, on the advice of the department, thinking the sun couldn't reach that deep, but it didn't work. The only chemical that will keep the algae out also will kill the fish. It isn't very pretty, but as he said, when you are fighting for survival, beauty takes a back seat.

Lincoln park has its pool. But the Mary Martin Community Center is a dilapidated shell. The park is, at best, austere.

The district used to get grants to provide summer recreation programs, track and field events, youth baseball, tennis tournaments, in the parks, but there are no recreation grants anymore.

The newest park, Jackie Joyner Park in Denverside, was given to the city by Jackie Joyner-Kersee in 1985, after her spectacular showing at the 1984 Olympics. It is near where she grew up at 1433 Piggott Ave. But the district has given up other parks: Bluff View, 22 acres in the Signal Hill area, abandoned in the late '70s; Oak Park, at 51st at Summit, given to a group, perhaps the American Legion, before Johnston was superintendent; Washington park, at 50th and Audubon, given to the Washington Park Volunteer Firemen (but the East St. Louis Park District still cuts the grass for the ball diamond and picnic shelters), one in Goose Hill, taken over in part by the East St. Louis

Lincoln Park Pool, Mary Martin Center in background

Housing Authority, one sacrificed in Alorton to the Bond Avenue overpass. Equipment in Alta Sita and other parks is broken, swings are without seats, teeterboards without boards, tennis courts without nets, with grass growing in the cracks in the courts.

Jimmy Connors learned his backhand at Jones Park, and his feet danced on the acclaimed clay tennis courts, now gone, while his father collected tolls on the Veterans Bridge. East St. Louis is not likely to produce any new tennis stars on the courts that are left.

The park district is not coextensive with the city limits, it reached out into other municipal jurisdictions. It is tax supported with an elected Board of Park Commissioners.

The seats in the concrete stadium at the once lighted softball diamond in Jones Park are empty now. There have been no games there since 1986. The softball players are "over the hill," Johnston said. The park district started charging $50 a game for lights — their actual cost — and the teams decided they did not want to play that badly. So the lights, like the water, were turned off.

Johnston has no major plans. He is hanging on, doing the best he can, fighting for survival — and when you are fighting for survival...

Twisted playground equipment in Alta Sita park

Fountain at the east baseball diamond always was clogged with rocks, seldom worked. Today it's off because the district cannot afford the sewer fee for the water usage

The Jones Park lagoon was a place to fish, a place to canoe with your girl, and wade if you tipped the canoe. Today it is shrunken and filled with growth

Weeds grow in most of the the tennis courts at Jones Park. Jimmy Connors perfected his game here while his mother coached and his father worked for the city on t he Veterans Bridge. Courts are not likely to produce any stars today unles they bring their own nets and dodge the holes

Aunt Mary's Parkway Inn gave way long ago to a Fina Station, but the war monu-ment remains at the east entrance to the park. But the flowers that used to spell out a welcome no longer or planted — there's nobody toi care for them, and no water for them

Those whose memories go back to Pittsburgh Lake can rmember when Grand Marais was a city park, the fish hatchery and fountain — we suspect at the site above — and the Lady of the Lakes Pageant, between lakes 2 and 3, born in the WPA Days. Then there were the motorboat races. And if you really go back, you can recall when you dressed in the weeds and swam there, whites on t he south side, blacks on the north, and there were drownings when some fool tried to swim across after downing a picnic lunch

The Sunken Gardens on Pennsylvania Avenue, once a place to display beautiful flowers grown by park district gardners

A pile of rubble remains near where Relay Depot once stood on Missouri Avenue, west of interstates

A camera tour of East St. Louis, the way it is, 1990

East St. Louis Radio Station WESL 1490AM
149 S. 8th St.

Before we go further analyzing the situation in East St. Louis with other interviews and our own observations, let's take a drive through the city and see what is here. Primarily we will be looking at houses and churches, business places, neighborhood by neighborhood, and whatever else we have missed in the presentations in the preceding pages and will omit in the topical pages to come.

The pictures you see here are typical rather than comprehensive presentations. Not even here can we present every house. What we show you, both good and bad, is just a sampling, There are other houses, churches, business places, just like, better and worse than those we have photographed.

We will begin downtown and move south into the traditional South End, then move east out Bond Avenue to Alta Sita, return to the mid-city, move out State Street to Hilltop and Loisel Hills, then north to Lansdowne and out Caseyville and Forest Boulevard to Kingshighway, and occasionally peek over the perimeter.

Drive south in Eighth Street to the old MacArthur Bridge approach, above, and you may think the road ends. But turn left around it and you'll discover Denverside, which dates to 1970 and the Model City Urban Renewal program. The city used its motor fuel tax money to install concrete streets and sidewalks and surface sewers as the "local share" of the cost. The area was cleared by the federal government for redevelopment as a prime residential area.The firehouse below at 1700 Central Avenue was built with Model City funds when Elmo Bush was fire commissioner. Meanwhile Rush City to the south has been bought up and cleared by a trust that rêsidents think is Monsanto Chemical Co., protecting itself from lawsuits over chemical leaks.

Apartment complex at 16th Street and Russell. The area includes fine homes, apartments, a school, and the Jackie Joyner playground pictured in parks section

This modernistic home is owned by East St. Louis Alderman Mike Cullen at 1424 E. Russell. The area has several homes with this general appearance, including one owned by Mayor Carl Officer's brother Edgar. Cullen is enlarging this house to the rear of the garage.

Largest home in Denverside is that of Rev. Norman E. Owens, 1601 Lawrence, pastor of Macedonia Baptist Church, 320 N. 10th St. There are fine homes east and west of his home

The view westward from Rev. Owens' home leads right through the Arch. The site is 10 minutes from the garages at Busch Stadium and has an excellent view of the St. Louis skyline. Bob Vancil's TIF housing plan, in later pages, provides for more homes in this area.

Solar panels heat this home at 1409 Gay Avenue

Home on Gay at 17th shows care with flag, hanging pots, shrubs. Other homes in block are similar

Home nearby at 12th and Colas is in sharp contrast

Sharon Thoele of Cahokia sells snow cones from the rear of her three-wheel motorscooter cart. She has been working the South End for four years. Sometimes her husband Calvin runs the route. Here she serves a church crowd after services. She says she has never been robbed or had any trouble. "Of course, they know I have a gun."

Liberty Church of God in Christ, 1408 S. 19th St.

Greater New Hope Baptist Church, 2240 Missouri Ave.

Mt. Zion Baptist Church, 2235 Bond Ave. Rev. John Rouse, minister

St. John's AME Zion Church, 1900 Bond Ave.

True Light Baptist Church, 16th Street and Tudor Avenue

Macedonia Baptist Church, 14th and Broadway, Rev. Norman E. Owens, pastor

There's room for a garden alongside this home at 10th and Baker

Weeds and brush hide the ugliness of an abandoned house at left. There are some houses with trees growing through the porch floor and roof. Below a homeowner keeps trash bags high above dogs at 1221 Russell.

Pilgrim Baptist Church, 15th and Gay, celebrated its 35th anniversary June 17. Rev. M. R. Lemons Badde is pastor

Church of God in Christ, Congregational, 10th and Bond, Bishop Hosea Slack

Market Avenue Church of God, 15th and Market. Just across the alley north of it is St. Paul's Baptist Church, which is putting on an addition

At left, St. Peter's Baptist Church, 805 S. 10th St. Below, Greater Liberty Church of God in Christ, 1408 S. 19th St. Churches are everywhere in East St. Louis, in storefronts, garages, houses, humble buildings, magnificent buildings. Phil Cohn of Cohn Realty, one of the city's biggest landlords, says there is an upsurge of religion in East St. Louis and it is making a difference among his tenants.

Purple thistles, beautiful but painful to the touch, grew everywhere in the city in the spring. They could be the city flower! Through the thistles, the Arch

Modest home, well-tended garden, reflects Bob Goodrich's concept of "pleasant slums." However, remains of house at left on 19th Street near Sauget and shell of a house below also are frequent reminders of the poverty of the city, especially in the South End. These houses look as though they simply wore out. Contrast them with some of those destroyed in Oak Park, in later pages

Home to someone, but a heavy snow could collapse the roof

Half a house is still a home in the 1200 block of Russell Avenue

One person referred to houses like these as similar to Appalachia

Both ends and the rear of this building, near the I-64 Fourth Street ramp, have collapsed, but people live here

And now, Alta Sita

Gunn's Midtown Lounge, 2700 block of Bond Avenue

B&M Liquor, northeast corner of 28th and Bond Ave.

Most old Alta Sita homes, though big and costly to maintain, are in good shape. There are exceptions.

The architects of these two houses, on McCasland, left, and at 2928 Bond, right, were at least acquainted. However, the one at left is well maintained, to the cacti along the drive, while the other suffers from what is called politely "delayed maintenance"

Former Aldersgate Methodist Church, 27th and Market, now Bride of Christ Church of God in Christ

St. Regis Catholic Church and School, 3500 Market Avenue

Unlike most of the town, there are a good many recently built homes in Alta Sita

Attractive frame home at 2701 Trendley

Two homes in the 3100 block of McCasland Avenue, one a triplex, show care typical of the neighborhood

Neat home at 2703 Trendley, above, features twisted brick porch roof supports. At right. Straightway Baptist Church, 3300 Bond Ave. Nearby, an exception in Alta Sita; half the house is gone, but it is occupied.

Stable neighborhood, but note bars on windows. Many homes have ADT signs

Home at left is falling apart, one on right, on McCasland, is vandalized

McCasland Avenue is boulevard with gates; undergoing street renovation

3600 block of Trendley is in Centreville Township, just outside city limits. House above at 3616 has entertainment deck over garage. Below the block from 37th Street. Residents say neighbors work together, have little problem with gangs or crime

Back to Midtown and east

Abandoned city garage — once Bi-State Garage — on Eighth Street, contains old city equipment from fire trucks to automobiles. It's for sale. East St. Louis abounds with abandoned buildings that would make decent business or industry sites

15th and Broadway once was the nerve center of the black community. This building is where Will McGaughy established his health services program, was booted out, and saw his successor charged with theft and the center closed. It has never opened again. Once it was a liquor store

St. Paul Baptist, 1500 Bond Ave. being enlarged

Wesley Bethel United Methodist Church, 1411 Missouri Ave.

St. Paul's Social Center, now the Boys Club, viewed across the lot where the old Rock Junior High School stood. The building we remember as the scene of professional wrestling matches has grown shabby in its old age

These homes stand across 10th Street east of the old East Side High School. They should be familiar to old East Side High grads. Let's see, June and Joan Helfrich lived along there someplace in 1942

The Kathryn Dunham Museum, the old East St. Louis YWCA at 1005 Pennsylvania Ave., is getting a badly needed facelift

Old mansion on Pennsylvania Avenue nearby is collapsing. In weeded lot next door sign says not to litter historic property

First Baptist Church, 1101 State St.

St. Luke's AME Church, 414 N. 14th St.

The old First Church of Christ Scientist, 612 Washington Place, is Mount Olive Missionary Baptist

Immanuel Evangelical and Reformed Church, 1301 Summit, now Mount Pisgah Baptist

Courtney Drug Store, above, 2701 State St., is a survivor — with wire mesh and other safeguards

Former Scottish Rite Temple of Free Masonry, left, today is GEMM (Gateway East Metropolitan Ministry — a cultural arts and media center

Bottom left is the State Street Square shopping mall at 1218 State St.

25th Street and State has a new look. H. C. Krumley Co. is the old State Street Theater, where the author watched Tom Mix and first saw, to his terror, Frankenstein. Kurrus Funeral Home was torn down to make room for the new National 24-hour supermarket, which in turn drew Church's Chicken next door on State Street. Across 27th Street the old Jeff Gates auto electric parking area is used to hawk shoes, clothing and cassette tapes by entrepreneurs.

These two houses on 25th Street are directly across from National's store. Developers hope the store will spur a desire to improve the neighborhood. House at left is boarded up

Peas-in-a-pod houses in the 500 block of North 28th Street. Even the flower pots on the porch posts are the same

Old State Street Methodist Church at 2901 State is Promise Center for Developmentally Disabled

When you get off the main streets through East St. Louis — the only ones most white people feel safe driving — you find the bulk of the well-kept homes. The homes on this page are typical of the midtown area — including the one boarded up with discarded sofas in the front yard. Many have been restored, sometimes imaginatively. The vertical picture is of a two-story on 24th Street that has a pot of flowers on each step. The house has been painted imaginatively, the yard landscaped. The house is turn-of-the-century architecture.

Former Beck Vanilla Co. plant is SIU Small Business incubator

Old Brichler Funeral Home is Muhammed Temple, 2216 State Street

Burke Funeral Home was Calvert Funeral Home, Firemen's Hall, now is boarded up

National Guard Armory same but fenced; used for surplus food distributions

Family Dollar Stores at 2318 State St., 8120 State and 1835 Kingshighway meet shopping need

Michael Collins express pride in city's athletes on back of liquor store at 25th & St. Clair

St. Joseph's School at 1501 Martin Luther King Drive is now SIUE Head Start center

Old Winstanley Baptist Church, 2801 State St., now Southern Mission Baptist Church

Illinois Power Co. — no East St. Louis address in phone book

Law offices of StateRep. Wyvetter Younge and her husband Richard Younge at 20th and State Streets

West of Law Offices, former Leon Davis Furniture Co. building stands vacant

Plumbers union office, East Side Health District and (not pictured here) East St. Louis Housing Authority offices are on 20th Street. Old Bell Telephone service building, Post Office sectional center and other good buildings stand vacant on 20th Street

St. Patrick's Roman Catholic Church, 33rd Street and Vogel Place

Old St. Joseph Church, now
Christ Redeemed Baptist Church

Haynes Miracle Temple, 823 Pennsylvania Ave.

Old State Street Mixon Buick building is leading eyesore as someone tries to box it in with used wood

Disposal of old rubber tires is a real problem, but not if you simply dump them in East St. Louis. Thirty-first Street looks as though it dead-ends against the I-64 highway, but it doesn't. This street is lined with old tires on both sides, then a block north truck loads are dumped despite hand-written pleas against dumping put up by neighbors.

Below, two blocks east these tires are piled in yard by garage

McAteers House of Lights once occupied this building on St. Clair Avenue near 33rd Street

The old Wagon Wheel bar and restaurant of a quarter-century ago still has a western look

Old St. Peter Kirche Evangelical Lutheran Church, built 1889, is now Southern Cross Lodge 112 of the Masonic Hall

Across the street from church at left, litter accumulates, so common a sight that after awhile you don't see it anymore

Oak Park — from 42nd to Harding Ditch

The old East St. Louis City Lines had a bus to 42nd and State, and beyond that, another to Edgemont. But Edgemont didn't really start until you reached the other side of the Harding Ditch. So for our purposes, we will name this section after Oak Park, a tiny park betwen 51st and 52nd Streets and Summit, next to a one-room Oak Park School, where Miss Myrtle McClinchie — Miss Mac — a saint of a lady taught the first two half grades in one-room. Her pupils included Rube Yelvington, who learned there it doesn't pay to chop down cherry trees just so you can confess and prove you don't lie

Apartments across State from Shop City fire-gutted and roofless

The old Oak Park School in the 800 block of north 52nd Street, is now a church — the Supreme Council of the House of Jacob, Bishop T. Malachi Pollard, pastor

St. Clair County Teacher's Credit Union at 5000 State St, directly across from East St. Louis Sr. High School. Miss Miller used to operate a neighborhood grocery at that site. When during the Depression our rented house burned — courtesy of kerosene, rags and a match — we rented the back rooms from Miss Miler for awhile. She drank Milller's beer, too.

The Yelvington's slept here — Big Rube and Toppy (as I was called then) and Carrie Elephair Haynes Yelvington — when I was about the size of the children out front. There was no garage attached to the side then. That was more than 50 years ago, and the house was 25 to 50 years old then. It has shrunk from the vision in my memory, but is in about as good a condition as I recall it. My dad always had at least two Model T Fords in the yard, each with one rear wheel jacked up so they would start easier when you cranked them. He was on the wrecking crew for the Terminal Railroad Assn., and being ready to go when he was called was of great importance to him. I think the used Model T's cost about $25 to $35. Ths house was at the corner of 55th and Ohio. The building below was across Ohio Avenue, and the owner let me help floor the upper level of his garage, and showed me how to blunt a finishing nail so it wouldn't split the boards.

Oak Park Baptist Church was built on Belmont at 58th Street. At first it just was a basement building, then the santuary was added. Now it is the New Bethlehem Baptist Church. The church has bought the property to the east and fenced a parking lot, has carpeted and air conditioned the building and welcomes visitors. For a short spell I was a church janitor here. The building looks better than when the congregation moved up the street and became the State Street Baptist Church.

Next door on the west are the remains of the Orphanage Apartments. Wilton and Marie Rice, parents of Attorney Bob Rice, bought the complex from a Pentecostal church about 1940, labored around the clock to turn it into an apartment complex of 23 units. They and Bob lived there. Bob's father sold the complex about 1980, after 45 years. Today it is gutted by fire and vandals and no unit is habitable

Guess who lived here at 53rd and Ohio? Every two or three years my mother would say she was "tired of looking at these four walls," and off we were. Siding, shutters have been added

Heine and Catherine Miller lived here. They owned Oak Park Market, where I drove a delivery truck.

Bill Turner lived here. He worked for the telephone company and was a deacon in the church, and made good dandelion wine

Yes, I lived here too, in the house with the awning at 646 N. 51st St. Next door lots were vacant

The "new" Calvert Nursing Home lies just north of the high school, with the entrance off Summit

Parallel to it on 51st Street, in the part of Oak Park cut off when Summit was paved, people dump

In the 800 block of 52nd Street, a house far newer than those I lived in is gutted

"State Street Baptist Church" is engraved over the entrance of this church on State at 59th, but the members followed Pastor Bill Fox to Fairview Heights and established Lake View Baptist Church

After fire, only the sign is left of the original Stop Light Restaurant at Kingshighway and St. Clair Avenue

A dream gone sour — wrong time, wrong place? The developer saw this as the Fairview Heights of the 1960s. The medical building still is operating according to Bob Kassing of First Illinois Bank, including a pharmacy and medical offices, but soon after Memorial Day financially troubled St. Mary's Hospital withdrew its clinic that it had operated there. Inset above left is the Shop City Red Fox grocery, in the building that once was Shop City Bowl. The northeast corner of the big paved lot, close to the new East Side High School football stadium, has been used as a tire dump.

French Village Drive-in was a family fun center as well as a petting zoo for teen-agers in the days before television came to every home, and the competition was compounded by the VCR. It was the East St. Louis drive-in, and makes our transition to the section on Edgemont; turn the page.

When whites already were fleeing the city, Loisel Hills was developed to let people live in the city but on the Bluffs. It is entered east of 89th Street, across from Loisel Village

All homes in Loisel Hills are in the six-figure class and are on large lots or acreage

Multi-level home hugs terrain

Smallest of subdivision homes impressive

Hilltop Place is a hidden alcove reached off Belleville's Lebanon Road. The elite area of the "old days," most homes are interesting and well maintained, but...

...there are exceptions

Just south of the 89thStreet entrance to Loisel Hills stands this interesting relic with a sign suggesting votes for "progressive leadership"

There was a time when Loisel Village had high-fashion shops. Not so today

Loisel Village is the older brother of Loisel Hills, and lies west of Illinois 177 (89th Street) These houses are typical, though in the upper picture the owner boasts more mature shrubs than most. Owners, most of them blacks, obviously take pride in their property and summer weekends find them mowing, trimming, pruning — sometimes painting. Most also avoid political involvement.

Trees, shrubs, trimmed lawns, all bespeak of a fine neighborhood. But when you look closely the ornamental iron tells that things are not always what they seem. Where else do storm doors have deadlocks? Fear is not so much personal as for property. Many homes have burglar alarms, ADT alarm services, ourside floodlights, sometimes motion lights turned on when someone passes close to the house. All this plus expensive insurance and high, high taxes. But pride of ownership is evident.

Not only in Loisel Village, but in the outer Edgemont area, most homes show care. Top photo, St. Philip Catholic Church, middle a well-maintained (and barred) home. At right, a small boarded up house, another of hundreds like it in East St. Louis. Here at least it has not been vandalized.

Home ownership here shows the same concerns as in any city

Housing is varied once you leave subdivisions. Older home lower right has failing roof

Edgemont Post Office, Edgemont Sports Store and Mirring Florists at 8700 State St.

Edgemont Bible Church began in building at left, now a shell; built beautiful church building above, then moved to Fairview Heights

The old First Presbyterian Church, and across the street the old Greek Orthodox Church, are serving different congregations, but look the same outside. Club 24/7 is the old Robert Hall clothing store. The Clyde C. Jordan Senior Citizen Center is the former Kenney's shoe store. Old White House Market is vacant. Master Guard storm doors (with deadlocks) is a thriving business.

Park N Shop Super Market, 7600 State St., once Harry Bise's grocery store

Krest Liquors at 6900 State St., at right, proclaims itself Democratic Ward Headquarters and has this platform on the front of the building, designed to appeal to the concerns of the citizens and thereby indicative of their views:

WE PROPOSE

1. To organize ward-wide for the purpose of keeping streets, alleys and abandoned buildings clean, safe and lighted.

2. To organize from a ward level to support those agencies responsible for our lives! Namely the police and fire departments.

3. To monitor and actively evaluate the use of our tax dollars.

4. To fight collectively with other elected officials to secure jobs and industry for East St. Louis.

5. To develop a prompt city-wide ambulance service.

OUR PLEA TO YOU IS THAT YOU

Care...When someone burglarizes your neighbor's home...tomorrow it may be yours!

Care...When your tax dollars are not paving your streets and keeping your sewer open!

Care...When your property is assessed triple that of anywhere else in St. Clair County, yet, you cannot purchase insurance except through t he Illinois Fair Plan!

Care...When your publc safety agencies are not equipped to handle their workload because of an equipment and/or manpower shortage!

Care...enough to make your vote count!

We care enough to ask for it.

Children's Center for Behavioral Development at 353 N. 88th St. is in Centreville, recently broke ground for a residential hall. A school for children with severe behavioral disorders, it serves the region

Business places you may recognize from 20 years ago. As elsewhere in the city, there are plenty of liquor stores and churches. Black congregations are proud of the edifices surrendered to them by the fleeing whites, and are grateful.

Homes and burnouts south of State Street and of Edgemont. Some or all of these are in Centreville Township outside any lingering constraints of zoning

And now, north of St. Clair Avenue

Back at the old East St. Louis Journal — before it was renamed Metro-East — City Editor Bill Gisinger used to refer to Lansdowne as the "silk stocking district," the "upper class" part of town. Tree-lined streets that look peaceful are filled at night with drug traffickers and violence — not as bad as it has been, but still far from acceptable. Abandoned buildings mar the neighborhoods where residents fight to maintain the value of their homes — though it doesn't really make much difference, no one will make a loan to a buyer anyway so they are stuck there forever. The North End probably has undergone more change than any other part of East St. Louis, so we might as well get the shock therapy out of the way and show you these pictures first.They were taken somewhere west of 25th Street and north of Pfizer Chemcial Co. (the old C.K.Williams, if you have forgotten.) Scenes like these can be found on isolated side streets where all dilapidated vacant houses become public dumps. We are including all the property north of St. Clair as the North End in our camera tour.

These houses are on Parsons Avenue east of 18th Street

Vacant House at 1214 N. Third Street, near entrance to old Hunter Packing Co. plant. Trees are growing through the porch roof

Home at 1705 Lynch Ave. , with Pfizer Chemical Co. in background. Chain link fence makes a substitute clothesline at modest but well-maintained home

Old Garfield School, built in 1929, in Goose Hill; concrete vault company uses premises in the rear

Section of house off Exchange Avenue in Goose Hill collapsing

Gethsemane Baptist Church, 1435 Baugh Ave.

School at 15th and Lake

Sign on Ninth Street welcoming visitors stands in front of a dilapidated vacant house, is overshadowed by thistles and boasts of 1979 state victories of the talented Lincoln High School girl athletes. No signs have been erected since, though the East Side High football team has won three state championships in the last four years and there have been many more athletic achievements: there is not even a sign that boasts that this is the home city of Olympian Jackie Joyner-Kersee! The state provides such highway signs for most cities

Lessie Bates Davis Neighborhood House, 1200 N. 13th St.

Fifteenth Street Baptist Church, 1314 N. 15th St.

View across street for Fifteenth St. Baptist, one vacant, one occupied

...And down the street

North End Missionary Baptist Church,
129 Exchange Ave., Goose Hill

Old Goose Hill school closed for lack
of pupils in the area

Old 15th Street Market;
neighborhood grocers ghosts of the past

House on Exchange Avenue
lots of derelicts in the North End

Kassly Funeral Home now Hillcrest Motel, police say used by women from the stroll but it was headquarters for Goose Hill Reunion

Old Sedlack Funeral Home at 15th & Winstanley now Doris Helping Hand for the Homeless; other houses in block generally well maintained

Homes in block by old Sedlack Funeral Home generally kept up

These abandoned houses are on Parsons Avenue just west of Jones Park

Top photo, Bethlehem Missionary Baptist Church, formerly St. Paul's Methodist, 1817 N. 39th St., lower photo Unity Lutheran Church, 4200 Caseyville Ave.

Former Holy Angels Catholic Church; the convent now houses the homeless

Above, Gallilee Central Baptist Church, 2334 Lincoln Ave. At right, Immaculate Conception Lithuanian Church, 15th Street and Baugh Ave., it's distinctive beauty unscathed

Colony Theater at 40th and Wavery still showing X-rated movies: police say it draws a good noon crowd of white businessmen and delivery truck drivers, and afternoon finds some of the same men cruising the stroll in downtown East St. Louis or what is left of Whiskey Chute. They point to the white traffic, including white men who proposition women going to work from Goose Hill in the mornings, when you tell them whites are afraid to come into East St. Louis. And most of the patrons of Faces on Collinsville Avenue are white. It all depends, it depends...

Convenience corner, also at 40th and Waverly

First street inside the city limits, north side, house is crumbling from "delayed maintenance"

The old Wurth Dairy on Bunkum — and we thought those were the days that would never end

East St. Louis Federation of Teachers Local 1220 Building, 3813 Bunkum Road

Stephens Hardware on Kingshighway (Ill. 111) in Washington Park another survivor. WashingtonPark suffers from many of the problems of East St. Louis including revenue, unemployment or underemployment, crime and to put it nicely, racial differentation

East St. Louis City Limits on Caseyville Avenue from Washington Park — the numbers are different now

Dr. Lillian A. Parks

School superintendent sees need for pupils, city to believe in themselves

They snickered when she said she was from East St. Louis, so she showed them she was the best

When Lillian Parks, fresh out of Lincoln High School, enrolled at the University of Illinois, new students were asked to stand up and identify themselves, tell their majors and their home towns. When Lillian said her hometown was East St. Louis, they snickered. "Even in those days," she remembers, "East St. Louis was kind of ridiculed, laughed at, always."

That experience made Lillian commit herself to excellence. She would make them swallow their snickers. She would be the best in her class, the best at everything she did. "It served for me, the negative was the positive. That was my attitude."

Today Dr. Lillian Parks is just as committed to bringing excellence to the East St. Louis school system, the first woman to be superintendent, an East St. Louis native, an East St. Louis resident, and one who believes in "showing them" the stuff you're made of, that East St. Louis is made of.

Her father Horace Adams was a fighter. He was a civil rights leader before it was the fashionable thing for a black leader to do. He was involved in politics — he founded the Paramount Democratic Club that turned the black Republicans to Democrats and welded together a political powerhouse that dominated elections in St. Clair County for many years. He was killed in an automobile accident in 1935 at the age of 40. She remembers the words that were written about him and to the family after his death: words like integrity and courage.

"The student population is dwindling. For many years it was stabilized, but in recent years we lose two or three hundred students per year. We have many students leaving. Families are leaving; they are moving to O'Fallon, Fairview Heights, Belleville and St. Louis County."

They are the middle income and lower middle income families that can afford to buy homes or rent apartments priced higher than in East St. Louis. But they also are escaping the intolerable property tax rate and the other costs of living in East St. Louis, like bars at the windows and doors, outside lights and ADT alarm systems. Dr. Parks knows about all that although she lives in the most elite residential area of East St. Louis, the Loisel Hills area.

Because of what has come to be called the black flight, the district had to close three schools this year, including Hughes Quinn, the original Lincoln High School, one through whose doors all African-Americans in the city once passed. Closing it was an emotional experience, but Rock Junior High School, the old East St. Louis Senior High School, had a campus, had room, and was adjacent to a new seventh grade building of 12 rooms.

Washington and Carver, the old Emerson, also closed. In some cases, the district did not have the money to do the extensive renovation necessary, and the declining enrollments gave the option of closing the schools.

Dr. Parks feels strongly about the educational atmosphere. That means making buildings safer and attractive. A sound, attractive building can provide the atmosphere for learning, she said.

The enrollment of East St. Louis schools in 1990-91 is about 15,600. An extensive early childhood program for four-year-olds and an enrichment program for three-year-olds accounts for 700 pupils this year. The losses are not as bad as in some other communities, including Granite City. Over 12 years, the district has lost perhaps 6,000 pupils. "We were maybe at 22,000"as the high enrollment.

The district has been working with the state on its finances. "We submitted a financial plan and they accepted it," she said, and this year, for the first time in memory, "we will not have to make a loan. We are very proud of that." The plan means simply that the district will have to live within its income. The plan anticipates that the "temporary" income tax will be continued. "For us, it must continue; one of our assumptions (for the plan) is that it will continue," she said.

About 89 percent of the district's funds come from the federal and state governments. Although East St. Louis taxpayers face a school tax rate above $7 — more than the entire tax bill for most cities in the county — the money from taxes would not meet the payrolls for more than two months.

Class size is mandated in a union contract and in some cases by funding regulations. Primary grades are limited to 30 pupils per teacher, and the district shoots for 25. In early childhood education, there can be no class over 20. In upper elementary, the classes go as high as 35 , though "we try to keep them at 30 to 32." On the state report card, overall the teacher-pupil ratio is about one to 23. "I'm very pleased about that."

That same report card shows the district does very well on the state reading test, but "needs some help" in scoring on the ACT (college entrance) tests. "The state averages about 18-19 (on ACT), we're averaging like 13-14, so we need to improve there. That's not to say we don't have those students who score very high, 32, 29, 28, but when we average them in with the others, we need to improve. "

"We have steady improvement with the California Achievement Test (CAT), our other standardized test. However, at the high school level we look at ACT."

The CAT compares the student achievement with similar grades across the country. The district achieved grade level at some grades several years ago, and is improving steadily, particularly in the elementary schools.

"Our goal is to improve our achievements, which also is to improve our self esteem, and the way our children feel about themselves. Oh, that's very important," she said. "I talk to them about it all the time."

"We hear all about the drugs and crime and the this and that, but I tell them about all the good people who come from here, an ambassador, from East St. Louis! How many people can brag about an ambassador, or an Olympic winner, or musicians or scientists or college presidents? I tell them they can be what they want to be.

"Somewhere we have got to stop emphasizing that our children are what we educators call *disadvantaged* or *at risk*. I don't use those words too often. I remind them that when I was at Lincoln most of the people there were poor, they were disadvantaged, but we didn't know that word then. Luckily, no one told us we were disadvantaged. Our teachers told us we were bright if we were bright, told us we were smart, told us about the African-American leaders and who invented what, and you know, we have to be told that. And that's what I tell the students all the time when I visit the schools, and I visit all the time. I have lunch with them and talk to them. We have some outstanding students here."

Her conviction, her determination, her enthusiasm, shine through her words.

But what," I asked, "happens when they get out of High School?"

"Many of them go to college, about 60 percent go to college or they go to other schools. We have a new relationship with Rankin Technical School now. They are offering scholarships; the PR group (public relations) that is offering scholarships to our students is Ron Thompson's company. We're going to send some over there because they have high standards.It's hard getting in there, and they have a 98 per cent rate of placement."

I said I still would hate to be an 18-year-old black in East St. Louis looking for a job.

"Still," she insisted, "If you want to make it..." But she agreed that you can't get a job at the corner store if the corner store is gone, and in most of East St. Louis, it is gone. If you want a minimum wage job flipping hamburgers, there are fewer than a dozen locations in the whole city, from the cluster of four or five fast-food restaurants at Seventh and St. Louis Avenue all the way to 89th and State. East St. Louis, she said, needs jobs.

Dr. Parks started her educational career as a teacher in 1954 — she's been in the district 35 years — at Dunbar School, taught at Lincoln from 1956 to 1966, was a consultant in Project Speak, a director, administrative assistant for secondary education, all in this district. When she left the University of Illinois she taught one year in Kansas City, then "came home in '54, been here ever since. I like East St. Louis, I love the education system.

"My friends in St. Louis say, 'Lillian, how can you live there?' I wouldn't walk any place at night alone, not just in East St. Louis, I wouldn't walk in downtown St. Louis. There are some places that are bad, you know that, but no worse than a lot of other places.

"What people never mention about East St. Louis, with all the negatives, is that there are good people here. And I've found that through the years good students, good church people, good mothers, good fathers, you don't hear about that too often, but they are here. I like my town, and I am hoping that one day it will come back."

"Is 'come back' the right term?"

"I can remember when Jones Park was beautiful; I can remember when the Sunken Gardens over by Lafayette, by Longfellow, were beautiful. I can remember when they swept the streets! I remember those things. I remember when people would walk past our house on the way to work at the Aluminum Ore, for example. I can remember the stockyards when they were booming. All those things I remember.

"I can remember when we would walk anywhere in East St. Louis; we'd walk to the park and stay there — *walk!* I can remember when downtown was Downtown and you went there to shop."

"Come back to what, Dr. Parks? The smoke-stack industries are gone."

"But some kind of jobs, if not smokestack jobs. What kind I don't know. I hear about modular housing. I keep hearing about those things. I keep hearing some pie in the sky kind of things, and I'm a realist. I'm not one of those persons who believes certain projects are going to turn everything around. I am not becoming cynical, but I am just watching progress or lack of progress.

"Jobs will help turn this town around, and I am hoping that perhaps there will be something that will come here to give us jobs. I know the service industry...they keep telling us the service industry is coming. Well, how much money do you make in the service industries? What are you talking about?"

I told her about SIU President Earl Lazerson's "three precursors" to a turn-around. She agreed, but singled out the special importance of leadership.

"I think leadership is the key in all agencies: government, school districts, the city. Respect, too. There is more to it than just jobs, responsibility. Our mindsets have to be changed a little bit, to believe in ourselves, have great expectations for our children, believing that we can succeed. Many people don't have that feeling. They feel that all is lost. They don't really see the future.

"Yes, leadership is important, that does include fiscal responsibility, it includes integrity, it includes believing in our leaders, too. I think that would bring a lot here."

She recalled the respect for her father, Horace Adams. He changed the political organization of the entire county. "I think that is what inspires me and my family to believe that you can do some things, and one of those things is to have a positive outlook. I don't have certain people on committees that I chair because they are negative, think all is lost, that nothing is going to work. We don't have time for that if we are going to move the school district.

"I'm hoping that within the next year or so we are going to see some changes. Some people are seeing things already in our buildings, but seeing some real changes in the system...Gotta do that! And it means having a board that is supportive of what you are doing and a staff that supports you, too. So I agree with what Dr. Lazerson said, but fiscal responsibility, isn't that leadership?"

She said there needs to be exhibited integrity in the models for the children, so that children know that if you work hard and are determined and you are not playing games you can move ahead.

While we read about the "breakdown" in black families, the absence of fathers, the ADC mothers "having babies to increase their aid checks," I mentioned my visits to Mt. Zion Baptist Church and of the strong sense of family discipline evident among the children there, and of an article I read about Jackie Joyner-Kersee and about the support network she had in her family and the community.

"You are right about the family, the importance

Workmen on a Sunday ready the Billy Jones School for opening in September 1990

of keeping together. Strong mothers have been there all the years; the mothers, they have kind of kept things going. We have mothers who wield strong influence on their children, but the family is where it is, where you learn all your values, you learn your attitudes at home. I'm always amused when parents say 'I don't know where she got those ideas.' I say 'She got them at home.' Family is very important."

We talked about the need for communication, and the imagined disagreements in turf battles.

"We have got to begin working together in a common cause. I am getting very annoyed with turf battles. Somewhere there's a little thing of jealousy going on. I refer people to First Corinthians 13: *Love knows no jealousies.* We have those that exist, 'You are outshining me, therefore I won't cooperate with you because you are continuing to outshine me, you are not supposed to do that.' I really have feelings that if we are going to accomplish some things we have to support one another. If you are right, I am going to support you. I've said that to some other people, too."

"You're tough."

"People say that I am. I have strong philosophies and I have strong views. I really do believe that students can do whatever they really want to do and it is up to us to equip and guide them. That's not just educator talk. That's my philosophy. I believe hard work does a lot of things too."

Dr. Parks said she has had good support from the state "because we have an open book here. We're not trying to hide anything. There are certain guidelines and rules that we must follow, and we are going to be in compliance. I don't want any school rated probationary or denied recognition. They come down here and meet with us on a regular basis because I invite them. They are demanding some things now and my only complaint to them is 'You should have done this years ago and our buildings, for example, would not be in the shape they are in.' But now they're saying we must improve them and we are improving."

She said she is getting good support from Martha O'Malley, regional superintendent of schools. "We're one of her schools and she supports us. The board has been supportive, too. There are not too many things that we have asked for that the board has said no. I am saying to them it is time we stop being ridiculed. I say to them that I don't want meetings to be circuses. If you have some arguments, let's deal with them back here and come out in an intelligent manner.

"I have strong feelings about people viewing us with an eye that says we are intelligent and we can do some things. Yes, I've been described as strong, but also as having integrity and also being a hard worker."

She said workers laughed at her "the other day" when she appeared at a school being rehabilitated and watched the workers. "I told them 'I want to see what you are doing, that's our money we are spending.' We've had some shoddy work in the past, shoddy. That's obvious. Nobody volunteers to do this work, they want top dollar, so we expect to get some quality work for that. You are going to see some progress here, and lots of it."

You know she means it.

Who are the role models for black East St. Louis children? What are the achievements that can be cited.

Dr. Parks reached into her shelves of books and came up with The Ebony Tree, written by Clementine Reeves Hamilton, a retired East St. Louis teacher, the first black teacher on the faculty at East St. Louis Sr. High School, who died in 1971. She had collected data and photographs for the book until her death, but had not published it. A committee from Delta Sigma Theta sorority, chaired by Dr. Parks, took over the work of publication.

The book traces some of the black history to the days before the Civil War and before the incorporation of East St. Louis as Illinoistown in 1961. As early as 1830 St. Clair County had 32 free Negro heads of families. They included Richmond Freeman of Rentchler Station, east of Belleville (last names often were chosen by ex-slaves, generally were descriptive, or from the families who owned them. Richmond Freeman was born of a free man. Part of that farm now is owned by Larry Reinneck, president of the board of Belleville Area College, bought from Maggie Freeman, an East St. Louis school teacher now deceased, whose pride in her students' achievements he recalls. Reinneck said a log cabin that was a Freeman home is imbedded in the house across the road from him, owned by Russ Erlinger.

Ebony Tree pays homage to John Robinson, former slave, credited with founding the first black school in East St. Louis, though he never learned to read or write himself. The account of that school, and all other accounts of black schools which this author has read, stress the eagerness of the black students to learn. That same attitude surfaces today in Bob Kassing's account of his work with Junior Achievement in this book.

The book deserves reprinting and updating.

Another book "Black Men Role Models of Greater St. Louis" by Sheryl H. Clayton (Essai Seay Publications, Box 55, East St. Louis, IL 62202) includes many East St. Louisans, including Dr. Parks' husband Alvin L. Parks, whose career as a junior high school coach included the beginning training of Al Joyner, who like his sister Jackie Joyner-Kersee, reached the Olympics. Certainly Jackie and Al are among the major achievers from East St. Louis. Dr. Clayton's book was based on questionnaires sent to prominent male leaders (She also has published *Black Women Role Models of Greater St. Louis*).

Dr. Parks lists as important achievers musicians Miles Davis, Diane Bolden and Eugene Haynes. Donald McHenry, former U.S. ambassador to the United Nations, also was an East St. Louisan.

Dr. Carrie B. Dawson was the first Negro woman to earn a doctorate from the University of Illinois and the second person in East St. Louis school district 189 to hold a doctor's degree. She was supervisor of elementary education.

Dr. Parks also recommends for any leadership list City Treasurer Charlotte Moore, "who has shown intelligence, determination and courage under often trying circumstances.' Charlotte Moore also is Dr. Parks' niece. And Dr. Parks should be on that list herself.

There are countless success stories, including from my own experience Lillian Williams, daughter of former Mayor James Williams, at the Metro-East Journal. Today she is an outstanding reporter at the Chicago Sun-Times.

There is not available a condensed typed list of academic achievers, though there are many. However, in sports, better records are kept. Richard Taylor, director of physical education for School District 189, prepared the following list of achievers from East St. Louis schools in professional sports ranks:

Football

Maurice McDonald, Continental League; Claude Webb and Darrick Glanton, Canadian; Alvin Randolph, Jim Long, Eric Wright (active) and Mike Majac, San Francisco; Gregory Johnson, St. Louis Cardinals; Kellon Winslow, San Diego; Ray Mays, Washington; Johnny Poe (active), New Orleans; Bobby Johnson (active) and Albert Dixon, New York Giants; Cleveland Cosby (active), Cleveland; Vic Scott (active), Dallas Cowboys; Shelby Jordan, New England Patriots and Kerry Glenn (active), Miami.

Basketball

Dave Winslow and Ray Mosby (active), Queensland, Australia; Dwight Jones, Italy; Benny Lewis Jr., Saints, Melbourne, Australia; Demarco Martin, Horsham, Australia; Joe Hurst (active), Hobort Devils, Tasmania; Terry Hamilton (active), Adelaide, Australia; James Garner, Art Easterly, Marvin Jones, Charles Harris, Harlem Magicians; Crystal Cole, Amsterdam, Holland, and Tina Hutchinson.

Baseball

Jefro Sam and Mark Chamber (active) and Don Johnson, Cleveland Indians; Roddy Johnson, Bobby Deloach (active), Russell Gaston (active), Alvin Bush, Cardinals; Barnell Richardson, Maurice Horton, Detroit; Art May, Boston Red Sox, Andy Walker, Clemme Cannon, Doc Connors and Will Cunningham, Chicago Cubs; Lawrence Moore (active) Cincinnati; Cliff Williams (active), Texas Rangers; Ron Stovall, Minnesota; Ted Savage, Philadelphia; Pat Owen and Larry Hopkins, Pittsburgh; Robert Jones, Baltimore and Ron Carathers (active), Melbourne Reds.

The bleachers are up in the new $4.7 million Clyde Jordan Memorial Football Stadium behind East St. Louis Sr. High School, visible behind the scoreboard. This picture was taken late in August. The contractor says it might be ready in October. At right, the single passageway through the bleachers on the home side; top level is the press and VIP booth. The school real estate tax rate, including bond taxes to pay for the stadium, is among the highest in the state. Below left, the entrance from the east will be lined with pillars.

Lincoln High School, 1211 Bond Ave., which also will play football at the new stadium

East St. Louis Senior High School extends from 49th to 51st streets on the north side of State Street

Historic Pasons Field, home of champions (west of Jones Park) where both schools play football in the meantime

The old East St. Louis Senior High School from Ninth to 10th at Ohio Avenue — today it is Rock Junior High

Hughes Quinn Jr. High School, once Lincoln High, at 1100 Broadway Ave., a school of many memories for the African-American community, was boarded up for the 1990 fall semester

Clark Junior High School, 3310 State Street

Martin Luther King Jr. High School, next to John F. Kennedy Elementary, 70th & Ridge

Lansdowne Junior High School, 3939 Caseyville Ave.

Jefferson Elementary School - the district's newest building at 1800 N. 25th. Landscaping incomplete

Above, playground entrance to Morrison School, 630 N. 59th St. Someone burns trash in two dumpsters at right. This area, once known as Oak Park, has been hit hard by deteriorating buildings.

Above, Alta Sita School, 26th and Bond; at left Attucks, 2600 Kansas; below Dunbar, 1900 Kansas. Inset, old School Board offices at Seventh and St. Louis Ave. The School Boad office was the first school building erected for Negro students in East St. Louis and served until 1908, with the board offices upstairs. It now is a shelter for the homeless.

Above, Lucas School, 1620 Russell, sign vandalized. Below, Lilly-Freeman School, 1300 Broadway; below right, Park Adult Evening School, 27th & Henrietta, abandoned this fall; bottom Miles D. Davis, 725 N. 15th St. Lilly-Freeman School was named after two women teachers, the first school named after a woman

Above, Harding School at 731 N. 74th St., still looks like a proud castle. Former Monroe Training School, left, where the author first smelled shellac, now closed and the target of vandals

John F. Kennedy Elementary School at 70th Street just south of State

Former Assumption High School, Kingshighway and St. Clair Avenue, above, a Catholic school, is being converted to a prison. Central High School for boys is long gone. St. Teresa's Academy for Girls, below, at 27th and Ridge, is a shambles in private ownership

City's TIF districts could help revenue stream, growth

Robert Vancil of Leroy, Ill., is an expert on tax increment financing (TIF), and he believes it can be part of the answer for financing city government in East St. Louis.

A TIF district is established when the city can meet criteria involving the economic need for development. It gives to the municipality all the taxes on the increased value of developments within the district: that is, the taxes that normally would go to the state, to the county, to the school district, to fire districts, and to all those other tax bodies on your property tax bill — if it is a real estate TIF district. But the revenues can only be used for developments within the district. These developments can be streets, water and sewer lines, street lights — improvements involving the infrastructure to attract more development. The city recently hired policemen from its TIF funds, and was immediately warned that was a no-no. But a police substation probably would be approved.

Robert Vancil

TIF funds also can be used to help a business — or a homeowner — pay the interest on the development up to a certain point.

We're trying to keep this simple, and in a way it is. But it also is complicated. When the TIF district is established, all the properties within the district and their assessed values are recorded. Distribution of taxes paid on these properties remains unchanged. However, as assessments are increased because of improvements, the additional tax money goes to the municipality for a TIF trust fund. But if a property decreases, it is not taken away, it just is not counted. That obviously is a good deal.

Now, there's more. There are different kinds of TIF districts. Real estate districts are one kind. There also are TIFs for utility taxes and for sales taxes. Or there were for sales taxes. The Illinois Tax Federation screamed the state was giving away the store when it enabled the sales tax TIF, and so it was closed — but East St. Louis got in under the wire. Most of the city of East St. Louis is in the real estate TIF. The downtown business section and the riverfront are in sales tax and utility tax TIFs. That means the city doesn't just get one-cent tax on sales, it gets all 6-1/4 cents on all increased sales. And it means it gets not only its three per cent utility tax, it gets the state's three per cent also, on all increased utility tax bills. And, ladies and gentlemen, the entire riverfront is in all three TIF districts for the next 20 years or so, according to Vancil.

One way of looking at it is that if the riverfront develops, the city will get and be able to spend for whatever it wants, including payback of the loans under the Distressed Cities Act, from the natural

Comtempri Homes of Pinckneyville builds this house to Vancil's standards

city tax increase, and it will be able to use TIF funds for the improvements necessary to serve the new businesses, like walks, lights, even local share to match grants of acceptable types. It could provide incentives for apartment houses, hotels, even amusement parks and shops at the landing for the gambling ship that the governor saw to it was authorized.

But that's still not all.

Vancil has worked out elaborate plans utilizing TIFs, community development block grants and revolving loan funds to find a way around the horrendous real estate tax rate that has just about frozen all new construction in the city. A $60,000 house should be assessed at $20,000 (one-third market value) and taxed at $20 per hundred equalized evaluation — theoretically the tax bill would be $4,000 a year or $333 per month. Put that together with the highest insurance rates in the state and a mortgage payment and you could easily be paying $1,000 a month.

Vancil's program of interest buy-downs from TIF funds, free site preparation and some other features can provide that $60,000 home for $500 a month with a 20-year loan, with the development by private builders. It would provide for the city to receive regular taxes on the property. One subdivision is in preparation now in cooperation with Target 2000, in the hope of drawing back to East St. Louis the school teachers and other professionals who have moved from the city.

Vancil says the Distressed Cities Act can stop the slide of East St. Louis into further debt, but it needs a revenue stream to pay its way out of debt. The various TIF districts all can help, but the housing can bring back into the city taxpayers, leadership and revenue. On each $60,000 house, he sees the city recovering in TIF funds $13,000 by the tenth year, $35,460 by the 20th. He lists as projects "on line" 240 units for Target 2000, 160 for Anna Estates, 36 at Mount Zion and 24 in Edgemont Court for a total of 460 new homes. He wants to make that 1,000.

In commercial development, the city received $507,000 in TIF funds for 1987-88, $680,000 the next year and will exceed $1,200,000 this fiscal year, Vancil said. "This increment developed while the total equalized assessment valuation decreased."

Vancil also has proposed that the city aggressively seek changes in legislation for TIFs in poverty cities like East St. Louis, and for the distribution of state sales taxes on the basis of population rather than where sales occurred (see article on page 104)

Elmo Bush in his living room at 417 N. 18th Street

Elmo Bush talks black

Elmo Bush has been many things. In 1966 he ran unsuccessfully for mayor of East St. Louis, the first black candidate, against Alvin G. Fields, who was seeking his fifth four-year term. In 1971 he was elected to the city council with Mayor James Williams, the first black mayor. Under the commission form of government, he was commissioner of fire, health and education. In 1975 he lost in the primary to William Mason for mayor, and became administrative assistant to the superintendent of schools, then Leroy Ducksworth. When Jerry Costello ran for County Board chairman, Bush opposed him in the primary. Bush supported Carl Officer for mayor 11 years ago, but when in the last election Clyde Jordan ran against Officer, Bush was his campaign manager. Obviously, Bush has been where the action is in East St. Louis.

Bush complains that whites want to pick the black leaders for the black community. Outspoken Bush has not been among those so chosen. He most recently said it to Carter Hendren, representative of Republican Jim Edgar who was seeking black support in East St. Louis for Edgar for governor.

"The ones the whites pick are the ones in their interest, not in the interest of blacks, They don't even wonder what the interest of a black man is. The Belleville News-Democrat in no way considers my interest as a black person down here paying $5,000 a year in property taxes.

Bush is supporting Edgar and has opened an office for him on St. Louis Avenue in East St. Louis. He said Neil Hartigan is a machine politician who opposed Mayor Washington in Chicago; that he represents Chicago interests, and that Edgar is a truthful man. Edgar is for continuing the two per cent sales tax increase, and without it East St. Louis schools and others throughout the state would be in a bad way quickly. Besides, he says the Democratic party, which he said spends $50,000 to $75,000 in East St. Louis every election to buy votes, needs to experience the return of a two-party system. He accused Hartigan of distortion trying to lay the tax on Edgar, when it was supported by Democrats and Republicans alike. And he says Hartigan says he would get money for schools somewhere else, but cannot, or will not, say where.

Bush was opposed to the state Distressed Cities Act as it was first reported, especially to the state-appointed board of overseers who it was reported would control the city's budget and spending. "They want me to give away management of my city that protects me, and have no recourse? The mayor is just going to cut ribbons? And I am going sit here and pay taxes to that body which is going to be an oversight body appointed from all over the state! I've got adequate evidence of what that is going to do to me. And yet they say 'You ought to be satisfied with that because these people are going to pay your bills. They're going to bail you out.' We went through that on the plantation in Mississippi. We didn't have to pay any bills, we had a company store, and we were in debt at the company store. We went down there this year, I just buried my brother who lived in a company town owned by U.S. Steel just outside Birmingham. I know my brother couldn't be caught buying in town or they would put him out of his house. He worked at the steel mill and he lived in a company house and he had to buy at the company store and the company provided a doctor and the company fixed the streets and the company came and repaired the tin roof on his house. The company did everything for you, so why should you worry? Why shouldn't you want this kind of bailout? 'You just go over there and get under a shade tree, get you a bottle of wine and a woman, that's all black folks want anyway. What more? What else could you possibly want?'

"Don't you see that when you're trying to put responsibility on blacks and you try to lead to further the black interest, whites see that as opposed to their interest? So you're not the guy they want leading the blacks. 'Here's the guy over here, he's the nice guy, that's the one you ought to have.' What you have to do quick is whenever the whites point at a guy and say he's all right, take another look at him.

"What's amazing people is that they haven't been able to get Carl Officer on anything. Now they've got Marion Berry up there and they want to know what 'Black America' is thinking about Berry. I tell you what Black America is thinking, and I'm not talking about those who write for the Washington Post. They're brain-fried worse than cocaine addicts; they don't believe it, but it's true. Here's a guy accused of (1) using cocaine and (2) lying to a grand jury by saying he didn't use cocaine and (3) having possession of some cocaine. Now, were he not mayor...Those charges would fit a thousand folks including some men in

Thank you Elmo Bush

When this author was the fledgling editor of the Metro-East Journal, he had to establish the newspaper as a regional voice to enlist the support of advertisers, most of whom already had left East St. Louis. And he had a moral and practical obligation to the citizens of East St. Louis, of whom an increasing percentage were black. As the new editor, hailed as racist in the Monitor, and following the racially-sensitive and humanitarian editor Bill Boyne, he had a mandate to establish positive relationships with the black community.

A major part of that program, which today he points to with pride, were the confidential calls to Elmo Bush to gauge the black interpretation of the editorials he wrote; not to check the position, but the presentation and the clarity of the position. The Journal editorials were not to please ourselves, or to put ourselves on record, but to influence others. Horseshoe Lake State Park, the State Office Building in East St. Louis, are among the results of those editorials, as were many more local decisions. During the Richard B. Ogilvie governorship, the Metro-East Journal's local editorials were the governor's daily fare.

Bush is an independent thinker with a keen mind. He kept our confidences. It is time to thank him for his viewpoints and his assistance back there as we sought to handle a sometimes delicate and demanding job.

Thank you, Elmo Bush.

congress.

"Possession? All they knew he had possession of is what they saw him buy with the camera, that's all they could ever prove that he had. They get spicy sex all wrapped up in it by getting a girl to say 'C'mon, we're going to get this coke and we're going to get high,' and he paid for the coke while she was in the toilet or something. You're showing here a private sexual encounter, a private illegal use of drugs by a private individual for personal use; it has no relationship to his being mayor at all. Nothing to do with his job. They haven't accused him of stealing money like they accuse most blacks. The only way to get him is to spend 50 million dollars to 100 million dollars to get a picture of him getting a little bit of crack. Is it right that he did it? No. It's not right that he did it. But is it worth to the American public what they are doing? No. What is more worthwhile is the $500 billion lost to the S&Ls, and you haven't spent as much to find those criminals as you have spent on this little unimportant mayor!

"Now, we are over here with Carl Officer. They have to come out in the paper and say 'We've got Joe Davis and we hope this is going to lead to Carl Officer.' Well, Joe Davis took a 30-year sentence. He probably shouldn't have gotten more than two or three. Then they get Kelvin Ellis. 'We know we got Carl Officer now. We're going to give him 40 years if he don't give us what we need to know about Carl.' C'mon, is that what you need to get rid of Carl Officer? (Actually, Ellis received a much shorter sentence).

"Why do you want Carl Officer out so bad? Are you that interested in these poor black folks down here; do you think we've got a black man that's really not for us? You know, frankly, I wasn't for Carl Officer in the first place; I was even Clyde Jordan's campaign manager in the last election. So I am not enamored with Carl Officer. But what's the big effort? Why this constant barrage of editorials? You know what they've done down here? They've turned all of us for him.

"There's not a man in East St. Louis that can beat Carl Officer today."

Bush said Officer says things in a flippant way that he doesn't mean, sometimes what amounts to private comments, and the press makes a big thing out of them.

"I went with Carl to a Catholic school probably 98 per cent black over in St. Louis. A college prep school. There must be 25-30 kids from East St. Louis that go over there. And there were some kids there that were questioning (City Attorney) Eric Vickers, they questioned me as superintendent of schools, they questioned (Mayor) Carl Officer. One little girl from East St. Louis said to Carl, 'Man, you're our mayor. We're over here in a school with most of these kids from St. Louis, and every day they're on us, everything that comes out in the paper that you say, they're on us. Everything about the city, they're on us. We defend our city, and we defend you, our mayor. Now, my question is, don't you think sometimes you could say some of the things you say in a different way, because you make it so hard on us to try to defend you sometimes?'

"I looked at that little girl, I couldn't believe that she had the tact and the delivery command to put it to him that way. And I thought 'I know that Carl is sharper than this. I hope he doesn't get angry with her and fire at her and try to make her look bad. I hope he doesn't do that.' But y'know, that father of his trained him much better than that. He looked at her and very calmly responded, 'Y'know, you're right. And y'know, I'm changing, I'm learning. When I became mayor I was 27, I'm 37 now. I've learned a lot. And I don't always mean what I say, but I need to learn to think first.' Those kids just ate that up when he took that approach with them. They loved him for it. They loved him in the first place. They identify with him."

Historically the state, with the exception of the Richard B. Ogilvie administration, has had an adversative relationship with the city, Bush charged. When the state came up with the interstate bridge plan, it asked the city to give it right of way right across the approach to the toll bridge the city owned, now called the Martin Luther King Bridge. The plan was to tie in the downtowns with all the interstates. How did that impact East St. Louis? It already was predicted that it would strip traffic off the Veterans Bridge, as it was then called, and that 20 years later the Poplar Street bridge would be so crowded the traffic would return to the Veterans Bridge. "But what was to happen to the bond payments in the meantime? They knew damn well there was no way East St. Louis could keep that bridge up with no tolls. No way. But when we defaulted on the bond issue, they called it bad management."

The state and county governments have worked in opposition to East St. Louis, Bush charges. He points to Gary Fears and Gene Graves, who gathered data while they were on the state payrolls. "They could have chosen to say 'Let's have a major strategy that is going to put these resources right across the river from St. Louis.'" Instead, Fears gathered the data from the state and sought to build a business campus in Collinsville at Illinois 157 and I-70, including the present Holiday Inn with a state loan.

(Graves was with Community Progress in East St. Louis, on SIU's payroll, and became director of the Department of Economic Development under Gov. Otto Kerner. He spearheaded many

Southwestern Illinois projects, including the Waterloo airport proposal, that would have benefited East St. Louis. Fears still has strong political ties, and we regard the location of the state office building housing the state police and highway departments, formerly in French Village in Fairview Heights, in Fears' development as more than happenstance.)

"Let me tell you something that happened while I was at City Hall," Bush continued. "We were putting together the application for the Jefferson Memorial expansion to the East St. Louis riverfront. (Carl Officer wanted to name it after the black woman who was Jefferson's mistress! The one he took with him everywhere. They were really shocked by that.) We put in applications for 100 acres on this side." State Sen. Sam Vadalabene came out with a proposal to build auditoriums on the campuses of colleges around the state and get the state to pay for one in Edwardsville. "I threw a monkey wrench in the damn thing. I sent to the legislature a resolution from the East St. Louis City Council saying that we would appropriate $250,000 from community development money to be the local share for the state to build an auditorium on the riverfront in East St. Louis. They weren't planning on putting in any money up there in Edwardsville. I wanted that auditorium built on the riverfront, I wanted it right next to the expansion. Put a tram across the river, people could ride over, there could be an amusement park, hotels. I was talking about an auditorium that would seat 20,000. If you have a method of transportation, rapid transit, 10 minutes across the river to downtown St. Louis, you could expand the kind of conventions St. Louis brings, use their facilities over there and the ones over here; then you are talking about major conventions you can't now handle. Now, where is the state in all this? Nowhere with us! That's what East St. Louis has been the victim of."

I told him about John Baricevic saying East St. Louis closed the doors on cooperation, refused to let the county trucks plow snow on the streets.

"Let me tell you one thing, that's bullshit! The county won't do what the county has a legal obligation to do. For example, go to county highway department and ask how many field trucks they have working. What is the mileage assigned to each one? What is the mileage approved to work in East St. Louis? How many miles of road do you actually take care of in East St. Louis? Nineteenth Street to Bond Avenue to Central Avenue is a county road put in to get the people out to Monsanto. I was out there when the street car barn was at 19th and Baker. There was a trestle over the railroad tracks. The streetcar went out Bond and turned on 19th Street, that was brick street. In 1936 the viaduct in 26th from Bond to Missouri was built as a WPA project.

"We lack cooperation? What is cooperation to them? Let the white folks come in and run it. They don't want to give anything to any black to run anything. Here is (School Board member Ed) Jucewicz raising hell about the football stadium. Ed runs the Boys Club, can't even make the financial report to keep the United Way money. Is he really for real about that? You got to be kidding." When bingo became legal, who got bingo? Bob Mays and Jucewicz were running it for the Boys Club.

"Clyde Jordan elected Jucewicz to the school board," Bush said. Clyde worked under Mayor Fields, learned the system. He set up a senior citizens organization and paid seven politicians $350 a month from federal revenue sharing funds to serve on the board. He gave the city money to buy motorcycles — his bodyguard was over the motorcycle patrol. And he gave Jucewicz revenue sharing money for the Boys Club. No reports were required. Now he's got Ed depending on that money. He runs Ed to take the place of Terry Jennings, a white with the Charles Merritts' faction. Jennings loses, and he has a token white on Clyde's payroll who votes aye to whatever Clyde puts up. Now he is arguing about the stadium, and he voted for everything plans called for, including the deletions. Jucewicz is a four-flushing phoney. You see him ride around with the Sunshine Van. It wasn't given him for a private use vehicle, that's what he uses it for, because he doesn't have a private vehicle. He's a white boy. If I was doing that, he would clobber me, like he tried to clobber me down there (on the school board).

Bush was fired as school superintendent after 11 months, which followed years as deputy and assistant. He bears no goodwill toward Jucewicz.

Turning our attention to housing: Why build more when there are homes boarded up all over the city?

"We always had too much public housing. We were sitting up here in 1960 with 23,000 housing units. About 5,500 for public housing. Now we are down to about 13,000 or little more housing units, with about 3,000 for public housing. Our problem with that is we've got too much public housing. We need to balance out public housing with private housing.

"When Clyde Jordan wanted to pass the school bond issue (which included $5 million for the stadium), he called a meeting of precinct committeemen. He told all precinct committeemen who lived in public housing areas that it would be OK to take the bond issue to their people to get passed because their people would not have to pay for it anyway. That's what happens

Elmo Bush

when you are dependent on that level of public housing."

He said the city needs more available private housing. Many houses have been torn down that should have been saved, he said, and neighborhoods have deteriorated under the pressure of people who want to make a living with a beauty shop or repair shop in their homes. In a town where people are fighting for economic survival, it is hard to enforce city planning. "The pressure is to provide jobs for people who stay here. So we don't abide by the rules."

"This house was built in 1916, and would have gone by the way of the demolition act if I had not come in here and tuckpointed and tried to make it a house, and keep it up." Bush's home is a beautifully appointed and decorated two-story brick with a large pavilion out back used for neighborhood parties and barbecues.

"Taxes here were $1,100 and I wasn't getting homestead. Now they are $771. I paid $10,000 for it. In this little block, most people stayed, their kids grew up here; we're being recycled and grand-children are taking over now. But we've allowed this town to be destroyed."

Looking at the future, even with a bailout act, Bush said "It is impossible for East St. Louis on its own to marshal all the forces together necessary to give new direction to East St. Louis finances. It's just too much for a town on its own. Who's going to do that?"

Bush said he is going to try to be available to help Carl in his next term as mayor. You can at least get his ear. "I helped him giving his state of the union address. One thing that came out was his olive branch, his willingness to sit and talk with people. I was one of the guys who insisted he go into negotiations with the state over the bailout bill. 'You sit down and share with the McPikes and Mattigans and governor's man, whatever. You sit there and you talk it out and you negotiate. Don't talk about caving in. What damn plan? Who do you owe? How much do you owe? When do you get the bill? People say you mismanage it. Challenge them to show you one damn thing you did that represented mismanagement. Challenge them. The Belleville News-Democrat said you mismanaged it, damn it, prove it.

"'Ask them about the state teacher's retirement fund? Did the state mismanage in borrowing from it? When are they going to pay it back?'

"Under William Mason the people with control over the motor fuel taxes let the city buy the land for the State Community College, use MFT funds for streets, sidewalks, offstreet lighting for the college, and turn it over to the state (as the local share), then the state turns around and says you have misused the money.

"Oliver Hendricks was on the board of aldermen when it was done.

"Some of this is a bunch of bullshit. Just because these people are white, you've got to tell them 'You're full of shit. Don't piss in my face and tell me it's raining. Let's call a spade a spade. Let's get with it and go on and talk from there.

"'If you want to deal about guaranteeing paybacks, let's come up with a plan to guarantee the paybacks. How are we going to get the revenue? You want us to let you have oversight to make sure nothing happens to hurt the payback. Earn your way for that, the way we do it in America. You hold the old carrot out there. You say you do so much, and you follow this plan, we'll go further. In a year's time we'll review, and if you have followed this plan and we'll go further. Let's set all this up, this recovery of East St. Louis. Let's do it in stages.' I say, I'm for even saying turn over the whole board and mayor too, if they don't follow the plan. That's what they are doing in fact...You can't give authority away, but that doesn't say you can't contract it.

"We have got to say that we have a joint interest in this, all of us, not just East St. Louis, and we're all for working together, because there isn't anything you're going to do for East St. Louis that Belleville isn't going to get some benefits from. I hear people like (State Rep. Ron) Stephens crying about state police down here in East St. Louis. I'd like to get in the legislature and put in a bill that the state police patrol no road except the state roads. You know what that would do to the rural areas of the state of Illinois? So why do they keep talking that bull shit as though nobody knows what the hell is going on in the State of Illinois. You know, they treat you like you're a complete dummy. And the News-Democrat writes like everybody is a damned dummy. Y'know?

"I just talked about how they came up on the campus and built the whole damned auditorium. They built a city up there. Who brought SIU to this area?"

There were not enough high school graduates from this area going to college, people who needed college, and Delyte Morris proposed a commuting campus in this area. They met at Morrison School. East St. Louis School District 189 gave the college the old East St. Louis High School, and SIU began using the Shurtleff College in Alton. Bush says Delyte Morris' brother's real estate agency in Collinsville bought the Edwardsville campus and "SIU moved the hell out of East St. Louis.

"Everybody used East St. Louis, then went on their way and talked about those 'dumb SOB's down there. If they had any kind of sense...they won't accept cooperation.' Who up there has ever shown cooperation? Republicans or Democrats? They play games with black folks. They all get white on us.

"You take running for county offices. The Democrats run a black for an office, we run a black for office, Republicans run a white, the whites will all vote for Republicans and we'll lose it. Then they bring all the white folks to us and these black folks vote for them. But they tell us they can't elect a black. That's what they say to us, and they say it so convincingly. 'We have troubles trying to elect a black, you understand that don't you?' Hell no, I don't understand it. Why, you bring me the damned stupidist people in the world that happen to be white and tell me I'm supposed to be for them because they are white. I look at these folks like Danny Costello, came off the levee board, and they elect him state representative, make him sheriff, make him, everything. He's a white leader! I look at the white leaders up there, Republicans and Democrats, just look at 'em, then see somebody like John Baricevic come along, he's refreshing. He gets to be chairman of something, that's refreshing, it really is. I look forward to a lot of it. The white folks have been very disappointing. I remember when the Democrats ran a black for circuit court, his name was Miller. Republicans ran a white man, named (Ed) Whiting. And the Democrats voted for Whiting.

Turning to school affairs, Bush cited his accomplishments in his 11-month tenure as superintendent:

"I laid off 116 people, cut the payroll by over $3 million. I negotiated under fire a contract that I wasn't supposed to negotiate: I came out of it not with a one-year contract, which I was ordered to do, not with a two-year contract, which was beyond what I was ordered to do, but a three-year contract, one per cent the first year, and the same year get $4.5 million more money from the surcharge on state income tax.

"Any time you've got a bad fiscal situation — control spending, increase revenue, and in the middle, keep control of what people are doing — you have to have a plan and stay with it. There's no other way. Control your spending. That means cut down people, amount of money. Everything that is going to cost you money, control it. Get people off your payroll, get away from retirement funds, life insurance, hospitalization. Everything you can move away and get good service, give it to the private sector.

"I negotiated a bill to get them a state loan. I wanted to get this board tied to a plan they would have to keep up.

"We were given a figure of a $17 million debt which turned out not to be one to two million low. Part was in retirement fund money, which had

> They tell us they can't elect a black. That's what they say to us, and they say it so convincingly. 'We have troubles trying to elect a black, you understand that don't you?' Hell no, I don't understand it.

been collected and deposited directly into the educational fund, rather than in the retirement fund and then borrowed. So there was no record of transfer. Some $3.7 million had been 'borrowed'that way — actually levied illegally in local real estate taxes. The auditors had never caught it."

The teacher pay was spread over 12 months instead of 10. This enabled the last two months to be paid from "next year's" taxes. Teacher rolls were declining with class size, and the district built up a $9 million surplus. "Clyde Jordan found out we had $9 million in surplus, he said 'Let's spend this money. We're not supposed to be making profits.' And he put on people; worst thing you can do. What he should have done was start remodeling buildings. We started hiring people, and that's what happened to the school board.

"In 1982 we had $10 million. From 1982 until now there was only one year we did not spend more than we took in. So the trend started with 1982. The auditor had to see it. The people on the school board had to see it, the state folks had to see it, the county superintendent was getting it; nobody said to these people 'What's going on, you keep doing this and you're going to run into trouble.' So finally we were out of money and had to start borrowing to make the 11th and 12th payment. The minute you start borrowing, you mortgage next year's money to cover this. I put that down as a liability. So that the year I went in there, I had $9 million we had to borrow to make the July and August payments.

"I wanted enough money to put that $9 million in place and I wanted to pay off the 11th and 12th the first year I get money, and money I get in August, use the next fiscal year. It was an argument that sold them. So when I came up and said I had a $6.1 million vendor debt, $3.7 million owed to retirement, $9.7 million, and I'm borrowing $9 million for two months, I'm looking at $18 million going toward $19 million worth of debt. I sat there and said the way out is to lower the cost, lower the number of people on payroll, cut down spending, borrow $9 million, use it to pay current debt. Give me four years and I'll pay out.That's what they are doing."

Chief of Detectives Inspector Lester James Anderson

Chief of detectives suspects plot to discredit department

You find out a lot of things about East St. Louis Chief of Detectives Lester Anderson very quickly. After he learned what this book was about and I convinced him to turn off the gospel program on his radio so I could record his remarks, he cleared the air.

"First of all you have to realize something. I am a born again Christian. I try to do my work as the Lord would have me do, even in this position. This position I did not want, I never wanted it, I've been offered it for years. I never wanted to deal with up here. I've always been a narc, I've been doing drugs for 20 years. I have 22 years next month (October), and I've never liked this up here.

"I didn't like the way the detectives acted. The detective bureau to me was always a secret society of big shots, you know. This job was offered, no, I was asked to take it. I turned them down four times. But I belong to a prayer group. They pressured me and pressured me, and I went on a 47-day — I hadn't had a vacation in five years. When Jesus found me I stayed out 47 days. This was last year. During that time I really did some soul searching. You know, when God's got something for you to do he's got a way of getting your attention. He got my attention, and almost destroyed me.

"I finally came to the realization that I had to put Christ first in my life. In order to take this position I had my prayer group to pray, and they said, 'The Lord wants you to take this job. And since that time, there' s like a full-time 90-degree turn up here in this detective bureau. We have harmony, we have camaraderie, you know. We are almost like a family and I like that. You can't come up here and see no playboy pictures all over the walls, there's no dirty talk.

"I've been here a year officially Sept. 1. I told

the chief, I told the mayor, 'You didn't put me in this position, God did. And only God can remove me.'"

Has there been pressure to remove Anderson?

"State's Atty. John Baricevic tried to get me out of here. Look at the things he said about me in the press: I was a crooked cop, I couldn't be trusted, I was this, I was that, and never in my life has anybody accused me of taking anything. The politicians have tried to get me out."

Baricevic said he wouldn't prosecute a case where Anderson made the arrest.

"That's what he said, but he's done it. They've done it. They can't stop nothing. Too many prayers go up. You can't go against what God's will is, I don't care who he is. Not even the Devil can do it.

"But I am encouraged, and I never did get discouraged. Now it took a lot of prayer."

The Belleville News-Democrat Sept. 23 headlined page 1 "East St. Louis is deadliest city," and explained that was of cities with populations over 10,000 and was interpolated to deaths per hundred thousand. The figure used was 134 slayings, "nearly twice that of Washington, D.C.'s 72 per 100,000 ... While Washington D.C.'s killing toll rated No. 1 last year among major cities, it fell to fifth place when compared with all U.S. cities with populations of at least 10,000," Rob Donaldson wrote in a copyrighted story.

"Asinine," Anderson said when he was asked about the story.

"It was obvious to everyone what was going on. It was something to humiliate this city again, to make us look bad," Anderson said. A lay person picking up the newspaper will see right there a dangerous city," and will not realize these are extended figures.

On Thursday Sept. 27 the East St. Louis homicide toll for 1990 stood at 40. In the same period last year there were 45. The homicides are down by five, or 11.1 per cent. Last year there were a total of 63 homicides.

What is the nature of the homicides? "Six or seven of the 40 homicides are 'drop-offs' (bodies from killings elsewhere and dumped in the city limits), maybe 10 or 12 are family-friend type, the rest are drugs, no doubt about it.

"We solve the murders. The murders we have problems with are the drop-offs." Anderson said the detectives solve 85, maybe 87 per cent of major crimes. "Whether the state's attorney goes along is not up to us to decide."

"How often are white persons driving through East St. Louis not involved in anything illicit themselves molested in any way?" we asked.

"None."

Murder victims usually know their assailant, he said.

"Even the one yesterday. This joker sold a woman a piece of rock, I mean a real rock off the ground, a woman he's been knowing all his life, sold her a piece of rock for rock cocaine for $20, then took her $20 and went and bought himself a real (crack) rock. When she discovered this joker had sold her a piece of chat, she came back and cut his throat. And they've been knowing each other all their lives.

"It's unfortunate that Baricevic is not always in his office. Scott Mansfield, (chief assistant state's attorney), you know what his comment is every time we bring a case up there for murder 1? He says 'Who cares?' 'Who cares?' This is this man's comment; homicides, drug cases, they refuse to go (prosecute).

"We had a white boy robbed up on the Hill, First and St. Clair, by a fag, a homosexual. He was up there trying to solicit himself some head, OK, then this homo beats him up, robs him and everything. He's all bloodied up, he cut his head. We got him (the perpetrator) in jail and everything. We put the case together, we got everything blah blah blah, take the case to state's attorney, last week. Know what the state's attorney said? 'Insufficient evidence.' Didn't even read it. The fact remains even though the man was doing what he was doing, it's still a crime. The next time this homo may kill somebody. Yet he's letting him go on the street.

"He (the victim) should have been charged too for patronizing a prostitute, male or female. But by the same token he was beat up, he was bloody, he got robbed, we got statements, we got witnesses. Who cares? Who cares? Who cares? That's the man's comment."

"What about the morale of the detectives?" I asked.

"I sit here and I thank God he gives me strength because I'm in constant prayer when this comes on me. I have to sit here when these guys come in, they've been busting their butts, they took all kinds of chances and they come here, grown men and women detectives, with tears in their eyes and say 'Can you believe what they did?' and I have to sit here and say 'Be encouraged, they're not gonna be like this all the time, just do your job.' I have to constantly tell them this, and then when they leave out of my office my inner man, my inner spirit grieves me. Sometimes I just shut my door and sit here in prayer. It hurts, man," and tears welled in his eyes as he grew silent.

How safe are the streets?

"It's just like years ago when they opened the Colony Theater (for pornographic movies). The white folks say 'I'm scared to go through East St. Louis, I can't go to East St. Louis, I'm scared.' What time is it? 12 o'clock? Look at the Colony

Theater during lunch hour, all those whites sneaking in the door, from all over, banks, stores, everywhere. Then watch them leave there and start patrolling Collinsville Avenue, Pennsylvania. You sit there and watch one truck or car run round the block four or five times lookin', lookin' lookin', y'know what they're lookin' for."

"I've seen them," I said, "some of them. God, they're ugly and dirty and they come out of hovels. I can't imagine..."

"Yeah, and half of them got AIDS," he said. "They don't care. The white boys pick them up in a minute. And when one gets robbed, he says he was just asking the time," Anderson said. "It's obvious what he was doing."

Anderson blames a downtown gay nightclub for a great deal of the police problems.

"It's just like when you turn on the lights and the roaches go scurrying. When St. Louis taverns close, they come over the bridge just like the roaches. Man, you can't even get down Collinsville Avenue after 10 o'clock on the weekend. It isn't our people, it's outsiders, and they wreak havoc. When the sun comes up they run back across the bridge, them that's able, then they talk about East St. Louis."

Have the state police helped? They have at least five cars in East St. Louis every night.

"They're not assisting the detective bureau, they are assisting the patrol division. We don't use them to assist the detectives, because our job is primarily investigation. Although we lead our own drug raids and from time to time we do go out and stage raids on corners and locations."

What about the HUD unit?

"What HUD unit?" he asked.

"The nine undercover state troopers assigned to the housing projects and paid with HUD funds?" I elaborated

"No connection. They completely cut us out of it. I did not understand it. I think it's still another part of policy to discredit the city, trying to say that we cannot take care of our own business. I was dead against it. They have lied about it from the offset. You know, ironically they got all that money and all that equipment, all this war equipment, steel helmets. I saw them out there, steel helmets, trucks, when they could have used that same money to help us hire some more policemen. They didn't make any impact in the projects because we had already cleaned out Orr-Weathers, we'd already done that.

"All I hear about is the state stats, but I've not seen anything. I'm still getting reports of shootings in the projects, I get reports of killings in the projects. What are they doing? I don't know what they've done, but they've got plenty of stats.

"It seems like everything is orientated towards a takeover. Everybody wants poor little East St. Louis. Everybody. I've said this, and I'll say it publicly, and I'll say it privately, you can oppress and depress a people for just so long. I'm telling you, and brother, I believe in the power of prayer, and a lot of prayers are going up for the city.

"I belong to a prayer group and Thursday nights we do intercessory prayers, and that's tonight. They're not going to be able to take this city. I don't care what they've got against Carl, I don't care what they've got against me, they're not going to do it."

Back to the troopers — they're harassing drug dealers and prostitutes, interfering with their business. How do you handle it? Do you harass?

"When the state police drive up to them, they laugh at them, they wave at them, and they stand there. Let me and my detectives go by there, and it's a different story. We're out of the car and got them up against that wall. And I leave word, 'I don't want you here.' They're gone!"

"That's harassing," I said.

"Yes it is."

"Does Baricevic object to that?"

" Yes sir.

"It's a constant struggle to see what is going on, to see that we are systematically being destroyed, y'know."

"Are you saying the whole city is being persecuted because it's black, by politicians, by the News-Democrat?"

"Absolutely...no, let's don't say it like that.

"I'm saying that we're not so much being persecuted, they're trying to eliminate us. What's left of Southern Illinois right now, what is left beside the riverfront.?

"What they done, they gave us this city to play with for 20 years, and we didn't do nothin' with it, because it was drained when you was here. We didn't have anything to work with when we got it."

"Amen."

"Just like Baricevic pressing charges on the mayor for sewer lines being busted when he had nothing to do with putting them in. It's like 'We let them niggers have it this long, now we will take it back.'

"What's happening is things are moving too slow for them. You got the state legislature (involved) now, the riverfront gambling, things are moving too slow. They've got to do some drastic takeover. They've got to have this area. Taxes...My father, 79 years old, mother 69, they went up the day before yesterday, because their taxes doubled. Doubled! The man is gonna try to tell them the taxes had to go up because they had to pay policemen's salaries, and I ain't had a raise in six years."

"Except for your promotion to inspector?"

"With the promotion, I make the same thing as a sergeant makes, and I've got five times more headaches. There was no raise..."

We were interrupted — a Little League coach wanted to talk with Anderson. He asked him to wait. The coach had taken over for Anderson who no longer could coach because of his job.

"I just like kids. My son," and he pointed proudly to a picture of a uniformed football player on the wall," is No. 1 high school quarterback in the area, leading passer in the state. He's Duby Anderson. He's not a junior, I'm Lester James, he's Lester Jay Anderson. That picture is his first sack."

"You have a brother who is a cop?"

"Vernon. I'm the controversial one. I'm the one been out here bustin' down doors for years."

I told him what Will McGaughy said about drugs and criminals and punks. Will said there are only 20 or 30 really bad guys in town, the rest are punks who could be straightened out if they had jobs. But State Police Capt. Bobby Henry said it is hard to get kids to switch when they can make so much more peddling drugs.

I don't know about the figures, but when it comes to jobs, he's absolutely right. Jobs are the key.

"Our drug dealers range from the age of 13 to 24-25; guys over 25, if they don't have a big bag themselves, are not into drugs, they are just users. They'd rather draw GA (general assistance) stand on the corner and drink wine, or prey on the women with all these kids. We have these outside groups coming in hiring these young kids, we can't do too much about it because they are under age. Repeaters from two or three years ago now are age 17, 18, and can be prosecuted. But a lot of them wind up shot, beat up, killed and what have you. I take the stand that when we have juveniles in here, we put the mamas in jail. Yes sir. I believe in locking mamas up."

"You charge them with contributing to the delinquency of their children? Don't you have to prove they know the kids sell drugs?" I asked, incredulously.

"I leave that up to the juvenile officers. I put the charge on them and let them tell it to the judge. Here's a kid out here 1 or 2 o'clock in the morning, isn't mother responsible?"

"Why don't you jail the fathers."

"Can't find them."

Scott Mansfied: I'm color blind

Scott Mansfield, assistant St. Clair County state's attorney, says that he is color blind when he prosecutes cases: blind to the color of the defendant, blind to the color of the victim. It's untrue that he says "who cares" about black on black crime.

"A lot of the cases we've gotten, especially in the last six months, are dope dealers killing dope dealers," Mansfield said. "I don't care if they are black or they are white, we don't have innocent victims here. And I can tell you the juries are not going to have much sympathy or much proclivity to convict when someone kills a dope dealer. If there's a 'So what?' attitude, a 'Who cares?' attitude, it is an attitude that dope dealers may be killing dope dealers and this is no great loss. It's not because they are black dope dealers. If a dope dealer kills a dope dealer, I'm not as concerned as when a dope dealer kills an innocent person in a robbery or as a bystander to a shooting. I'll prosecute it nonetheless, but there are degrees of concern when you get to these kind of things. We're getting a lot of bad people killing bad people."

Mansfield recalled the case of the man allegedly beaten and cut by a homosexual. Mansfield said in contradiction to Anderson's statement, he reads every report sent to him. Actually, Mansfield said, the accused was a transvestite. The victim said he was an ironworker from Granite City driving home to St. Louis and on Route 3 in National City (at the First and Last Tavern, First and St. Clair, frequented by gay men prostitutes and women prostitutes) and picked up a hitchhiker, that there was no sex involved, and the man suddenly turned on him, beat him and cut him.

The transvestite said he was picked up at the tavern by the ironworker who asked him to perform a sex act and said he would give him $20. The transvestite performed the "head" but the ironworker refused to pay. The transvestite said they got in a violent argument and maybe he stuck the guy a little, "I don't know." Mansfield said the injuries were not serious.

"Maybe I made an error in judgment," Mansfield said, "but if I did, I can live with it." If the case had gone to trial and the ironworker had realized he would have been accused of having sex with a transvestite, he probably would have said "forget it" anyway, Mansfield said. In all sex cases, if a victim admits he was seeking a sexual liaison and says he was beaten and robbed, "I'm more likely to prosecute than the guy who says 'My car broke down and I'm an innocent fellow who's down here all by myself and these bad people are trying to take my money.' Well, he's lying already. In this case, I felt the victim was lying," Mansfield said.

"Any time I decline a case, every department, not just East St. Louis, or any other assistant state's attorney declines a case, any police department is free, and it doesn't hurt anybody's feelings, to take the case to John (State's Atty. John Baricevic). Most of the time John upholds our decisions, but the are times when John says 'no, go ahead and charge it.' He doesn't say we're wrong, he says 'Well, it's a matter of opinion.' So apparently they weren't that concerned about the case either," since they did not appeal to John.

The following was taken from the Belleville News-Democrat of Tuesday, Oct. 2, 1990.

"An East St. Louis man pleaded guilty Monday to murder and was sentenced to 11 years in prison. Walter C. Rice, 21, of 1301 Russell Ave., pleaded guilty to second degree murder in the drug-related shooting death Dec. 7 of Vincent Vance, 33, of 1506 Tudor Ave. St. Clair County Associate Judge Jan Fiss sentenced Rice to 11 years, a term negotiated in a plea bargain.

"In the plea bargain, Asst. State's Atty. Len Cleary agreed to reduce the first-degree murder charge for which Rice was indicted in march and recommended the 11-year sentence. Cleary said the charge was reduced to second-degree murder because Rice acted under a sudden and intense passion provoked by Vance.

"Rice's attorney, Asst. Public Defender Lloyd Cueto, agreed to the prison term.

"On Dec. 7 Rice shot Vance in the chest at 13th Street and Piggott Avenue in East St. Louis, Cleary said. Rice had been selling crack cocaine to people driving by the intersection, Cleary said. Although Vance's sister would testify that the shooting occurred when Rice tried to rob Vance, Rice and other witnesses said Rice shot Vance when Vance tried to drive away with several rocks of crack cocaine instead of picking just one to buy, Cleary said...Rice pulled out a pistol and shot into the car as he was running beside it, Cleary said."

And in the same issue:

"An East St. Louis woman was charged this weekend with first degree murder in the killing of a man whose throat was cut last week in Lincoln Park in East St. Louis.

"Cynthia Little, 31, of 539 Veronica, was charged with killing Shelby Brown, 29, of 1059 Liberty Ave., in East St. Louis with a broken bottle, the court record said.

"Little, who also was known as Lois Little, was being held in the St. Clair County Jail in lieu of $200,000 bail."

Mansfield said he was disappointed that Chief of Detectives Anderson felt as he said about Mansfield. "I thought we had a working relationship," Mansfield said. "The office and Lester Anderson have had our differences, I never thought we had made up and everybody loves each other, but I thought we'd gotten to the point recently where we had a working relationship that lets us all get the job done...where we were getting on with the business of police work and the prosecution was getting done."

Mansfield said that he often finds when he rejects a case because of lack of evidence or shoddy police work the black policemen want to blame it on race. He said he marvels at the belief by some blacks that there is a great conspiracy against East St. Louis by the whites in the county. "I marvel at it, but then when I think about it realistically, I can see where a persuasive black leader could convince a lot of people that it is a fact."

Undercover state trooper 'narcs' work city's housing projects

The HUD Squad is not a common household name to police TV show devotees, but it is nine men doing one heckuva job cleaning up drug sales in the East St. Louis housing projects.

The men work undercover as part of the undercover unit headed by Capt. Phil Kocis, commander of Zone 11 of the Division of Criminal Investigation, Illinois State Police, headquartered at Collinsville. The cost is picked up by the Department of Housing and Urban Development (HUD) to attack drugs in public housing.

The statistics are impressive. In the five months between May 1 and Sept. 1 the nine-man crew has handled 221 cases, made 222 arrests, 1,509 for dealing or possession of controlled substances, found 47 persons wanted on fugitive warrants, made one armed robbery arrest, arrested 23 for weapon offenses, possession of syringes and obstructing justice, seized 43 weapons — every kind imaginable, and has seized 1-1/2 pounds of cocaine.

They also have collected $27,319 in drug money.

Since all the coke was seized in street sales, that's a sizeable amount. Most of it is in crack.

The nine men tend to travel together. Their job is to arrest street sellers and to break up street selling, not to track the sources or infiltrate the

State Police Capt. Phil Kocis, seated, and Capt. Bobby Henry

drug trade. In essence, they make drug buys, then arrest the sellers. Working under cover, they may become the target of crime. The first day the men were at work in East St. Louis, one of them found a gun at his temple and was robbed.

There also are five marked state police cars in East St. Louis at all times, and East St. Louis police also help; the backup of the HUD drug unit is excellent. They work with the Housing Authority. It uses the arrests to evict families involved in drugs. "Our job is to get the drug dealers out of the projects; what they do is administrative," Kocis said.

The statistics for buys and arrests are falling off, Kocis said. "I don't know whether we are solving the problems are they are getting familiar with our operation." Housing authority spokespersons say the unit has made a marked difference.

Kocis agreed that stopping street corner dealing means less crime. People who come to East St. Louis to buy drugs are at risk. While dope dealers don't want their customers to get hurt, to be frightened away, there always is someone around eager to take the dope buyer's money away from him. They get robbed, they get murdered. One man brought his girl friend with him on a trip to buy drugs. He was robbed, locked in his trunk and his girl friend raped.

As far as gangs are concerned, Kocis said "There is no similarity to the organized activity that occurs on the West Coast or Chicago or even St. Louis. There are no real gangs in East St. Louis, just guys who decide to wear their hats backwards and call themselves gangs. "Oh they have some affiliation I guess, but they are just individual thugs, they're not into perpetuating the organization or anything like that."

"I would think that all drugs are the result of syndicate distribution. It has to start as an imported product in quantity then it breaks down further and further. Also the people we see are more likely dealing for another individual, perhaps who is capable of dealing in multi-ounce quantity. But I don't know that we've had too many folks that can handle kilos or that type of thing, because that's pretty big money."

The HUD squad works with other drug units, including the Federal Drug Administration, but the HUD men are in the city more than any other drug investigators.

Capt. Kocis said the officers' job is to make

arrests for drug dealing, not to give administrators evidence to throw families out of the projects. Of the practice of expelling families who are involved in drug activity, he said "I think it's a great idea, but our purpose is not to document things for HUD and throw people out. We are there to make criminal cases."

Throwing people out on the street does just move the problem around, he said, and "I don't know what the long range effect is. However, they're not going to be dealing in the projects, anyway."

Kocis said the project will end sometime. He doesn't know how long it will continue.

Newspaper reports quote Ron Grimming, deputy director of Illinois State Police, as expecting the contract, signed April 25, to last a year. However, Housing Authority spokespersons say they have applied for HUD funding for two more policemen, these to be city policemen to serve in uniform for a visible presence.

State police patrols first of kind

State police patrols in East St. Louis began in July, 1986, on the orders of the governor and at the request of Mayor Carl Officer who said the city needed help because it could not patrol the interstates. The assignment is unique in the annals of state police history. Capt. Bobby Henry, District 11 commander of the Illinois State Police, recites that mission and its accomplishments.

"I think we have had substantial impact on the city. I think the things that prompted us to go in there were the high incidence of crime, some of that crime spilling out onto the interstate highway system that traverses East St. Louis to the extent that we had people who would bump the side of the car or rear end you.

"The thing we're all told to do if we have an accident is pull over and exchange driver information, right? Wrong! This was the time for rape, robbery, sometimes a combination of the above. We thought there had to be something done. At that time the governor approved the Illinois State Police at the request of Mayor Officer to come into the city.

"During that time frame we have made a substantial number of criminal arrests. We had gang members blatantly and openly wearing their colors on the street. We have pretty well been able to inundate the gangs; many of the gang members are locked up now and serving time in the prisons througout Illinois. You don't see any colors being worn on the street. Things have tightened down, you don't have the armed robberies and shooting and problems on the interstate system. We have made a sizeable number of arrests.

"Since July 21, 1986, through Sept. 9, 1990, we have made 5,156 criminal arrests, from murder on down to lesser criminal offenses. We have written 26,725 traffic citations, we have issued 454,237 written warnings for lesser traffic violations, a total of 71,96 total contacts.

"I think that with the aggressive enforcement posture that we have taken and the thrust of the gang crimes unit that we had down there for awhile, and now we have the housing detail working the narcotics and the drugs...yes I think we have made East St. Louis a better place to live."

Sixteen officers work usually five cars in East St. Louis. The men ride one man to a car and back one another up closely. "Do they still need five cars on the street, or are that many needed to protect the policemen?" I asked.

"We need that number for officer safety. We probably would have scaled down and adjusted the officer allocation before if we could, but in all honesty the 16 are approved by the governor and we are locked in at 16, even if you or I thought we could be out of there with five. We would have to have the approval of the governor before we made any change in our commitment to East St. Louis."

Last year, the year before, shots were being fired all night long. Henry said he hasn't seen much of that this year.

When there is a police call, an emergency call, all five state police cars are likely to converge, along with city police and other police. "We almost have to operate that way," Henry said. Troopers ride one man to a car and it is a "pretty high risk operation."

"City police I think are doing better," Henry said. "For a long time there those guys weren't getting paid. How long can you expect a guy to work and keep his chin up with no pay? It's tough to keep motivation up. They are taking a more positive and aggressive approach. What we saw recently with the guys volunteering their own time to come back for a sweep of street corners, they are to be commended for that. In time I think we'll see even more improvement in the turn around of the problem."

The "bailout" funds are to go in part for the police department. Will they help?

"We hope so. Time will see the answer.

"This is one of the most challenging assignments of my career, to maintain a specialized detail in an area like that for this length of time. Never in the history of the Illinois state police has that been done. Sure we went into Cairo, and we went into Waukegan when they went on strike. Of course you know what the problem was in Cairo. But historically, this is a first.

"We have taken over 300 weapons out of traffic stops in East St. Louis just with those 16 troopers. So you know that doesn't occur every day. To have that level of intensity with the types of weapons we've taken, the variety of weapons, Mini Macs, Mini-Uzi's, automatic type weapons that these officers know they are faced with, and they know we are dealing with people on their way to prison or have gotten out of prison, street smart and tougher to deal with ... It is a high risk area."

"Is East St. Louis really all that dangerous, especially in the daytime?" I asked.

"I wouldn't recommend it. You know, why drive across a bridge that you know is not safe to drive across; if it is approved for 2,000 pounds, why see if you can drive a semi across? If you know there is a problem, and I know a lot of people do, and you'd be surprised at the number of young ladies, young girls, in the 18, 20-year bracket, coming over from Missouri by themselves into areas such as Rush City to buy drugs. It's almost like hanging a sign around their neck 'Rob me, beat me, rape me' type thing. They just don't realize the severity and magnitude of it.

"I don't think it is as bad, especially in the daytime, as it was.

"My wife worked down there in one of the governmental buildings for awhile and I was never comfortable with her working there. She no longer works there and I am very, very happy."

Capt. Henry said he thought East St. Louis is off on a more positive avenue now. "I hope they continue to do that. When you look around on the west side of the river, St. Louis is all developed and you have to go a long way to get out of the developed area. You circle on this side of the river and everything within that circle is developed other than that one area. That area is a prime area, prime property.

"It is a shame they (East St. Louisans) don't really take the bull by the horn and take the leadership to move that city ahead. It could again be the place to live and the place to shop. Look across at the St. Louis side, there's no reason this side can't mirror what you see on the St. Louis side. We may not see it in the length of time that I have left, but I think it's got to come back. Because it's like a big eyesore or a big cesspool sitting in the middle of a total economic developed area. I don't see how it can continue to sit there without getting cleaned up and shaped up."

State Police Sgt. Roger Hayes had told me that police are only dealing with two per cent of the population, the other 98 per cent are generally law abiding. He said he had been flagged down to be told by East St. Louisans they were glad state police were there.

I don't like the ticket, but I'm glad you're here — Traffic Offender

"I used to ride the streets down there myself, be down there with the guys and know what they had to cope with and that sort of thing, Henry said. "I've even issued tickets and had people thank me and say 'Well, I really don't want the ticket but I want to thank you for being here'."

Township Supervisor Will McGaughy said there are only 20 to 30 "bad guys" in the city, the rest of the trouble makers are "punks" who could be turned around if there were jobs, I told Henry.

"He's simplistically stating it. He's on target on some of it, with the job aspect. But if those kids really wanted a job, they could find a job, I think. The other aspect is how can you and I convince some of these kids to go out and work for a minimum wage job when they know they can make $100 or $200 a day in the blink of an eye selling drugs? What I am saying, I'm not condoning what they are doing, but it's hard to convince those kids to work for minimum wage when they know that $100 to $200 dealing drugs on a street corner is very easily achieved.

"I can take you to St. Clair Square Mall Friday night, Saturday, Sunday, and I can point out these kids with a thousand to two thousand dollars worth of jewelry around their neck. The average kid, unless their parents are rich, can only be doing one thing to afford that jewelry. Do your children run around with that kind of gold around their neck? How do they get it unless it is gotten illegally?"

Roger's percentage may be a little bit low, but the basic concept is good, there are a lot of good decent people, especially the older people, who live in East St. Louis. That is their home. None of us want to give up our home, none of us want to be relocated to other parts of the country or other towns that surround there and give away everything ... this is home, this is where I want to be. There are good decent people trapped there; they are trapped there due to shear economic necessity.

"That's the thing that keeps us going, whether its two per cent bad or 10 per cent bad, I think it is lower today that when we first went in there. We bust them, all the time. Unless it is really an unusual drug seizure, the courts usually give probation for the first time or two before they ever get the court's attention to tighten up a little bit and give a more serious sentence."

Sgt. Roger Hayes

One night with a state trooper

The shift activity ended with a high speed race from downtown South End to 68th and State Street for a call that shots were fired and a man was down. Illinois State Trooper Sgt. Roger W. Hayes whipped across town to I-64, out to I-255 and south to the State Street exit, which poured us right into the Clark Station. We were there f-a-s-t, but the "down" man already had been taken away in an ambulance and there were several police cars on the scene.

But among the simultaneous chatter on the police radios was something about a shooting a block away. Sgt. Hayes cruised to 69th, met another state patrol squad, listened, heard someone calling, finally pinned down the direction and drove there. A black male in blue jeans and no shirt said there had been a drive-by shooting at the house. He had seen the car cruise west slowly, went out and sat on a wooden trim to a flower bed and watched for the return. The return was accompanied by at least 10 shots, he said, so close that he could feel some of the bullets pass his back as he crouched down. A policeman and I found five nine millimeter casings in the street. Sgt. Hayes found a bullet hole in the frame of a storm window. The rest of the shots may have gone toward the garage alongside the house.

East St. Police arrived with us, continued the investigation. The woman of the house said her son had been missing for 24 hours, she was going to the police station to fill out a missing persons report. Earlier in the day two young women, strangers, had run the doorbell, told her the house would be shot up. City police said the missing man had some drug involvement.

Sgt. Hayes cruised for a little while looking for a car with a sagging rear bumper that matched the description of the car from which the shots were fired. We sped to catch up with a vehicle that aroused suspicion, but it contained a family with two children. It was 1 a.m. and Sgt. Hayes radioed for the other state police patrols to meet us at city police headquarters. En route we came upon a drunk staggering wildly and five feet from the curb. We pulled alongside, I rolled down the window, and the sergeant suggested he would be safer on the sidewalk. "I waited 30 minutes for a bus," he said slurring his words, then I went to the bathroom, and when I came out he wouldn't let me on the bus. Now you tell me I can't even walk in the street." He uttered some unintelligible curse words. Sgt. Hayes shook his head as we proceeded to police headquarters and ended the patroling — Hayes had to return to District 11 headquarters in Collinsville to complete his paperwork.

Bullet hole in storm window frame

It was a Friday night, and Sgt. Dave Jung, public information officer for District 11, had arranged for me to ride with Hayes. We started at 7:30 p.m. at the city police headquarters in the back of the new city hall. We quit about 1 a.m. I had chosen Friday as the night with the most activity, but for a Friday, it was quiet.

We drove only a few blocks at twilight when Hayes noticed a car with one headlight, and the driver doused the lights. Suspicious, Hayes pulled him over. The man's driver's license was suspended in 1988 and never reissued. The car was not registered. Hayes handcuffed him, told a young lady in the car the bail would be $100, and we returned to the police station to place the man in a holdover cell.

Paperwork was completed, and we pulled out in time to hear that an officer needed assistance at First and St. Clair, at the entrance to the Stockyards. It was the canine handler, L. H. Parker, who had stopped a stolen vehicle with two men in it. He said he had not made a distress call, just a request for a standby, but there were two policemen from National City, two state police cars and two city police cars on the scene. The troopers ride one man to a car; it is good to know backup is so swift. Hayes, who formerly was a dog handler, said Parker should have turned the dog loose, he wouldn't have needed any more help.

Parker spent most of the rest of his shift handling the case. The driver said he was just driving and the motor had been running when he got in, the passenger said he had been the driver but asked the other man to drive when he became sick, and that the car was stolen by someone else. The ignition as punched out. There was confusion over what charges to file. Hayes told him to be at the county jail at 9 a.m. Saturday to meet the assistant state's attorney, and what work to do before he went. Parker made note that Saturday, Sunday and Monday he was supposed to be off, and that Saturday was his wife's birthday. "Look at all the money you'll make," the sergeant smiled.

We had seen a few prostitutes at the tavern at First and St. Clair, one with a foot in a cast Hayes said has AIDS. We returned to the corner later while cruising, drove around the First and Last Chance Tavern. Hayes explained that the first time he did that the owner came out to ask what was wrong. When he explained he just was cruising the owner said thanks, that the car ran off the "he-shes" that were ruining his business. As we drove through a strip of Pennsylvania Avenue that was simply a trail through the head-high weeds, Hayes said National City policemen said they found three to seven looted and discarded wallets here every Monday morning. Two things bring white men down here at night, drugs and women, he said.

Hayes said there were perhaps a dozen women prostitutes working the area around Eighth and St. Clair, sometimes out of a motel on Ninth Street. Near Eighth and Pennsylvania we passed two sitting in front of a hovel. The building was unsafe enough. The women looked worse. I expressed my astonishment that they could draw any johns. He agreed, pointing out the news stories currently in the papers about a new strain of gonorrhea that is resistant to medication. Still, they come.

We drove through the various housing projects, not nearly as dangerous as they used to be, still places to be careful. In Villa Griffin, a resident flagged us down.

"A guy was fighting with his wife, man, and he slammed her up against my car and put a dent in it."

Hayes told the man to call city police to have a report made.

About that time three cars with white occupants cruised through the project. "Speak of the Devil," Hayes said. It was the HUD Squad — a squad of eight undercover agents paid by the housing

Sgt. Hayes books motorist

authority to investigate drugs and gangs in the projects. They asked Hayes if he was riding with a partner. "Reporter" he responded. "Ask him if he wants to ride with the *real* police." "Ask them," I said, "why they have to ride in groups of eight and you go alone?" (For the answer, see interview with Capt. Phil Kocis).

Alongside Alta Sita Park a juvenile, maybe 15, dipped slightly as he we approached. Hayes stopped, opened his door, picked up the can of beer the lad had put down (which I had not seen). The boy turned, expecting to be called. "Just keep walking sonny," Hayes called as he poured out the beer.

Back on St. Clair Avenue, maybe about 30th street or thereabout, we pulled behind a tavern. A young man dropped a plastic medicine container and started sauntering away. "He dropped it." Hayes summoned him back, had him face the wall while he knelt and fished up the bottle. The youth insisted it was medicine, and that he had not dropped it. Hayes explained he was going to cuff him, then he would test what was in the bottle, little round balls. If it wasn't crack, then he'd be freed.

Hayes opened the trunk, and as the youth stood by, tested the balls with chemicals. It was not crack, but neither was it a pill. Hayes cut it in two with a key. "What is this, soap?"

The youth insisted that it wasn't his, that he had not dropped it.

Sgt. Hayes checks on bottle of 'drugs'

Hayes rephrased his questions. "Whoever was selling this stuff, what was he getting for it?

"$20."

"Anybody complain about the stuff."

"Not that I know of."

Hayes unlocked the handcuffs. "Do me a favor, tell me your whole name so next time I see you I can call you by name."

He did.

"Your middle initial?"

He told, and we were on our way again.

We passed the old Waverly Theater, still showing X-rated movies. Patrons approach from the north, off Black Lane.

We drove around Lansdowne Towers, back northwest into streets full of garbage and trash. "It's really disgusting when you remember this city 30 years ago," Hayes said.

I asked him about the gang signs. Was that "fun stuff" or were the gangs still active? Either left over or fun stuff, he said. The gangs are about gone.

We drove by Roosevelt Homes. Hayes said that for awhile the homes were almost all empty, and inside, holes were knocked in the walls between apartments. "You'd chase a guy into an apartment and think you had him trapped, and he'd come out at the other end of the building." Fenced, they were being rehabilitated, part of a $40 million overhaul of East St. Louis public housing. "Roosevelts are shut down right now for remodeling, only a half dozen occupied there. The DeShields stay pretty busy. Gompers stuff has been picking up lately. Orr-Weathers is still busy."

The marked cars and uniformed men patrol one to a car. They look for street corner drug dealers, try to harass the prostitutes to keep their business cut down, and answer calls along with East St. Louis police, usually as backup, take charge when East St. Louis is busy elsewhere. They also make traffic stops. Hayes said most people appreciate the troopers, even flag them down and thank them for being there. He estimated that the police deal with two per cent of the population. "Most of the problems we have are drug related, and problems with prostitutes." He has not experienced racial resentment as a white trooper in a town almost completely black.

We passed a state trooper standing beside a car with a flat tire with a white driver on St. Clair Avenue. The driver was calling for help on his cellular phone.

At Orr-Weathers, he said, two years ago a white "buyer" would be surrounded by guys trying to sell

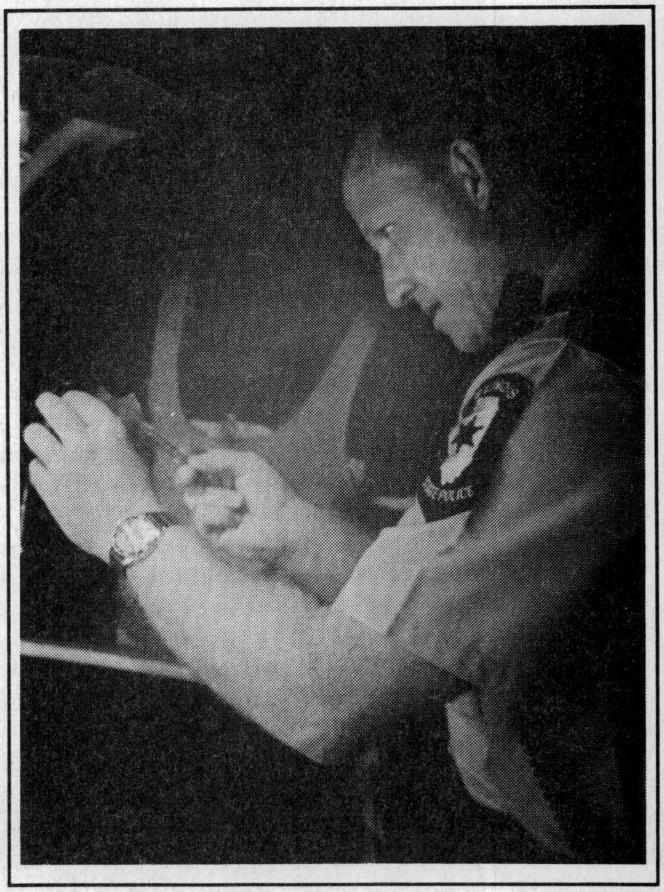

Hayes tests sample for crack

crack, and there were lots of robberies, ripoffs. They'd just as soon steal it from you as sell to you." The HUD undercover unit has moved the dealers out of the projects and with the marked cars off the street corners and into houses. The result is a reduction in street crime, Hayes said.

We drove past 27th and Ridge. "First part of the year we were getting at least one shooting a week on this corner." It has quieted down. He flashed his spotlight on a burned building. "That was a crack house we raided. Two weeks later it burned."

Taverns are not a problem, though there is drug dealing in some of them. There's little trouble there. Hayes said he only had a couple of calls to taverns in a year.

There was another man down, shots fired call at 24th and Bond, but apparently it was a false alarm.

When we returned to the police station Hayes checked to see the plight of the early arrest. He still was in the holdover. Hayes filled out the prisoner's court date, warned him that the sergeant would be most unhappy if he did not show up and released him. He was grateful.

Golden Gardens warns away drug dealers, but police say one of area's biggest distributors is headquartered there, just south of city limits

State troopers say this house was burned soon after it was raided as a crack house. It is near 27th Street and Ridge Avenue

Public policy to heal the wounds of city still sought by Sen. Simon

U.S. Sen. Paul Simon has bills that will be passed someday, including a full-employment bill, job training act bills, and perhaps bills for his dream for the city, a $60 million world-class museum, but East St. Louis needs can't wait. It needs any help that can provide some economic stability, Simon said.

"Way back when" Simon wanted to put Southern Illinois University's Metro-East branch in East St. Louis rather than Edwardsville. "I think my idea was right, but I didn't have much support at the time. But what you need is some kind of anchor to start building an economic base. If we can have my idea of developing this museum that would be world class, would attract people from all over the world, that would be tied into the riverfront complex, then you generate jobs, and all that needs to be done. You generate a lot of tourist jobs; tourist jobs frankly frequently require less demanding skill levels than a lot of other kinds of jobs."

Simon, a Democrat from Makanda, south of Carbondale, is a former Troy resident. He and Illinois' other senator, Alan J. Dixon of Belleville, served together in the Illinois House of Representatives and Illinois State Senate. Dixon and Simon were elected to state offices, Simon lieutenant governor under Gov. Ogilvie. Simon's wife Jeanne was a state representative; they met in the Illinois House. Simon moved to Makanda to run for the congressional seat vacated by Kenneth Gray. Unhappy with having to spend so much time campaigning every two years, and wanting to be able to spread his sphere of influence, he ran for the Senate and upset Republican incumbent Charles Percy. Meanwhile, Dixon had been elected to the Senate, so the two are serving together again. Simon ran for this party's nomination for president, unsuccessfully, in the last presidential election.

A long-range goal is educational, particularly attacking adult illiteracy. "When I mention long-term, it is really not quite as long term as a lot of other things. That's something where you can have, I think, a fairly rapid increase in improving things. Illiteracy is a long-time concern of Simon's.

President Gorge Bush this year signed into law new Simon-authored legislation that expands a movement he began six years ago to promote the use of libraries in tutoring adults to read and write. The new legislation will equip libraries with the latest literacy teaching materials. Public and private literacy programs still reach only about 19 per cent of those in need, Simon said.

U. S. Sen. Paul Simon

"One of the things we clearly need is for the governor of Illinois to really take an interest," he said. "There is always a pre-election interest in East St. Louis, but not much post-election interest."

On a more immediate basis, Simon has been involved in individual problems, including the federal takeover of the housing authority, hospital financial difficulty and an earlier dispute over payback of federal funds used to build the city hall.

East St. Louis desperately needs to build confidence in its integrity among federal and state agencies and others outside the city that could give help, Simon said.

Simon took time from a busy schedule, involved in the federal budget crisis and concerned about the Persian Gulf, and on weekends campaigning for re-election to his senate seat, for this quick interview. Whatever the action that will help East St. Louis, Simon made it clear he stands ready to lend the power and prestige of his office.

Two years ago Sen. Simon wrote a column about Jackie Joyner-Kersee and her pride in East St. Louis. He recalled it during our interview, and later sent me a copy, which follows:

Jackie Joyner-Kersee, winner of two gold medals at the Olympics in Seoul, is being called the world's greatest female athlete by newspapers everywhere, but I think she is doing something even more important that winning gold medals in Seoul.

Jackie Joyner-Kersee deserves a gold medal for citizenship. Let me tell you why.

When she entered the stadium in Seoul for the closing ceremonies on the shoulders of her husband, Bob Kersee, she carried a sign: "I Love East St. Louis, Illinois."

Today, East St. Louis, is a city of devastation, of crime, of unpaid city employees, of intense poverty — but also a city with marvelous people. It is a city that many, black and white, have fled and forgotten.

Jackie Joyner-Kersee wants to return to reopen the Mary E. Brown Community Center where she ran her first track meet at age 9 and where she long-jumped 16 feet 9 inches at age 12. (Her gold medal winning jump in Seoul was 24 feet 3-1/2 inches). She has signed a sponsorship contract with Seven-Up to help fund a foundation to reopen the center for young athletes in East St. Louis.

Jackie, now 26, grew up in poverty. Press accounts say she sometimes ate bread and mayonnaise for dinner and the family used to collect plastic tubs of water in the kitchen because their pipes froze frequently.

She remembers her mother telling her, "Don't get pregnant at a young age, and make sure you finish school." Jackie graduated from UCLA with scholastic honors and in the top 10 percent of her class. Her mother died of meningitis in 1981 at age 38 but Jackie says she feels her mother is with her in spirit.

Says Jackie, "I have this burning desire to get out there and do my best. It's as if I'm keeping it all in a little bottle, and it's all going to come out when I do the best I'm capable of doing."

East St. Louis has so much potential, and the people there have so much potential.

The former U.S. ambassador to the United Nations, Donald McHenry, grew up in East St. Louis and has done much to help that city.

Katherine Dunham, the ballet and dance pioneer who received the Albert Schweitzer Music Award grew up in East St. Louis and still maintains a home there. She has also done much to stimulate young people to take an interest in culture and in their African-American heritage.

Jackie Jyner-Kersee is a great athlete. But she is an even greater person for remembering her roots and for striving to see that more of the talented young people in that depressed city have a chance.

Jackie Joyner-Kersee

America is one family. When anyone in that family hurts, ultimately all of us hurt.

People in East St. Louis are hurting and Jackie Joyner-Kersee wants to help heal the wounds.

She needs to be joined by public policy that does the same.

Sen. Simon is willing to chair a "summit conference" on East St. Louis after the elections. City, county, state and federal officials all agree the city cannot solve its problems alone. Such a conference would be a working meeting at which the problems could be considered one by one and authoritative officials including the governor, federal department heads, the county board chairman, city officials and the state and federal legislators could commit to programs. It would not be an opportunity for anyone to grandstand.

The meeting would have to be preceded by a planning conference and supported with "white papers" accurately defining the problems, sponsored by someone like SIU-E and requested — sought — by the mayor and aldermanic council.

Rev. John H. Rouse talks with the children of his church

Each black mayor has inherited his problems

Rev. John Rouse is pastor of Mount Zion Baptist Church at 2235 Bond Ave., with 2,600 members on its rolls, including the mission at 425 N. 88th St. It probably is the biggest church in East St. Louis. As pastor, Rev. Rouse sees an obligation to care for the welfare of his flock — or his constituency if he is being political at the moment — and be concerned about the physical well being as well as the spiritual well being of the people of the community, and that includes the service of their government.

Rev. Rouse was a member of the Task Force on Municipally Distressed cities that wrote the Distressed Cities Act, known popularly as the East St. Louis bailout plan, and also chairman of the Governor's East St. Louis Financial Advisory Board. Both organizations ended their responsibility with the passage of the new act and its approval by Gov. Jim Thompson. Rev. Rouse said some people are surprised at what the committee found — and didn't find.

"The first thing we found was that no money had been stolen. Many people had thought that was the reason the city was in debt. It was found each of the black mayors simply inherited the problem from the other and when Williams (the first black mayor was James Williams) became mayor, he inherited the problem from Alvin Fields. We don't have records back that far, so we don't know what the situation was under his administration.

"Each mayor took over with a large deficit; and we were able to show where they had spent money illegally, so to speak. They received money for one thing and they used it for another. For example, HUD money was used instead of fixing streets to pay policemen. So the monies were not stolen; the priorities kind of dictated where the money went. That was one of the things we found.

That was the biggest problem. It surprised a lot of folk that nobody was stealing the money. You've always got some petty theft. Y'know you have a couple of situations where people in departments were getting away with money from demolition and so forth. But overall, from the general fund, money was not being stolen.

"I think we did a pretty good job. We put together a program that I feel can help other municipally distressed cities in this area and can even be a model for cities in the nation."

But the act does not provide for a revenue stream to repay the loans.

"No, it does not," Rev. Rouse concurred. "The city is required to put together a program that will enable them to repay, if bonds are floated, they have to pay off the bonds; if the city receives that $4.5 million loan, the city will be responsible for repaying that. It is hoped the city will be able to generate the revenue through the riverfront; we have the riverboat gambling bill that they are hoping will provide enough funds to retire the indebtedness."

"What would Frank 'Buster' Wortman think about the city being financed with gambling?" we asked.

"I think he's probably turning over in his grave wishing he was here," Rev. Rouse said, laughing. "I remember him when I was a youngster.

"As a minister I cannot say that I support that (riverboat gambling)," Rev. Rouse said. "However, it is something I know is about to happen and if it does not happen on the east side of the river, it's going to happen on the west side. And I'm like this, if I have to be poisoned, at least let me handle my own poison. This is why I would prefer that this community rather than St. Louis would have it, because it's just as easy to cross that river to gamble as it is to stay on this side, and if we are going to pour arsenic in the water on the west side, we're eventually going to get it over here. Let's just handle it over here."

"Are you among those that think there is a white conspiracy to discredit East St. Louis to take it over again from the blacks?" I asked.

"Yes, I definitely believe that, and it is more than just a belief. I have had some friends of mine, in Belleville, in Collinsville, a couple of people from outside the area, who said that if enough pressure was brought to bear, East St. Louis was going to cave in and there are folks just waiting to move in. The riverfront is the big thing. I'm not saying they want to take over the city government; they just want that riverfront, because that's a billion dollar gold mine."

"What is so wrong with, say, St. Louis money developing the riverfront? What's the problem?" I asked.

"There's nothing wrong with it. I have no problem with that. If the mayor would say to certain entities, 'OK, we will develop this riverfront together,' with some of the powers that be, politically and businesses, we would not have the problem that we are having now. But the mayor has determined that riverfront will be controlled totally by East St. Louis, that is the problem. He's not sharing power, he's not sharing wealth. Consequently the outside forces are stopping him from developing that wealth. If he could put a marina there, if he could develop export-import facilities there, if he can get the gambling, if he can develop some of the businesses and the hotels, and the city and the local blacks are controlling...then you see where I am coming from. (Some people think) There's too much money for a black community to be in total control of. I've been told that."

"You can use somebody else's money and still maintain control," I suggested.

"That's what they are concerned with, that control factor. I'm not too sure the mayor hasn't over-reacted to a certain extent. There are people who would like to invest and not have control. But you do have some people who want to control, they don't want to lease, they want to buy and they want to own. If they have the right people in office, they think they can get this."

"Are you supporting anybody in particular for office?" I asked.

"In order to maintain my ability to move amongst whoever is elected and try to do things for the city, I am staying somewhat independent," he responded. The minute I back one man and he loses, or I back one man for mayor and the township is against him and he wins, then there are certain offices I am going to have trouble getting into. I think my being able to talk to people regardless of who is in offices is important, especially when I look at my congregation. These are the people that I represent. I have a constituency just like a politician, and when problems are there, if I need to go see the mayor, I don't need the mayor refusing to answer my phone calls or refusing to let me in to see him because I didn't support certain people or him for election. I need for him to say 'OK Reverend, I know where you stand, I know why you are here, what can I do?'"

But Rev. Rouse strongly urges his church members to be politically active, and arranges for them to register to vote at the church.

Recognizing Rev. Rouse's concern with the total lives of his church members, we asked him to rank the problems of that "constituency."

"Right now, believe it or not, ranking with economics, underemployment and no employment, I think one of the major problems I am having to confront even in my church is the drug situation, crack cocaine. The number of drug addicts I have in my church is almost unbelievable, and they're not all from the poor community either."

They talk to him about it. "Yes, most of them want help, you know. I don't know too many that are satisfied with being a drug addict. They want help and they come to me under the cloak of confidentiality. I try to make them aware that you have to acknowledge that you are a drug addict, to go out and really get the help you need. You've got to have a support base, and the support groups...

"We are organizing one now. We have been relying on community-based organizations to provide that kind of service. We're finding a need because of the proliferation of addicts to try to develop additional support groups. We want to establish one in the church as well as establish a couple of others in the community. The problem is one meeting a week many times will not do what has to be done. If we can get five or six different programs so you have one on Monday and one on Tuesday, whenever that person has a problem — like alcoholic's anonymous...it's rough on a man to have to wait for meeting time to get some help."

The church feeds the hungry every day, an average of 60, sometimes it drops to 35-40, sometimes it will jump up to 80 or 85. There also is a grocery pantry that serves 325 families per month.

Rev. Rouse agrees that the true unemployment rate in East St. Louis could be as high as one-third. "It could be 33 per cent. You can't depend on Employment Service because you have so many people in East St. Louis looking for jobs, so they are no longer registered with the employment office."

A great many black leaders say they believe there is a conspiracy of white people to discredit East St. Louis, as expressed by East St. Louis Chief of Detectives Lester Anderson, in order to facilitate a white takeover. Rev. Rouse is among them.

"I feel that attitude does prevail. I talk to a lot of people in Belleville and I get the feeling that 'We'll let the drugs proliferate in East St. Louis.' You can go to a pawn shop outside East St. Louis and buy a gun real easy if you live in East St. Louis, and I've heard people say 'Well, the fact is if you all kill each other off we don't have to worry about you.' I believe that he's (Anderson's) right there. It may not be an overt action, but I believe that thinking is there. Every time something goes down in East St. Louis it either becomes a joke, you'll find them laughing about it, or they just don't care. I feel this is basically the attitude of the judicial system in Belleville toward East St. Louis."

Whether there is a legally-defined conspiracy, no one seems to contradict that such attitudes do exist and that the black flight from East St. Louis and continued mismanagement could have the same result as a conspiracy.

"I think you have to believe it and they (white leaders) don't want to be caught up in it. I think ultimately it will happen. I have seen master plans for East St. Louis. I have heard people talk about what it ultimately will be. And when they talk about these things, the blacks are not included. The blacks are looked at as more of a labor force that will be available. But in terms of ownership, entrepreneurship, they are not considered."

Rev. Rouse questioned whether the state Department of Community Affairs and regional planners are doing all they should to develop East St. Louis. "Can you conceive or perceive of a city as strategically located as East St. Louis that cannot get any businesses to locate there? It either means that the state government through economic develop-ment commissions for the region, for the county... somebody is not really working to pull things into East St. Louis. Why is that?"

Rev. Rouse said his commission found many little things the state could do to help the city. "The taxes we pay help buy the state police cars. The state could say 'Here's 20 cars we have pulled off the road, take them.' That's cheaper than putting the state police in the town, but they won't do it...My concern is that they are looking at one man, Carl Officer, and they're letting him blind them to the needs of the general population.

"My concern is for East St. Louis," Rev. Rouse continued. "I am here because I want to be, and not because I have to be. Sometimes East St. Louis does discourage me, but I bounce back. Sometimes the situation can almost send you into a state of depression. But I can see good people here. I can't conceive of walking away from them. I am saying that same thing to the political powers. We've got some good people that deserve better than they are getting."

All you read about the city is critical, he said. "We are still turning out some strong students, some of the best athletes in the country, have one of the best music departments, and all of the kids that go out of East St. Louis to colleges and universities, they don't flunk out. But nobody really makes a noise about that. I think that's pathetic.

"I'm afraid some people in East St. Louis are letting other folks paint a dark picture, and when you do that, self esteem drops. You find you have people ashamed to say 'I'm from East St. Louis.' And that's bad. If we are going to rise above the situation, we've got to believe that we are capable. Too often the media content is negative. They do very little to highlight the good things that come out of a bad situation, but that doesn't sell papers."

Oliver Hendricks

Hendricks' formula for recovery: New leadership

"Well, the city is at its lowest end right now. I know that it will come back. We just have to change its leadership. Once we do that, we're going to have a city. And the reason I say that is the people haven't left, the people are still here, the East St. Louisans are still here, and they just want this city to get off its behind and dust itself off and come on with it."

The speaker is Oliver Hendricks, a deputy sheriff until 1969, an employee of the Illinois Department of Revenue ever since, chairman pro tem of the East St. Louis Board of Aldermen. And he has a single idea to solve the problems of East St. Louis: change the city's leadership, get rid of Carl Officer.

The city primary is in February, the election in April. East St. Louis is the only municipality in the county whose candidates run on Democratic and Republican tickets. It is up to "the organization" — the Democratic Party in East St. Louis — to choose one person for mayor, one for treasurer and one for clerk, to clear the field of competing candidates, to defeat Officer, he said. Officer won over Clyde Jordan four years ago with the precinct committeemen supporting Jordan.

"This is a different ball game now," Hendricks said. "We have lost everything we could lose. We've lost the community block grant, the housing authority, the city hall, our land, you name it, we've lost it." (A circuit court judge awarded the city hall to a claimant who said the city had not met its obligations to him. See "Update.")

Wally Spiers of the Belleville News-Democrat agrees. In a column Oct. 1 he wrote, after commenting on the loss of city hall, "The city is about as close to ruined as it can get. It cannot even hold onto its buildings." But he also predicted Carl Officer "will skate away from under this crisis as if it never existed...Officer thrives in the chaos.

He has been sued, questioned in front of grand juries, hounded and praised. He has crossed state's attorneys, governors, political parties and lived to brag about it. He went to jail for contempt of court for not speeding along sewer repairs in the city. So far Officer has survived the fall of his grandiose riverfront plans and an investigation by the Internal Revenue Service. He survived an attempt by a hostile city council to take away his power to appoint department heads.

"Officer stands — above all — as a controversial figure, a stance he apparently likes. He shoots from the lip, then stands back while the fur flies. 'Bankers come in from Belleville and steal us blind,' he said at the beginning of his administration 1979. In 1989 he called Gov. James R. Thompson — the same governor he endorsed for re-election in 1982 — Pontius Pilate...He survived — and that is the point. Other politicians survive by being effective and doing a good job. He survives no matter what.

"If the people of East St. Louis do not like Officer, they can throw him out in 1991," Spears wrote. "Officer swept to his first mayoral victory in 1979 with 91 per cent of the vote. He won re-election in 1983 with slightly more than 80 per cent of the vote. He won re-election in 1987 with 60 per cent of the vote, and several opponents split the rest. Is there a downward trend there? Do not hold your breath. The man is a survivor."

Elmo Bush, first black to run for mayor, former council member, former school superintendent, and former campaign manager for Clyde Jordan when he ran against Carl Officer, said there's not a man in East St. Louis who could beat Carl Officer right now," and ironically, he blamed the News-Democrat for that. (See Elmo Bush interview.)

But Hendricks said the time is now for Officer to be replaced. It has to happen, he said, or there will be no city. The federal, state and county governments will dismantle it piece by piece, and there will be no East St. Louis.

Like a pitbull with his teeth sunk into a shank, Hendricks sees only one solution to all of the city's problems: Replace Carl Officer with new leadership. New leadership can develop the riverfront. New leadership can solve the crime problem. New leadership can solve the drug problem. With new leadership doing the right thing, schools improving, services provided, business and industry will come back, will take another look. There will be jobs. With new leadership, people will feel safe to come into East St. Louis to ride Metro Link. The rift with Carl is not the problem; the city needs new leadership that other governments and other people can trust, he said.

With new leadership, Hendricks sees a bright future for the city. The Distressed Cities Act in place, in part through the lobbying and the strong stand of the aldermen, will provide the oversight commitee and fiscal responsibility. "Everything is in place for us to move forward."

We've been in charge here for 20 years...This is our mess that we need to clean up. Yeh.

Hendricks does not believe in the "white conspiracy" theory.

I don't believe that. I don't believe that. No. You have to go back to the 60's for that kind of stuff. We just have to do our own thing." He said that when you foul up, you always have the tendency to blame someone else. "I'm not blaming them," he said of whites.

"We've been in charge here for 20 years; blacks have been in control of the city 20 years, Williams four, Mason four, Carl 12, so that's 20. This is our mess that we need to clean up. Yeh!"

The average citizen doesn't care about politics. They want good police protection, fire protection, their streets and alleys clean, like in any other city. But when they drive over the same streets dodging the same potholes year after year, they get fed up. The business of city government is delivering services, and "we haven't done that," he said. There are more tax protests than at anytime in history, Hendricks said. That says that the people are fed up, and he is sure they will vote for new leadership.

Yes, there are people strong enough to lead the city and strong enough to win the election against Officer, Hendricks believes. He won't say who they are, but he says he knows individuals whoc an do the job.

The city acts like the "richest poorest city in the nation," he said. "Carl says we can do this and we can do that, when we can't even pay the light bill. You have to live within your means. You have to run this like you would your household. If you haven't got enough money for pork chops, you have to eat bacon, and if you can't buy light bread, make corn bread. It may not be just what you want, but you are surviving. Then you can get yourself back on your feet and do the things that need doing. That's our problem. That's been our problem."

When there's new leadership, then is the time for a coming together of all the people in the federal, state and county governments concerned with East St. Louis and the new leadership to map a plan to turn East St. Louis around. Then it will happen, he said, but only with that new leadership.

Sen. Kenneth Hall amid walls of photographic memorabilia

Sen. Kenneth Hall optimistic for first time in 22 years

State Sen. Kenneth Hall is more confident of the future of East St. Louis than any time in the 22 years he has been a state senator. "I think we've turned a corner now," he said with unabashed optimism.

"I feel good in this respect. At long last we're going to have a fiscal officer who will oversee our finances, the money that comes from the state to this city, and he'll have the oversight of five people, I think very good people. I think we've turned the corner now where you're going to have fiscal responsibility."

He was talking primarily about the money from the $34 million state "bailout bill" which he championed through the legislature, which was blocked for some time by State Rep. Wyvetter Younge with additional demands, and opposed verbally by Mayor Carl Officer. As a leader of the black caucus and its ties with the Chicago vote, and as the chairman of the Senate Appropriations Committee, the 72-year-old Hall had the clout to convince a skeptical legislature that it needed to pass the bill. But it would not without a unanimous consent from the mayor, the council, and most importantly, the member of the House representing the district, Rep. Wyvetter Younge.

"If any money comes to this city, it's going to be money that's going to be spent properly, and I think it will be a boon to this community. So, it's long needed. I see maybe a resurgence of this city, along with the State Community College, with the proper people in place, bouncing back to be a catalyst also. The legislature is very unhappy with the situation now, but I see us correcting a lot of those things (that give the city an image of fiscally irresponsibility) and I have confidence we're going to emerge."

The State Community College has a new board president, Warrington Hudlin, who was helpful in getting the college established, and is seeking a new college president. "Can you imagine, after 20 years those fellows still don't have their act together," Hall had commented a few weeks earlier while he was battling for passage of the bailout. The college was established by special legislation authored by Hall, the only one in the state that was directly state supported. It has a new campus, but enrollment has dwindled.

Before the bailout bill was passed, Hall had expressed fear that the people of East St. Louis would accept high taxes, limited police and fire protection and decaying streets as the best they could have, and his concern over the dearth of leadership and the unwillingness of those who could make a difference to be politically active.

Hall is a "different" black leader than most. He was a friend and political associate of the last white mayor, Alvin G. Fields, and Fields once told Hall that he was Fields' choice to be the first black mayor of the city. Hall also was the choice of the county Democratic party, but Hall was happy in the legislature. He was raised in the Catholic faith, very close to the church, a marked minority in black East St. Louis. He is widely accepted by the white power structure, and when members talk about the "good blacks" they know in East St. Louis, Hall's is likely to be the first name off their tongues. But he walks his own road. He has few good words for Wyvetter Younge, whom he sees as almost scuttling the bailout bill, nor Mayor Carl Officer, whom he sees as abrogating the authority of the Aldermanic Council in attempting one-man rule of the city, and failing to provide fiscal integrity for the city. Officer, who is not inhibited in name-calling, places Hall with Aldermanic Council President Oliver Hendricks among his list of foes whom he charges would sell out the black interest of the city.

Hall is a hard worker at whatever he does. During school breaks over Christmas and the like he worked as a dining car waiter from Chicago to San Francisco and to Los Angeles. "A quarter looked as big as a cart wheel in those days, and I worked hard for tips." Out of high school, he worked as a timekeeper and first aid man for the Works Progress Administration, under Franklin Delano Roosevelt's presidency, for $81 a month. He was elected to the East St. Louis Park Board for two six-year terms, for 11 years he was a deputy sheriff. He worked for the Aluminum Co. of America Research Division in the "miniature plant" located behind the now-gutted research headquarters building. He served two terms in the house, 20 years in the senate with two terms to go. He and his wife have raised four sons, all successful.

The walls of Hall's East St. Louis office are covered with pictures of Hall and distinguished Americans from presidents to prize fighters and other athletes. He has a number of scrap books with clippings about his successes as a legislator and community leader over his 24 legislative years. They virtually are a history of the city.

Hall says he is sometimes kidded by fellow legislators about living in East St. Louis. He said that he tells them that once you have drunk the waters of East St. Louis, you can never leave — you always come back.

Hall is concerned about the revenue stream required to repay the state's "bailout bill" loans. The city was guaranteed a riverboat gambling license to help repay the loans. Since the riverfront is in the city's tax increment financing (TIF) district, and parallel retail development of restaurants will add disproportionately more to that revenue stream than otherwise possible (See interview with Bob Vancil).

Hall thinks Target 200 and its chairman Willie Nelson are "on the ball" with the planned housing development, involving TIF, and that the plan to finance a new housing plant is all right, but he would prefer to see an Illinois firm handling it rather than a Philadelphia company.

The high cost of sewage treatment by the American Bottoms plant is untenable and something is going to have to be done by the state or federal governments. "It was a federal program forced on us," he said. The bill for disposal is twice what the residents pay for the water. "It's got to be looked into." It is on his agenda.

Light rail will be important to East St. Louis too, he said. And when the bailout is fully in place, "the policemen will get cars that will run and there will be more police and fire manpower... We have to do something to bring insurance rates down so people can afford to live here.

"For the first time I am beginning to be optimistic, for the first time since I have been in the legislature. I think we're trying to see some light at the end of the tunnel."

Hall said he missed the old Metro-East Journal, and the city needs a newspaper that will serve an advocacy role. During the bailout legislative deadlock, the Belleville News-Democrat played an important role, he said, and when it editorially asked "Where are the people?" to support the bailout bill, the people came forth. "It really stirred some people," he said. "There's nothing like the press, and I told them so."

Warrington Hudlin

Hudlin determined to prove SCC can play major role

The State Community College District 601 in East St. Louis is 20 years old "and they still haven't got their act together," State Sen. Kenneth Hall remarked recently.

But Hall's good friend Warrington Hudlin, 68, now president of the SCC board, says he and his new board are changing that, and by June everybody will recognize the change, "We will have quality."

. Hudlin, a successful insurance man with offices in First Illinois Bank Building and at 24th and State Street, was a member of the steering committee for the establishment of the college. But he watched in dismay as the college was made a political tool, was launched without proper preparation and even was looted. But last January Gov. Jim Thompson said enough is enough and removed the whole board, changed it from an elected board to an appointed board, and Hudlin was chosen as chairman. Now, after 20 years, he has a chance to correct the situation.

He has set his goals: A quality administration and faculty whose credentials meet the job descriptions and who will attract students; a new strong emphasis on vocational education for those who do not want to go to college, while keeping the transfer program intact; cooperation in training for business and industry; innovation in job training and programs to attract students.

State Community College is the only community college in the state that is not supported by local taxes, and some legislators are murmuring about that, saying the district must fund sources to help pay its own way. But the district was created by the state legislature because Belleville Area College District and the Lewis and Clark Community College District had been allowed to annex all the tax-base, especially industry, without taking in the poorest population in the area most in need of a junior college. BAC had been allowed to wrap around the American Bottoms to rip off industry-packed Monsanto (now Sauget) with its 100 or so people, without taking East St. Louis. Lewis and Clark had come down to take in the heavy industry of Granite City and Venice, but stops short of Brooklyn. The alternatives were to force BAC and Lewis and Clark to take the "undesirables" or create a state-supported district. The legislature and the Illinois Community College Board (ICCB) took the latter course.

"Now they are saying to us 'You've got to find some taxes.' I talked to the legislators, I told them 'You know what you did. What do you mean how much time? Twenty years ago there was no tax base."

But Hudlin sees the riverfront as providing that tax base eventually. He has hope for the city, and for the college's role in it. "Before we pass on, you're going to be surprised at how much East St. Louis has changed," he said.

Looking back at the college's beginning, he said the legislation was signed in June. "There was no building, no staff, no nothing. Two months later here they were (in the rented Spivey Building) calling themselves a college. Now that's ridiculous. With no planning, no nothing."

Of the people chosen as administrators, only one or two had any college experience, and that at the lowest levels, he said. The dean of instruction two months earlier was an elementary school teacher, "and she became a dean. I don't know how she was baptized into all this information. The man in charge of business wasn't even a senior accountant.

"Our community college board did that. It put the college in a bind right off. And the worst thing, they let Wendell Wheadon talk the state into having an elected board, and it became political. This is one time the governor should have appointed the board so he would know there was a level of competence," Warrington said.

Warrington has a sister who was a dean of nursing at Southern Illinois University at Edwardsville. "SIU had formed a dean's committee to come down to community college to help them, but Wheadon chased them away. The ICCB should have said, 'No, this is wrong, wrong!' But they went right ahead with the program. I've always been unhappy about that," Hudlin said.

There have been cuts in staff, and the teachers have been told there will be no more classes with just six or seven students. The instructors know that their jobs depend on the college's ability to create student growth. The enrollment is only "a couple of thousand," but it is up 22 per cent from last year, and Hudlin sees that as only a beginning.

How much time does Hudlin spend working on college matters? "I think about it a lot," he said. "At first I said I wouldn't go over there, they might think I was meddling. But I found out that really you have to meddle. I also have to have enough presence over there so the word will go out, that I want no politics."

Hudlin said he found sincere people on the faculty, but their resumes did not fit their requirements. "They were sincere people, but they just didn't know. We are rapidly putting in people whose resumes fit. It's not hard to do, but it is hard in our town because of politics. Look at the stadium out there (at East St. Louis High School). Awful! Awful! Awful!

"We've had to move people. We'll have to move more. The job descriptions and resumes of some of the people who held them had very little in common. Most of these have resigned; some have gotten better jobs. We had people who just didn't fit. They're the ones who kept making the same mistakes year after year after year."

The day of the interview a new director of vocational education had been hired. "We're going gung ho on that," he said. He said he had talked with SIUE President Earl Lazerson and they agreed that vocational education should be SCC's special niche. New deans have been hired, with one new dean and a new president to go. The contract of the existing president, Richard Bonner, is up Dec. 31. Applications for his successor were to be cut off Oct. 15. But already, there are many good applicants. Only persons who have been deans will be considered. Some applicants have been vice presidents. "Some are so good I wonder why in the world they would come."

Hudlin resisted pressure to replace Bonner immediately a year ago. "We didn't even know what all the problems were," he said, "so it seemed to me that you ought to at least know the problems before you went out to hire someone, in case you wanted to look for certain strength to match the needs."

"We were severely criticized because each year the auditor made a report with 20 or 30 exceptions, and many were repeats. Since the president hadn't moved, didn't recognize the necessity or didn't elect to do it, the first thing to do is change the president, get a new leader. If it is so bad the whole board is removed, then he has to change," Hudlin said.

Hudlin believes the college can reach the unreachable, those who think they can't be taught, with the proper faculty and recruitment. He recalls his days in the service in World War II when a soldier claimed he could not remember the 10 General Orders. But he could recited over 30 verses of the Sanctified Monkey. And those who couldn't learn math, but could keep track of all the bets and the payoffs in a craps game. There are ways to

State Community College, 601 James R. Thompson Blvd.

reach them, he said.

In vocational education, he wants students to build houses for practice and demonstration. He wants to see unwed mothers trained for high-paying construction work, highway work. And he wants to find the unemployed or underemployed, to recruit them off the streets, and bring them to the college so that they can become earners. He already has talked with lumber companies about the houses, with Rev. Buck Owens, the street minister, about recruitment.

There are teachers in East St. Louis who are outstanding nationally, including Ron Carter of the Lincoln High School music department. Carter has different students each year, different levels of skill, of aptitude, but each year the jazz band sounds the same, and it is nationally recognized. Coach Bob Shannon at East St. Louis High School has different football players every year. They are not all stars when they come in. But they are stars when they play, and he wins state championships one after another. Hudlin wants junior college courses that these people can teach, and bring those who want to study under the masters to the college.

Riverfront gambling may cause more problems that it solves, in Hudlin's opinion. But the college has sent a couple of faculty members to Las Vegas to learn how to train gambling house employees. Whatever the needs in business or industry, the State Community College will be prepared to meet the needs to train workers, he said.

Hudlin is hopeful for the city. The impossible happens. "I went through a period when I was not optimistic. Yet when I see what many of our young people have done, including my own sons..."

He was talking about Warrington Junior and Reginald who on their own managed to go to Yale and Harvard, and who recently produced a movie "House Party" for Tri-Star Productions, now available on video cassette. The movie cost about $2,300,000, made $26 million. They have been signed to produce two more for Tri-Star and a TV movie for NBC. They always identify themselves as from East St. Louis, Hudlin said proudly. Hudlin's third and oldest son Christopher is with Hudlin Insurance, and operates the office at 24th and State.

As for East St. Louis physically, the opportunity is the riverfront. Hudlin said he can't understand how Mayor Carl Officer could have messed up so completely on developing the riverfront. Millions have been lost. Somehow it will have to be wiped off. "I don't know how you can do something like that." The important thing, he said, is to get started. "I would like to see Malcom Martin do his thing." Martin is a St. Louis attorney who years ago tried to locate the St. Louis Transportation Museum on the riverfront. Now there is talk of an ethnic museum. Such a museum could be started with a central unit with each group allowed to add on its room, he suggested. He said Martin saw such a museum in Mexico that was successful.

Billions will be invested in the riverfront, depending on who comes, he said. Those billions can restore East St. Louis' tax base, and the college can pay at least some of its own way.

East St. Louis in the news

Nothing is static in East St. Louis. Buildings we photographed in June were burned down by the end of August. Housing projects with gaping windows were boarded up. The Hughes Quinn Junior High School was closed and boarded. The adult evening school was moved and the old Park School site boarded up. The sidewalk project on Missouri Avenue from Collinsville Avenue to the Federal Building progressed. Vandalized schools were repaired. There hardly is a day that East St. Louis is not on the front page of the area dailies. Then there was the ridiculous news St. Clair County Circuit Court Judge Roger Scrivner had given City Hall to a creditor!

To keep this book as current as we can, we capsulate the news that has occurred since we began preparation of this book last Memorial Day and is not covered elsewhere.

•Sept. 27 Judge Scrivner awarded East St. Louis City Hall and the Alcoa property deeded to the city to Walter DeBow, who was awarded a $3.4 million judgment against the city in 1985 for permanent brain damage suffered when the man was beaten in the city jail. That award also was by Judge Scrivner. The city issued $5.2 million in bonds to pay DeBow who would receive more than $4 million in annual installments including interest until the year 2003. DeBow's attorney Clyde Kuehn went back to court arguing that the bonds, not marketable, were worth only $2.8 million and asking the judge to award DeBow the real estate to make up the difference. Eric Vickers, attorney for the city, said the city has never missed a monthly interest payment of $20,000 on the bonds, already had paid DeBow $656,000 in bond money in the last three years. Judge Scrivner authorized quitclaim deeds transferring the property to DeBow, and Kuehn in turn "sold" it to a blind trust. A quitclaim deed quits the claim of the issuing party, but does not necessarily negate the claims of other parties, a question that has not been raised. The city hall cost about $10 million, was financed in a major part with federal funds, and the other land has a possible value of $5 million. The award of property valued by the city at $15 million is in addition to the bond obligation, which continues.

Oct. 5 Vickers struck back and at a press conference announced he was seeking a federal court injunction prohibiting the transfer of the property ("You cannot give away city property because it belongs to the citizens") and seeking $125 million in damages ($25 million actual, $100 million punitive) from St. Clair County Circuit Court, contending the court and Judge Scrivner engaged in racially motivated actions against East St. Louis; filing a motion in circuit court to reverse the decision and that he was asking the U.S. Senate Judiciary Committee, headed by Sen. Joseph R. Biden, already investigating charges of harassment of black officials, to investigate racial actions against Carl Officer and the city.

The action by Vickers reportedly was taken without consultation with the aldermanic council, which President Oliver Hendricks was quoted as saying planned action of its own.

Who cares about the citizens, Carl? Who cares? Who cares?

With no one — including Judge Scrivner — showing any concern for the citizens of East St. Louis or that the legal mumbo-jumbo failed to pin responsibilities for any action on any person or officer, but would tend to damage institutions and citizens instead of those who might be responsible for any misdeeds — or even identifying the misdeeds — Mayor Officer added to our sense of outrage at the tragic comedy when he posed for a photograph in the Post-Dispatch dressed in a french-cuff shirt and wearing a tie, "slam dunking a toy basketball" at his desk, with five golf clubs leaning against the wall. The display evidently was intended to show his personal disdain for the whole mess — but also indicated a lack of concern for the image of his city and the harm done to his people! Sorry, Carl, we have tried to be understanding and impartial in this book, but we couldn't contain that editorial comment. You must see yourself as you appear to others. Why didn't you hold the press conference in a partially burned building in the South End surrounded by jobless people to show who really is hurt by these legal shenanigans? Who cares? Who cares?

•State Rep. Wyvetter Younge has gotten the question of city manager government on the city ballot for the April 1991 election. Also on the ballot is a proposal to stagger the terms of the aldermen — they now all expire simultaneously. Some council members said they will not support the proposal because Younge did not consult with them in advance. Especially critical was Percy McKinney.

•Gov. James R. Thompson signed the Dis-

Gateway Community Hospital joins the ranks of abandoned buildings, could come down

tressed Cities Act in East St. Louis Aug. 30 and appointed Southern Illinois University-Edwardsville President Earl Lazerson, 59, chairman of the five-member East St. Louis Advisory Authority to oversee the city's finances. Other members are Ron Bean, 47, executive director of the Illinois Development Finance Authority; Ronald Thompson, 41, president of the GR Group Inc.; Claudia Thomas, 72, retired East St. Louis teacher and Rev. Jerome Jackson, a minister at the Southern Mission Baptist Church. Thompson urged the city to create the revenue stream to repay the $34 million loan from the state, $4 million for infrastructure and $30 million to refinance debt, but gave no specific suggestions as to how the tax-poor city could achieve that payback. Nevertheless, Mayor Carl Officer praised Thompson: "This man has the heart to help." He said to the governor "I share with you a renewed vision."

•It would take 10,000 truckloads to haul away trash strewn on city streets, alleys and vacant lots, according to the Metro-East Church-based Citizens Organization (MECCO). The city discontinued providing trash pickup in 1987. Ken Mensing of the Illinois Environmental Protection Agency said it would take four trucks operating eight hours a day nearly a year to clean up about 120,000 cubic yards of garbage and trash. MECCO hopes some of the state loan money from the Distressed Cities Act will be used for cleanup.

•The St. Clair County Board Taxation Committee voted Aug. 2 to discontinue payment on maintenance and security bills at Gateway Community Hospital — formerly Christian Welfare Hospital — in East St. Louis. Meanwhile, many employees still are owed as much as six weeks back pay. Since the owners also owe the IRS, few expect to get any of the pay.

Trash dumped on vacant lot in Oak Park

•Circuit Judge Jan Fiss awarded a $2.7 million punitive judgment against Samuel and Larry Ferguson, owners of the former Morris Paint & Varnish Co., and ordered them to pay $900,000 for a state cleanup of hazardous waste at the plant.

•State Rep. James F. Keane, chairman of the Legislative Audit Commission, said legislation will be introduced next spring to place State Community College under Belleville Area College or SIUE if it doesn't correct its financial problems before then. An audit showed the college gave $100,000 in grants to students who were not eligible, paid employees who did not work, allowed students to register and get their grades who had not paid tuition or fees. More than 70 discrepancies were found in the latest audit in June.

•Three homeless shelters in East St. Louis in June received grants from the Illinois Shelter Grants Program: Call for Help $25,752; Catholic Urban Programs $7,535 and Second Chance Shelter $65,878.

•Financially pressed St. Mary's Hospital announced 60 layoffs effective Aug. 24. In June, 20 were laid off. President Charles Windsor said 20 more may be let go. The hospital had 500 employees, but has only about 100 patients. It is East St. Louis' largest private employer. Sixty per cent of the hospital's patients are eligible for Medicaid, another 23 per cent for Medicare. The Department of Public Aid has said it will raise payments for Medicaid patients to give the hospital another $2.45 million a year. The hospital planned a 20-bed inpatient drug and alcohol abuse center to open in October.

•The Post-Dispatch reported the Illinois Environmental Protection Agency has scheduled cleanups at the former Lansom Chemical Division, where more than 100,000 gallons of waste oils, sludge and solvents, including PCBs, are stored; the Lefton Iron and Metal Co., scrap salvage site with soil contaminated with PCBs, and Wastex, Inc., a defunct blending operation with storage tanks containing liquids contaminated with PCBs and 7,000 drums with waste oils, solvents and sludge.

•Alderman Percy McKinney, 44, one of the more vocal members of the council, announced Aug. 30 that he will run for mayor. Gordon Bush, a member of the St. Clair County Board of Review, said that he has re-election to win, but then he will look at a race for mayor. Incumbent Carl Officer's aides and Township Supervisor Will McGaughy already have said Officer will run and he has had one unofficial fund raiser. The filing deadline is Dec. 17, the primary will be Feb. 26 and the general election April 2.

•Aug. 27 the News-Democrat reported that the City of Centreville donated three used police cars to the East St. Louis Park District, which embraces the city. The donation means that the park district's four park policemen can each have a car, Leonard Johnson, parks director, said. The park district also includes Washington Park and Alorton.

•East Side Health District employees volunteered to distribute 2,200 free condoms to East St. Louis prostitutes after an outbreak of a penicillin-resistant gonorrhea. East St. Louis policemen say some of the prostitutes, including homosexuals, are known to have AIDS. The East Side Health District reported Aug. 27 that it had given out $7,000 worth of condoms since January.

•The East St. Louis School District voted to pay McIntosh & Co. $70,000 for patching and plastering jobs in 1986-87 less $15,000 for an exterior veneer on a north wall of Rock Junior High School. It fell down a year after it was applied.

•Police Lt. Robert Dean told the News-Democrat that TIF (tax increment financing) funds have been used to provide off-duty policemen at $18.75 an hour patrolling in the downtown entertainment district (Collinsville Avenue area) which attracts 2,000 to 3,000 visitors on weekend nights. Later the city was warned this may be a questionable use of TIF funds. The city had been spending about $2,000 a week on the program for about a month, Dean said Sept. 3.

•Sept. 6 the News-Democrat reported police volunteers on their own time collected at least $1,000 in suspected drug money and made 56 arrests during a "sweep" of street corners the previous week. Chief of Detectives Lester Anderson said "We think the riff-raff, deadbeats and some of the drug dealers have gotten the message. If they think this is the end of it, they're wrong." Anderson lead the detail of volunteers from the detective, patrol and canine divisions for two nights. Shots were fired at policemen once but no one was hurt. Nine officers volunteered Thursday, the first night; 13 Friday. State Police Capt. Bobby Henry praised the sweep, said it showed the policemen's dedication and determination, but said the state patrolmen were not told of the plans.

•The Post-Dispatch Sept. 9 reported that dead people are voting regularly in East St. Louis; that there are more voters than adults in the city; that there are a minimum of 2,717 and a maximum of 12,735 "phantom voters." East St. Louis has not been conducting the legally required canvass of voters every two years. James Lewis, executive director of the East St. Louis Board of Election Commissioners, said the canvasses were delayed for financial reasons, and with approval from the State Board of Elections, according to the Post. State's Atty. John Baricevic has charged that East St. Louis has not been required by the state to meet its legal obligations in many areas, and many of the city's problems are a consequence. While the Post disclosure raised a hue and a cry and some News-Democrat stories, there was no indication the rolls would be cleaned up before the November 6 general elections. State's Atty. John Baricevic said that there would be vote fraud even with the rolls cleaned up. Gubernatorial candidate Jim Edgar chided his opponent Ill. Atty. General Neil Hartigan for not cleaning up the mess, and clucked in amazement at Baricevic. The board did remove the names of voters who had died in Missouri and asked trhe city for $10,000 to purge the voter lists. Similar articles could be found in the files of the old East St. Louis Journal 20, 30 and 40 years ago, when thewhites were in control.

•Mayor Carl Officer, Centreville Mayor Riley Owens and Washington Park Mayor Sylvester Jackson met to consider supporting Ted Farmer for County Board chairman because they question Baricevic will represent the best interest of blacks, the News-Democrat reported Sept. 2.

•Legislation to permit East St. Louis to levy a land tax was considered as part of the Distressed Cities Act, and evidently discarded. It would have taxed land on its best use, rather than on its use. Thus owners of vacant land would have been taxed most heavily, spurring development. The tax method was taught in economics classes at the University of Missouri in 1950, but has been adopted in very few places.

•State Community College received a $91,400 grant to enclose a second-floor walkway in its library with Plexiglas, decreasing the noise level in the rest of the library.

•The Illinois State Board of Education approved the financial plan of School District 189 as "financially acceptable." Supt. Lillian Parks testified that the district had a deficit of $17 million when the state declared it in financial difficulty in December, 1988. By the 1989-90 school year it was down to $9.5 million. By the end of this school year it will be down to $2.4 million and by the end of 1991-92 down to $1.1 million. But she told us that this depends on the continuance of funds from the "temporary" state income tax increase. Parks and the district were praised by State School Supt. Robert Leininger.

•Unofficial census returns gave East St. Louis 40,253 residents, down almost 15,000 from 55,200 in 1980. St. Clair County also dropped, from 267,531 to 261,084. The figures are not final and are subject to adjustment.

•Gov. Jim Thompson in September signed legislation that assured East St. Louis of a gambling boat when it found a qualified applicant. An application by Riverboat Development Corp. is being reviewed. The company promised to hire 500 to 1,000 residents and train them at the State Community College, and to generate $4 million to $7 million for the city annually, including a set-aside of 50 cents for each patron in a special fund to be administered jointly by the city and the developer.

•A "Focus" article in the July 1 News-Democrat on SIUE President Earl Lazerson noted that during his administration, SIUE appropriated $445,600 for an optometric clinic on its East St. Louis campus in 1989 and had completed a $1.3 million dental clinic there in 1990.

•At its first meeting, the East St. Louis Financial Advisory Commission voted unan-

Truckload of tires dumped at abandoned house

imously to withhold state loans until the city submits budgets and a financial plan to the authority. The aldermanic council slashed the budget over the objection of Mayor Officer to show the oversight group it's intent to cooperate.

•On the crime front, Carl Lawson was sentenced to death by Judge Michael O'Malley for the brutal knifing and killing of Terrance Kevin "TJ" Jones, 8, son of his estranged girl friend; city policemen said Lawson was a distributor of drugs and the founder of one of the East St. Louis gangs. State police said the stab wounds were in the shape of the gang's symbol. "He has shown no mercy, neither will I," O'Malley said. O'Malley sentenced Derrick Brown, 30, to 35 years for stabbing to death his girlfriend Genelle Howard and burying her body in a shallow grave in his back yard at 764 N. 72nd St. Brown's attorney said his client has "strong provocation," he was in love. He stabbed her 13 times. O'Malley sentenced Mark Wysinger, 19, of 1941 Gay Ave., to 30 years for the shooting death of Louis Dooley, 46, of Edwardsville during a robbery. Dooley was shot in the back of the head as he fled after being robbed. His body was found in a trash heap at 14th and Wilford. Both Brown and Wysinger pleaded guilty.

•Alderman Percy McKinney wants to rename Lincoln Park after the late boxing trainer Theodore "Pop" Myles. Meanwhile Jackie Joyner-Kersee wants to help reopen Mary Brown Community Center in Lincoln Park, where Miles trained his boxers. McKinney remembers timing boxing matches at the Pop Myles Athletic Club on Goose Hill.

What happened to East St. Louis? How did it get into such a mess?

What has happened to East St. Louis?

The next few pages will try to reconstruct what happened, albeit in what has to be vastly oversimplified terms — oversimplified for time and space reasons, and for lack of in-depth research. But I lived through many of those years, and was more of a professional observer than your average resident. However, I'll admit that in almost a quarter century reporting and editing on the East St. Louis scene, from 1949 to 1971, I still never saw the forest for the trees.

When East St. Louis was platted back in the 1860s it was in effect a subdivision. There also was Illinoistown. Illinoistown, from which the Piggott Ferry carried pioneers westward across the Mississippi, was a rowdy, boisterous place. Travelers to as far away as Indiana said they were ashamed to say they were from Illinoistown, so bad was its reputation. So when the town was incorporated the name *East St. Louis* was chosen over *Illinoistown* to change the image of the city. So much for the reputation of East St. Louis.

In the "good old days" the blacks — they were still called Negroes then — "knew their place," and it was south of Louisiana Boulevard, west of 26th Street, east of about Eighth Street and south all the way to Monsanto (now Sauget). East St. Louis had gone through a race riot in 1918 when "the boys came marching home again, hurrah," to find many of their jobs taken by blacks who had migrated to the city during World War I. As best I can gather, the basis for the racial strife then — and really all through history — has been economic.

East St. Louis was an industrial giant — only it really wasn't. Most industry was outside the city limits. The Stock Yards incorporated its own city, National City, and Macon Toberman was the almost-immortal mayor. The stock yards industries, including some that spilled across First Street into the East St. Louis city limits, employed well over 10,000 workers. That included Armour and Swift, those two with as many as 8,500 employees, and Hunter and Circle and other independents, the Yards company itself, and the Stock Yards National Bank which employed dozens of youngsters as runners and gave many present-day bankers their start. Monsanto Chemical Co. was in its own village, along with Moss Tie and American Zinc, Midwest Rubber, Phillips Petroleum, Socony Mobil — and I am naming those I can easily remember. Aluminum Ore Co. built its huge complex in Alorton, just outside the city limits east on Missouri Avenue. Still, there was in the city Certainteed Roofing, Obear Nester Glass Co., American Steel, C. K. Williams (Now Pfizer Chemical), Key Boiler Works, Walworth Valve Co., Beck Vanilla Co. even at one time Continental Can at the south end of Collinsville Avenue.

If you couldn't find a job in East St. Louis, you couldn't find a job anywhere

It was said that if you couldn't find a job in East St. Louis, you couldn't find a job anywhere, and so it was for a long time, but changes were happening.

When I came to the Journal in 1949, not so very long after World War II, the civil rights movement was gaining steam. But there still was residential segregation, enforced by social and political means. I can remember as a child when a black family moved north across Louisiana Boulevard, and crosses were burned in the yard. When the word got around — and it did like the proverbial wildfire — whites came from all over town to see the phenomenon. The streets were jammed with cars and pedestrians, some simply standing and staring at the house. My father and mother drove to see this with their very own eyes, and of course took me along. I did not really understand what was happening, however, until I began work as a reporter, and another family moved across that line. A city official picked up his phone, called the superintendent at Aluminum Ore, and asked him if the offending black worked for him. A check of the payroll revealed he did. The black was told to move back or lose his job. He moved back. The system worked.

The black area was staked out sometime after World War I. By the '40s the population grew more dense. Factors included the availability of jobs, blacks came to East St. Louis looking for work.

In Mississippi, one in 10 residents was white! The blacks did not have the vote. Living conditions were squalid, educational opportunities sparse. I cite Mississippi because I looked the figures up there long, long ago. Doubtless the situation was similar throughout the South, but I drove through Mississippi to visit my father's birthplace in southeast Arkansas, and so saw the squalor. Human living conditions couldn't have been much worse anywhere. So those who could sent their children to live in East St. Louis with aunts, uncles, even "foster relatives" to give them an opportunity for future better than their parents had. It contributed to the population and the school enrollment, all in the South End.

Then the civil rights legislation came along. The blacks won the vote. That winter I drove through Mississippi on my way to Hamburg, Ark. The cotton still hung, unpicked, from the plants in the fields along the highway. The next summer, the cotton picking machines came in droves. The minority of whites in Mississippi suddenly were outnumbered 10-1 at the polls, but the blacks to a great extent were illiterate, certainly unschooled, and incapable of marshalling their electoral power. In the meantime they systematically, it seemed to me, were driven from the state by the elimination of their jobs. Before the civil rights reform, they dragged huge cotton sacks through the fields, on their knees, picking cotton protected by needle-like spikes on the bowls. To get ready for cotton picking they soaked their fingers in turpentine to toughen the skin above their nails, where the dried bowls gouged until their fingers bled. But once the blacks had the ballot, the cotton picking machines, previously rejected as inefficient, suddenly appeared on every farm. And the blacks had to find work elsewhere — work or relief.

The East St. Louis police blotter told the story. Place of birth: a city in the South, often Mississippi. I served for a good many years on the county advisory board of the Illinois Department of Public Aid. Its rolls were swollen with relief recipients from the South, driven out by economic pressure after civil rights legislation, ill-prepared even for the back-breaking work of the smokestack industries, and choosing Illinois because in public assistance, we were among the more liberal states — certainly far more liberal than Missouri. Many went to Chicago, but we were closer to the South. So East St. Louis acquired more than its share of problem people from the troubled south. The South End — the contained ghetto — was straining at the seams.

Meanwhile, industry was going through changes. The Aluminum Ore Co. was located in Illinois refining bauxite from South America and Arkansas into aluminum ore to be shipped elsewhere for fabrication. It built a reduction plant at the mine mouth in Arkansas. Then it tried shipping bauxite from South America in small freighters with a shallow enough draft to sail right up the Mississippi to East St. Louis. At least one round trip was made — probably two — before that was given up as not cost effective. So the whole reduction plant was moved to the Gulf Coast — and though we are not privy to any company records, probably to an area with lower salary costs.

Armour and Swift plants were old and inefficient. They closed rather than rebuild, moved to more efficient plants in the Sunbelt states, where labor was cheaper. New marketing techniques broke their dependency on locations next to the stock yards.

The heavy industry had responded to World War II with maximum production — the cost was not important. But now competition forced industries to look at their efficiency, and to decide whether they would rebuild or requip ... or move. A factor was East St. Louis' tough organized labor climate and its reputation for jurisdictional disputes among construction crafts. The Sun Belt beckoned.

What began as a trickle turned to a tidal wave of departures and plant closings. The city of jobs suddenly had no jobs.

The railroads were big business in East St. Louis. The Terminal Railroad Assn. was successor to the Wiggins Ferry Co., and controlled the riverfront, owned the Eads Bridge and Union Station in St. Louis. East St. Louis was second in the nation only to Chicago as a major railroad terminal. Front Street was lined on the east side with railroad freight houses. The Alton & Southern was thriving as a major switching operation. Its employees made up a significant portion of Alta Sita. The Missouri Pacific yards at Dupo were the heart of that community. Then came trucks and planes and buses and the railroads shriveled up and died, and with them thousands more jobs.

It is my opinion that if you could factor in all the spin-off jobs lost when heavy industry and the packing plants left the greater East St. Louis area, that between the end of World War II and 1970, almost 45,000 jobs were lost.

That's what Phil Cohn meant when he said that East St. Louis should not want to return to the '60s, as some suggest, because the city already was critically ill — only it didn't realize it. But the blacks still were pretty well bottled up in the South End, the numbers swelled by a high birth rate encouraged by public aid practices, by immigration encouraged by public aid and — though segregated schools weren't all that great

Commission form of city government invited graft for the good ole boys

either — educational opportunity. If our nation had given blacks more welfare and educational opportunity then, it would be far better off today, but East St. Louis did not need all these poverty-stricken people to add to its burdens.

Looking at the political picture, East St. Louis was ruled by a white often bipartisan political machine, the good old boys. It would have been hard for any of them in the political climate of the day not to have been involved in some way in the spoils of office, because there were plenty of tempting opportunities to pick up money on the side. Gambling and prostitution — once the federal ended prohibition — were the biggest pots at the end of the rainbow, and the system was intertwined with Frank "Buster" Wortman, the mobster who with the help of police kept the other gangsters out of town. The city had the commission form of government, which meant every council member was a commissioner responsible for a segment of government — police, fire, finance, streets, etc. Each had his own little kingdom, and payoff and kickback opportunities. Suppliers undoubtedly held out bowls of sweets for the commissioners to taste as the very minimum of "perks."

Our interview with Charles Merritts Sr. will give you some feeling for what went on then. It wasn't necessary to tap the public tax till, you could become a millionaire — some did — with sideline payoffs that the commissioners still could spend tax money on improvements. But political patronage made the political system go 'round, and waste was rampant. The city found itself in financial trouble. All those industries were not in the city, were not taxpaying. I have seen the finance commissioner, after a bout with Capt. Charles Cadell and the Fire Fighters Local 23, hold his head in his hands and weep, because he didn't know where the money was coming from to pay salaries.

And those sideline payoffs were declining, too. Why, it wasn't hardly worth being a city official any more! In 1949 Sen. Estes Kefauver brought his traveling TV show to St. Louis — television was in its infancy and KSD was the only station in St. Louis, I believe. He spotlighted organized crime and its links to the political system, and embarrassed the East St. Louis police department and commissioners, citing the betting parlors run within sight of City Hall, and wide open gambling and prostitution throughout the city. Charles Stewart, investigative reporter for the East St. Louis Journal, had led the Senate committee's chief investigator (was his name George White?) throughout the area serving subpoenas on gaming operators to be questioned by the panel. One of the volunteer witnesses, by the way, was a young newspaper publisher from Troy, Paul Simon, who testified about gambling and prostitution on Collinsville Road. The Journal did a feature story on him, and Russ Maxwell photographed him sitting on a big dictionary so he could reach his typewriter — little but mighty.

East St. Louis came to its darkest financial hour. Firefighters Local 23, AFL, was holding the council's feet to the fire, prohibiting politics in the department, demanding fair wages and working conditions, and threatening to shut down city government if their demands were not met. (The policemen, many of whom owed their jobs to political appointments, refused to go along.) There was no money to meet the pay demands.

Let the trumpets blare, the flags fly, (sound cavalry horses hoofbeats in the background) the bankers came riding to the rescue. They invented a system to bypass tax referendums to give the city more money, and the banks interest payments. They called the system *judgment funding bonds*. You see, the legislature permitted taxes within certain basic ranges. To raise them, you had to have a vote of the people. That is, you usually did. But if there was a court judgment against you, then you could issue bonds to pay the judgment, and raise taxes to retire the bonds, all without a referendum. The judgment funding bonds indebted the taxpayers for 20 years at a time — and the taxpayers had no recourse to limit taxes. Each year new ones were issued, piling them up, tax upon tax. This is the device that plunged East St. Louis into long-term debt, and helps keep it there today! And it came from the bankers. No politician was smart enough to think of it.

To get the judgments, those whom the city owed gathered their bills together and filed suit collectively. The city agreed not to fight the suit. To laymen, that sounds like collusion, doesn't it? But that is the way it worked. And the judges were — and are — part of the political system. Who was to complain?

When we interviewed Bob Kassing, president of First Illinois Bank, he complained that the city does not fight judgment suits against it, and taxes go up and up. When I remarked the banks invented the system, he objected that it was meant for a short-term solution; instead it has become a long-term problem.

Revenue bonds also were not subject to the debt ceilings, so there was no limit to the depths the city could plunge financially.

All this is history. All this is accurate generally if not specifically. And all of this happened before the white flight: the whites were in control, and while some blacks were bursting out of the tight confines of the ghetto, the white flight was barely discernible.

On day I received a telephone call from a news source with the housing authority. He advised me that the federal government was going to provide funds for "turnkey housing" to be scattered throughout the city. If I would buy some vacant lots, I could be assured they would build houses on them and I could make a little money on the side.

Somebody made a lot of money building marginal housing for the housing authority. And real estate agents and developers made a lot of money building and selling houses in west Belleville to whites who fled when one of these turnkey houses, or other kinds of federal housing — and there lots of kinds — was built in formerly all-white neighborhoods and occupied by blacks. They became part of "block busting" and turned the white flight into an exodus.

The Civil rights movement in East St. Louis unleashed activists, some thugs and angry young men

The civil rights movement went into high gear. What happened in East St. Louis was a microcosm of the nation. "Militant" was the key word. It began with sit-ins at the banks, included an axe-handle march for jobs on construction projects at Scott Air Force Base. Whitey was on the run, scared, feeling outnumbered. And the blacks didn't let up the pressure. I took my son to a basketball game between Lincoln and O'Fallon at O'Fallon. We sat in the stands on the Lincoln side. The referee made a questionable call against Lincoln. The whole black side stood in the bleachers, rising in unison, stepped forward one seat, and sat down again. They didn't say a word. There was a concerted gasp, and absolute panic registered on the faces of the whites on the other side of the gym. I don't know how the move was orchestrated, but it struck fear deep in the hearts on the other side. The blacks laughed.

The ranks of the militant blacks were infiltrated by thugs, punks, who were in the action for the money and goods they could steal. Some were robbers. Others established themselves as militants, then sold out and took jobs at fat salaries with white companies as advisers on how to keep peace with militants. Then there were angry young men who did not know what they wanted, except it should be their way — the War Lords and their followers. Against this mix, the few whites who did seek to understand what was going on were perplexed. They could do nothing right. While there was a revolution going on, it was for varied reasons and toward varied ends and sometimes there was no reason at all, just anger.

War Lord leader Sweed Jeffries taught me the basic, and I mean basic, meaning of words like candor and truth and honesty in reporting, and I appreciate that. I looked hard for him when I started this book but I could not find him. The Globe ran a page one report on "snipings" in East St. Louis which contributed to the fear. Almost all "snipings" were domestic disturbances, black against black. Sweed could background almost every shooting. At the Metro-East Journal, I tried to keep a balance in the news. I initiated a "news threshold" so we didn't even report domestic incidents short of deaths. And we strove for accuracy and fairness. One anxious night when a policeman shot a fleeing black kid in the back as he crawled over a fence, killing him, we let the police keep it secret for 24 hours. We didn't really know what happened, but we knew something happened and we were silent, a little while. We didn't want to add to the problem, but we did tell the story, and I think, fairly.

An irony of the militants' actions was that they were directed against their white friends, perhaps logically so, even if unfairly. The neighborhood grocer who was first to hire blacks to stock shelves or even operate checkout lines — the same one who extended credit and called his black customers by name and who had not fled when the neighborhood changed — was the "softest" and therefore the best mark for even greater demand. And there were greater demands. The store of the grocer I have in mind eventually was torched.

At the Journal I hired a black librarian. I also hired Lillian Williams, whose father James later was to be the first black mayor, to write obituaries and serve as my secretary. She now is a star reporter for the Chicago Sun-Times. Bill Gray, black, editor of the Menard Times prison newspaper, had been writing to me. We were able to get him released from prison to be a reporter. Black reporters were hard to find. We hired a black from Iowa — who had no accent as I recall — who left us for a high-paying job with Sun Oil Co. He wrote back he spent his time at a desk reading Playboy —

he was the token front-office black. It was too bad, he was a better newsman than that.

I had a hard time getting reporters to work in East St. Louis. I hired Bob Goodrich, white, now a reporter for the Post-Dispatch in Belleville. One of the first stories he wrote — call it "enterprise" — was on discrimination by the Belleville Board of Realtors. Many of us are not always sure of what is right and wrong. I am sure many of the old political leaders took their payoffs and considered themselves public servants. I've always felt only preachers and Mormons were certain of right and wrong. Recent revelations about nationally known preachers just leaves the Mormons. Bob is Mormon. I wasn't going to reject a morally right article on discrimination. But the Real Estate Board members were among our best advertisers. I had a problem. Yes, we ran Bob's story, but as I recall I had him balance it with a story about the pressures that home sellers and apartment owners put on the Realtors to keep blacks out. That is the kind of basic honesty Sweed taught me — the whole story, not just one side.

Sweed taught me by visiting me, usually backed up by a group of other angry young men, who somehow had swelling muscles. One time they came in overalls and no shirts, and I swear they had oiled their skin so the light would glisten on the rippling muscles. Sometimes they began with threats, so he could establish his toughness, but he had brains and we talked out our problems. That was good — I was short on muscles.

One of our "shorts" drivers on Saturday night stopped for the stoplight at Tenth and State. A black man held a gun up to the side window and fired a shot through the car, just in front of his face. The driver came back to the office, left the keys and a terse note on a desk and quit.

There was violence. People were hurt. Homes were burglarized, people were robbed and terrorized and some were killed. The quip "they all look alike to me" took on another meaning as the whites were afraid of all blacks and joined in the flight, contributing to the problem. There was no way to stem the tide.

We had a janitor who lived near 15th Street and Broadway. In those tense days I worked until midnight almost every night, and I drove him home, to 15th and Broadway, almost every night. I never had a problem. I carried a hammer on my car seat, I drove defensively and I knew what I would do if I were accosted, but I never had to do it.

Elmo Bush said many white businessmen in those neighborhood stores found a way to retire; they torched their own stores and headed for the hills with the insurance money. Perhaps some did. Perhaps many did. But the bottom line was that neighborhood stores just about disappeared. If an East St. Louisan wants to buy a spool of thread today, he almost has to go to Fairview Heights to find it. If he is a high school kid looking for a part-time job, there is no corner store to hire him. You'll find the determined black kids at work in Fairview Heights, too, despite transportation problems.

Whites who could sold their houses for peanuts and ran. Thefts and vandalism soared, sometimes in the guise of black militancy. At a bachelor party for a young friend I said I thought East St. Louis would come back, and it was smart people who bought property there. A man called my hand, said he would sell me two houses in Lansdowne for $2. I borrowed $2 from a friend Joe Haas and paid the man. In a week or so he sent me the deeds. I drove down to see one house, a frame house on a raised corner lot. It stood four-square solid, even the paint was good, but the furnace had been stolen, the plumbing and the wiring ripped from the walls. The house had been rented; the renter moved out while the owner was away on vacation, and when he returned it was stripped. At that time East St. Louis was said to be tearing down abandoned houses and putting liens on the property of the owners, including their homes, if they lived in St. Clair County. I could see no way of restoring the house without standing guard every night, and if I tore it down for materials they would be stolen before dawn. I sent back the deeds. East St. Louis police were not able to deal with crime, and theft and vandalism of property went unchecked.

The worst crime was black against black, and protection raised the cost of living in East St. Louis

The worst crime was black against black, and people with property had to install bars on their windows, buy ADT systems, build garages, hang floodlights around their houses — or move out. Many affluent black East St. Louisans joined the flight, to Fairview, Belleville, O'Fallon, as far as Mascoutah.

Mayor Alvin G. Fields, the symbol of the white machine and an effective political leader, retired. Elmo Bush had been the first black to run for mayor, but he was defeated. Sen. Kenny Hall could have had the job, but declined it. Republican Jim

Fiscal responsibility now is required? Will it lead to new fund sources? To recovery?

McRoberts, who had masterminded the election of Dave O'Neal, a Republican, as sheriff, was political counselor to Jim Williams who became the mayor of an even-then bankrupt and corrupt city. He had one big thing going for him, Gov. Richard B. Ogilvie was behind him 100 per cent. But Williams wouldn't play politics. "Hell, I'd give him anything he asked for," a disappointed Gov. Ogilvie told me one time, "but he didn't have the backbone to run the city." Maybe the anatomy was off, he didn't have the stomach.

Politics is a game of IOUs. You don't win supporters because of your principles, but rather for the favors you do for your supporters and for other politicians. Even Abraham Lincoln knew that. Williams didn't. The black leaders who held hands with Al Fields played that game. They included Sen. Hall and Oliver Hendricks, chairman of the board of aldermen. The No. 1 Fields apprentice was the late Monitor publisher Clyde Jordan, who had hundreds indebted to him.

Mayor Carl Officer still hasn't learned the lesson. That's why some feel the city lacks leadership prospects now, and say the city hasn't had a strong leader since Jordan died. Jordan could get what he wanted from others, including the political party. Which party? Both parties. He distributed political funds to precinct commiteemen of both parties! He supported Republicans for governor. Officer flips off the committeemen and the professional politicians (and a lot of others) at all levels. He says he doesn't need them. Maybe he doesn't, but maybe the city does.

Tax rates have gone up and up, and have hit $20 per $100 assessed valuation, the highest in the state. The figure is unreal, almost impossible to accept. Fairview Heights replaced Collinsville Avenue as *the* shopping center, and city sales tax revenue plunged. Attempts to provide patronage jobs in the school district and City Hall shoved both deeper into debt. Police ran radar to arrest motorists and collect fines for the city instead of solving crimes — and sometimes still went unpaid. Taxes for judgment funding bonds all go to principal and interest on the bonds; there is no operating money.

With an estimated 14,000 residents living in public housing, the tax burden is shifted to the remaining 26,000 — if the census figures are correct. Unemployment figures are meaningless: a study years ago showed less than half the households had a regularly employed member; there is reason to believe that the figure today is worse. Forty per cent of the rsidetns draw public aid. True unemployment may approach 60 to 75 percent. As the photographs have shown, there are many fine homes, and if the residents pay fair share taxes, they are making huge tax payments. It costs a lot of money to live in a poor city! The blacks who can are fleeing the city, too.

East St. Louis critically needs jobs and taxpayers — taxpaying business, industry and workers. It has a reputation for crime, poor schools, poor city services and high taxes that frightens away business, industry and workers.

The school district has been working with the state to learn to live within a budget that depends on money from the "temporary" state income tax increase. It is doing well. It has as superintendent Lillian Parks, a home-grown educator with knowledge, a strong will and a high sense of values. The situation is promising.

Gov. Jim Thompson appointed special committees to investigate the plight of East St. Louis, which proposed the $34 million loan program — inaccurately called a bailout — which is in place now. The plan has a watchdog element in a special committee to oversee the use of the state funds headed by SIU-E President Dr. Earl Lazerson. He is a no-nonsense administrator. The committee is expected to introduce a new level of financial responsibility in city government. But the city must also develop an "income stream" to pay off the debt, provide services and prevent a recurrence of the bankruptcy of the city.

As you have read, State's Atty. John Baricevic points out quite accurately that neither Mayor Carl Officer or anyone else can operate a city without funds, and it cannot increase taxes already the highest in the state. That is the problem in East St. Louis at this instant. What now?

Observations

It's an open secret how to turn East St. Louis around. Everybody knows. Everybody

It's an open secret. Everybody knows what must be done to turn East St. Louis around.

Everybody knows.

Asked the question, everybody agrees.

East St. Louis' problems are everybody's problems. They are the problems of the city, of the county, of the state, of the nation. And they are strikingly common in innercities across the nation.

Everybody agrees.

But we fight about bailouts, and paybacks, and most of all we fight about the black egos and white greed, black indolence and the white conspiracy, and black and white racism.

Yes, especially racism.

Problems of unemployment, of hunger, of hopelessness, of ignorance, of fear, of lawlessness and of the fight for self respect — all the problems that walk hand in hand with poverty and become so enchained with poverty that to try to pull one from the mire you must pull all — these the human problems go unresolved while we argue about race and prestige and priorities.

Prejudice is old fashioned. Prejudice is illegal. Prejudice is out of date. We accept the Declaration of Independence, that all men are created equal...

But now the cry is "racist." We hear it in East St. Louis, and across the nation.

Nationwide, it doesn't mean prejudice in the old sense, it means favoring race, putting race first, of thinking black or thinking white, putting one's race first rather than condemning the other, per se.

So we have black television programs, and black theater, and black caucuses in congress and the legislature — and there even are those who think we must have black East St. Louis. And they are black. They want that black city, control of that black city, even if they must pay the price of enchaining the people with the unemployment, the hunger, the hopelessness, the ignorance, the fear of lawlessness, that all walk hand in hand with the poverty of the city.

To some black East St. Louisans, the only blacks that count are those who have retreated to the ghetto, who have dug in in East St. Louis and drawn in the black city limits around them, cloaking them, giving them the brotherhood of race. When the county hires blacks, for instance, from Lebanon or Mascoutah or Belleville, they don't count, they don't constitute integration in the work force because those are white blacks.

And in O'Fallon, and Fairview Heights, and in some parts of Belleville not too gripped by fear, there is a twisted racism that sees itself as white, including the black colonels from Scott who live next door, the black state troopers, the black school teachers, the black doctors and nurses, the blacks at McDonald's and Kentucky Fried Chicken, they all are white to some whites because they live on the hill or work on the hill. Those who live in East St. Louis are black because they live in East St. Louis. Of those who live on the hill, whites can say "Some of my best friends are black."

And some whites can claim black friends from East St. Louis, who are "different" from the others.

And if this sounds stupid, it is. But it is the reality of much of the thinking that stands between the problems of East St. Louis and their solutions.

When can we approach a problem as a people problem rather than a racial problem? Some say never. If never, then we must learn to find a solution so that this preoccupation with something called racisim will not destroy opportunity for all of us.

Tom Wobbe of the Southwestern Illinois Metropolitan and Regional Planning Commission stands in a meeting room of 7 West in Trenton and talks about the need for a downtown beautification program. You are what you are perceived to be, he says. "Beauty is good business. Image becomes reality."

We all know that, Tom. We can remember when sports teams were required to wear crewcuts and dress jackets. They acted as they looked, and became credits to their schools. We have seen the book "Dress for Success." Cities, too, need to dress for success.

So who is doing what about the appearance of East St. Louis?

Drive down the streets of East St. Louis, and you will see ample evidence of pride. You will find trimmed lawns, flower beds, flowers in pots on the front steps and the porch railings. You will be impressed that so many families do care about the quality and appearance of their homes. You will have a warm feeling toward them. Already these are "different." You have never seen their faces, but you know they are "all right," despite, or perhaps partly because of, the wrought iron bars on their doors and windows.

But what about the city as a whole, the burnouts, the piles of of old tires and rubbish in dead-end streets, the old sofas and TV sets rotting in vacant lots? What do they say about East St. Louis? What do they make you think about the people who live in these neighborhoods?

We are told in the preceding pages that Jerry Costello, as County Board chairman, with the cooperation of the Operating Engineers Union, offered to send county graders and backhoes and bulldozers and trucks into East St. Louis to help clean up vacant lots, level burnouts and abandoned houses, but nothing ever happend.

We are told the county offered to hire up to 500 youths in East St. Louis in a carbon copy of the St. Louis Operation Brightside. Nothing happened.

We are told that in a snowstorm, the county offered to clear East St. Louis streets, and was told by Mayor Carl Officer that if the equipment came into the city, it would be confiscated and never seen again.

If these instances are true, who is racist? Who is putting race above the needs of the people — all the people? For the problems of East St. Louis are the problems of us all. All taxpayers in St. Clair County pay more in county taxes because East St. Louis is able to pay less. All of us suffer the lack of business, the lack of jobs, because the reputation of East St. Louis frightens away employers from locations 10, 20, 30 miles or so from East St. Louis. Whether the reputation is true or false is irrelevant, it is there, it is effective. It costs us all.

State's Atty. John Baricevic says the most confirmed white bigot should be able to see the importance of solving the problems of East St. Louis.

But racism — our fear of black East St. Louisans, fed by the press and especially the television stations — denies the whites (whether their skin be black or brown or white or green) who live above the bluffs the cultural and social benefits that would come from the riverfront of a normal community.

But everybody knows that. Everybody.

We on the hill talk about *them* in the American Bottoms.

Will *they* just go away? Can we ignore the problems of East St. Louis and wait for the black flight to vacate the land, to leave only the weak, the old, the very ignorant? Is doing nothing an answer?

Nobody really believes that. But while we argue about causes and effects, about *their* motives and what *they* are trying to do to *us*, we do ignore those problems, and the black flight continues.

Is there a great white conspiracy to suck the blacks out of East St. Louis with Section 8 housing on the hill, by keeping East St. Louis as a municipality on its financial knees, by denying normal services, by not prosecuting black crime when the victims are black, and at the same time by being too hard on black criminals when vicitims are white? Is there a great conspiracy to take East St. Louis away from the blacks so the whites can move back and take over the prime location across from the Arch and in the center of the nation? These all are charges. There are people who believe them. But there is not one fact, one iota of evidence that there is such a conspiracy, says State's Atty. Baricevic.

Yet while we argue, while we exchange charges, while we accuse and deny, the black flight continues, and the white monied interests look longingly at the opportunity to make a buck, and the Post-Dispatch writes exposes about white speculators and land buyers — including among those whites the black professionals who could live next door in Fairview Heights or O'Fallon or Belleville or maybe even Powder Mill Woods.

The very thing the East St. Louis blacks fear as the white conspiracy could come to pass, not because it is a conspiracy, which we know is not true, but because the bickering and arguing wastes time and the people who could make a difference in East St. Louis, who don't want to walk hand in hand chained to the friends of poverty, move out.

Not all East St. Louisans are poverty-stricken. Not all are uneducated. Not all are ignorant. Not all lack taste. This image of East St. Louis is unfair. And it is untrue.

There are thousands of East St. Louisans who are affluent — affluent enought to pay tax rates four times the average rate above the bluffs for nice homes. Affluent enoug to pay high "pool" insurance rates because companies will not write regular policies in East St. Louis. Affluent enough to pay exorbitant insurance rates on their automobiles because they live in East St. Louis. Affluent enough to add expensive ornamental iron to doors and windows as protection against burglars, chain link fences and deadbolt locks, and to provide a place to lock up yard tools. It is expensive to live in a poor city.

Yet, as we have shown you, there are countless homes that evidence pride of their owners in flower pots on the steps, flower beds in the yards, manicured shrubs and lawns, fresh paint and sometimes novel and attractive decorative treatments.

To be affluent, they hold down good jobs, many in St. Louis.

They furnish their homes tastefully with fine furniture, oil paintings, decorating schemes that reflect the magazines they read, decor that would make many of the readers envious, as they did me.

They are not a people apart. They are Americans with American appreciation of culture and American pride in their homes.

Unfortunately, some tell us they avoid politics and politicians, the very system and people who must be made responsive to bring about a significant difference in East St. Louis.

Economics is color blind. Investors look at bottom lines, at the rate of return on investments. White Americans own companies, buy stock, wheel and deal. But more and more, so do black investors, and their dollars are just as acceptable in the marketplace. The only color the financial marketplace is aware of is green. The money men may be good neighbors, they may be good employers, but in the free enterprise society, they are out to make a buck.

There are some who think that is bad.

There are some — nations of them — who have just decided that free enterprise, open markets, profit, are not all that bad. Walls have fallen, fences have been torn down, and a global economy born.

Yet there are some who would rather cry out against the profit motives of investors than join in the competitive society and make a buck.

Yet East St. Louis needs nothing more than the economic climate for investors to make that buck, for the investors to establish businesses and industries that pay taxes and provide jobs. The fact that the owner makes a dollar does not make the corner supermarket a company store; that he provides jobs for blacks does not make this a plantation economy. Blacks are moving up the ladder in business and industry, are holding responsible positions — but they can't move up until they get in, are hired.

Philip Cohn, with perception far beyond his 28 years, a product perhaps of his close association with many of the poorest of East St. Louis residents, says to try to build an ecomomy without attacking the problems of illiteracy and ignorance is to build a house on a foundation of toothpicks.

Earl Lazerson, president of Southern Illinois University at Edwardsville, says it more analytically, but he says every student in the East St. Louis schools must be guaranteed the best education possible.

Without education, the jobs created by business and industrial development in East St. Louis will go to outsiders who are better equipped to handle them.

Young Cohn would have incentives offered to business and industry tied to the hiring of East St. Louis residents, including training them to hold the jobs if necessary.

We understand the riverboat gambling bid contained just such promises.

The East St. Louis junior college can certainly fit into such a plan, tailoring training to specific jobs under contract.

But the jobs and the training will not come if we fight "white" money and insist on the black brothers running everything.

On the other hand, whites must trust black leadership.

How can it do that?

Elmo Bush, whose brain cruises at high speed, says we have to sit down together and talk and talk and talk, and agree that when we disagree we'll come back tomorrow and talk some more, until we not only understand one another but build confidences.

"All those blacks want is money throwed at their problems, with no strings attached." How many times have you white brothers heard that? How many times have you white brothers said that? (C'mon, black brothers, if you can have a black brotherhood of man, why not a white brotherhood too?)

Yet the black brothers to a man say that while they do not want whites taking control from them, they do not object to audits, to fiscal controls, to reports on government funds.

State's Atty. and probable future County Board Chairman John Baricevic says that the state and federal governments have had the opportunity to stop misuse of federal funds, that they have refused to conduct the audits they are required by law to do. He cites the alleged misuse of state motor fuel tax money and says that if that had been stopped when the first dollar was misapplied, the recent fund freeze halting badly needed road work would never have happened.

Elmo Bush says that first "misappropriation" was to provide site services for the State Community College, and that the state applauded the use as a way to get the junior college program started, almost 20 years ago. Now the state is saying that was wrong.

Who is "the state?"

Who in state worries about principles when expediency is around?

All of which is history. It is a waste of time to talk about it. Instead we need to talk about the now and the tomorrow, and talk, and talk, and talk, as Elmo says, until we can agree and understand one another about audits and fiscal responsibility.

Bob Vancil, consultant financial expert who is planning East St. Louis tax increment financing programs, says that he has seen many municipal governments and that measured for fiscal responsibility, East St. Louis is not much worse nor better than most others, but in East St. Louis the financial resources are so thin that the results of any mismanagement are dramatic.

Everybody agrees that East St. Louis cannot bootstrap its problems. U.S. Rep. Jerry Costello says that Gov. Jim Thompson himself could not provide city services any more than does Mayor Carl Officer without financial resources. Everybody knows that.

Any solution requires the cooperation, the working together, of the city, county, state and federal governments. Everbody says that. Everybody knows that.

No solution to any one problem in East St. Louis will work without jobs. Township Supervisor Will McGaughy says confidently that there are only 20 or 30 really bad criminals in East St. Louis, and everybody knows who they are. The rest of the crime is by hangers-on, punks. Most of these mothers' sons could be straightened out if there were jobs, but without a future, without hope, they sink...

And his son breaks in: "Sucked back into the whirlpool."

He means the whirlpool of drug abuse, of usually petty crime, or serious crime, to support that drug habit.

The No. 1 problem in East St. Louis is the need for jobs.

Well, not everybody agrees on that. State Rep. Wyvetter Younge and County Board Chairman Francis Touchette agree that you can't treat one problem at a time, you have to treat them all at once, and Wyvetter puts it, "It is as simple, and as difficult as that." If people are to work, they must have skills, and they must know how to work.

There are two and three generations of relief recipients in East St. Louis, of men and women who have never worked, never held a job.

"Yes," says Phil Cohn, and there will be four and five if we don't do something about it."

Everybody knows that.

Let's move on more quickly.

East St. Louis needs:

1. Jobs.

2. Quality education, broad for today's youngsters, market oriented for the older workers, and all coupled somehow with training in living skills that builds personal pride.

3. Business and industry to create those jobs and to provide a tax base, an income for the city.

4. Fiscal credibility to give the assurances necessary to bring in those businesses and industries.

5. Quality city services, especially fire and police.

6. An improved infrastructure: streets, sewers, water supply, utilities.

7. A massive city cleanup campaign.

8. Supportive financial programs with an emphasis on rehabilitation, through the banks or from new sources.

It is hard to say any of these things should come first. The need for all is critical. The remedies are as intertwined as the problems.

Many, if not most, believe that East St. Louis' future lies in riverfront development; that what happens here will ripple across the city.

Not many think riverboat gambling in itself will be an answer to fiscal problems. But most believe it will help the city economically, especially, says U.S. Sen Alan J. Dixon, if it brings accompanying developments including restaurants, nice bars, gift shops. An amusement park also is proposed.

Most think an extension of the Jefferson National Expansion Memorial to the East St. Louis riverfront could trigger major investments if— and a big "if" —the city could demonstrate fiscal integrity and provide city services including especially police protection to reassure visitors.

And many think that light rail, definitely on its way, could give this whole effort a major boost, especially if the city could concentrate development efforts on the station areas at Fifth Street and Missouri Avenue to provide the perception of safety and, Heaven help us, beauty!

Put all three together with the state program to loan the city money to restore city services and to refinance its debts, and some very intelligent use of Tax Increment Financing incentives, and bring in the schools and junior college, and get everybody working together, concentrating on the programs instead of worrying about who or what race gets the credit, and East St. Louis could enjoy the greatest success in its history.

Oversimplification? No, we didn't say it would be easy, or simple.

There is truth that in adversity there is opportunity, and wise is the man — or city — who can see it and take full advantage of it.

No city in America has more opportunity right now than East St. Louis.

The spotlight of the nation has been focused on its problems by television.

The attention and power of the state has been turned to address the city's problems.

Dreams long regarded as just fantasies are coming true: light rail, the national park, a regional airport, and now a gambling boat with millions in revenues.

A powerful politically astute team in congress dedicated to solving problems at home can do more than any we have had in the past.

If we can:

1. Use the energies wasted in blaming and claiming, turn them into planning and working;
2. Learn to communicate;
3. Put need above race;
4. Do it...

We can cash in on opportunity.

If we continue to quarrel, blame, play to the crowd, invite criticism, worry about racial implications, we can retard progress and make the black community's worst fears come true.

East St. Louis has a powerful young leader in Carl Officer, and the politicians say he is looking at four more years. He is quick, intelligent, charismatic, and flippant. He plays to the applause of the oppressed who have found a spokesman to put white power in its place. It's fun. You can see whitey turn red with anger. But often it closes the door to opportunity. Opportunity can knock more than once, but not forever.

If someone can help Officer harness his intellect and charisma with a vision, and a plan to make that vision come true, and if he focuses on those goals and uses his resources without concern for race, he can see East St. Louis turn around, and go down in history as the greatest mayor the city has ever had.

Or perhaps the problem is one of execution of his will.Over and over we have heard that Officer has agreed to programs, but then nothing has happened, the ball has been dropped. He praised the president of a bank for offering to have sidwalks, the city's responsibility, repaired at the bank's expense. The bank agreed to pay the check, within certain limits and with approval of the contractor. Nothing ever happened? Why?

Perhaps city manager government that can provide a vertical follow-through for Officer's and the council's plans. Perhaps city manager government will be voted in with Officer's re-election, as he and Rep. Wyvetter Younge want. Perhaps there will be a search until a fully qualified man is found. And perhaps with that support Officer will be free to dream a dream, to draft a plan and make it happen.

On the other hand, if he fights cooperation and wants to cut his own way through the jungle. If he rejects the paths leading toward his goal, cries racism every time he is frustrated rather than seeking a solution, he can commit the city to years of painful distress. He can bring about the loss of any hope for East St. Louis or for the blacks here who deserve an opportunity to participate in a sound economy, deserve jobs, deserve education, deserve a future.

Everybody knows that.

Dear Reader,

Two months later than I intended I have closed this book, proud of what it is, dissatisfied because of what it could have been and isn't. The more you explore East St. Louis, the more there is to explore. There are many other persons I would like to have talked with.

I did not mean this to be a people book. It is about programs and government and social trends that affect and reveal people but not intimate people stories. The Belleville News-Democrat in September did a four-day series on the people of East St. Louis, talking with 50. It was a commendable effort, but too short-lived. There are a thousand stories of heroism among the people fighting for survival in a city they are too proud, or too poor, to leave.

There also are available now, as never before, the stories about what really happened, the stories behind the news in the 1940s, '50s and '60s. I would love to talk to some of the policemen and tell how it really was in the days of slots, gambling and prostitution.

Ed English, whose father was police commissioner in the 1950s, is collecting the happy stories of life in East St. Louis in that era.

I have enjoyed writing this book. I hope you like it, because I would like to write more, and Top's Books would like to publish more. If you would like to know what we do, send your name and address to Top's Books — the address is up front — and we'll keep you informed, including about Ed English's book.

Rube Yelvington